Life History and Narrative

Qualitative Studies Series

General Editor: Professor Ivor F Goodson, Faculty of Education,
University of Western Ontario, London, Ontario,
Canada, N6G 1G7

Life History and Narrative

Edited by

J. Amos Hatch and Richard Wisniewski

 The Falmer Press

(A member of the Taylor & Francis Group)
London • Washington, D.C.

UK	The Falmer Press, 4 John Street, London WC1N 2ET
USA	The Falmer Press, Taylor & Francis Inc., 1900 Frost Road, Suite 101, Bristol, PA 19007

First published in 1995

A catalogue record for this book is available from the British Library

Library of Congress Cataloging-in-Publication Data are available on request

ISBN 0 7507 0404 7 cased
ISBN 0 7507 0405 5 paper

Jacket design by Caroline Archer

Typeset in Graphicraft Typesetters Ltd., Hong Kong

Printed in Great Britain by Burgess Science Press, Basingstoke on paper which has a specified pH value on final paper manufacture of not less than 7.5 and is therefore 'acid free'.

Table of Contents

DEDICATION

To the qualitative researchers who serve as reviewers for the *International Journal of Qualitative Studies in Education*. Their generous, but necessarily anonymous, contributions are deeply appreciated.

Life history and narrative: introduction

J. AMOS HATCH
RICHARD WISNIEWSKI
University of Tennessee
QSE Executive Editors

Planning for a special issue of the *International Journal of Qualitative Studies in Education* (*QSE*) on life history and narrative, and for this book, was begun at the 1992 meeting of the American Educational Research Association. That decision proved to be timely. Since that time, the visibility of life history and narrative work has increased, and its importance has been more widely recognized. A call for papers was issued early in 1993, and over 40 manuscripts were submitted for review. Regretfully, many high-quality papers had to be rejected because of space limitations. We are very pleased, therefore, that this volume includes all of the articles in the special issue along with two additional chapters, including our summary chapter. The book represents some of the best thinking in life history and narrative inquiry. It advances an understanding of the many exceptionally difficult decisions that need to be made in conducting this type of research.

The lead chapter, "Narrative configuration in qualitative analysis" by Donald Polkinghorne, is helpful in situating narrative inquiry in relation to qualitative research in general. Polkinghorne provides a set of definitions that will be especially helpful to researchers new to narrative work. He draws several distinctions (e.g., between narrative and paradigmatic cognition, and between analysis of narrative and narrative analysis) that help clarify theoretical and methodological issues at the heart of this type of inquiry. Polkinghorne also includes criteria for developing and judging narrative analyses.

"Fidelity as a criterion for practicing and evaluating narrative inquiry" by Donald Blumenfeld-Jones makes a case for applying criteria used in judging art to the evaluation of narratives. Linking narrative inquiry to art making, Blumenfeld-Jones establishes the importance of connections between reality (objects) and interpretation (art forms or narratives). He argues that fidelity and believability (rather than truth) are appropriate criteria for judging both art and narrative inquiry.

Catherine Emihovich presents "Distancing passion: narratives in social science." Emihovich links emotion and reason through narrative voice (including discussions of power relations and ownership), textual organization of narratives, and the politics of metaphor. She argues that how knowledge is framed determines its importance and that narratives can free social scientists from conventional rhetorical forms. She also discusses postmodern ethnography as potentially nihilistic and offers collaboration, consensus building, and the inclusion of multiple voices as ways out of existential dilemmas associated with postmodern social science.

"Audience and the politics of narrative" by Jan Nespor and Liz Barber examines the place of audience in collaborative narrative writing. The authors describe their experiences writing a book with parents of children with disabilities. Calling their collaborative work "resistance narratives," Nespor and Barber demonstrate how issues of authorship and voice were redefined through a focus on the audience for the narratives being written. They conclude that examining assumptions about the audience for their text shaped the book into a political act within a local setting.

Thomas Barone's "Persuasive writings, vigilant readings, and reconstructed characters: the paradox of trust in educational storysharing" addresses the issue of trust and distrust in educational storytelling. Acknowledging the poststructural-ist concern for hidden power relationships related to authorship in narrative work, Barone argues for the development of "emancipatory-minded storytellers" and "emancipatory-minded readers." He asks: Can stories stand on their own, or must they be accompanied by scholarly analysis? Using examples of epiphanic moments from emancipatory autobiographies, Barone argues that some educational stories should be sufficiently trusted to be left unaccompanied by critique or theory.

Nancy Zeller applies theories and techniques from the genre of new journalism in an effort to improve the writing of narrative qualitative research reports. In "Narrative strategies for case reports," Zeller contrasts the time and space conditions of two writing modes (narration and description) and provides sample narratives to demonstrate the application of narrative techniques from the new journalism. Techniques adapted for writing better case study narratives include: scene-by-scene construction, characterization through dialogue, point of view, full rendering of details, interior monologue, and composite characterization.

Ivor Goodson's "The story so far: personal knowledge and the political" warns that life stories, in effect, may be disempowering the very people we are seeking to empower. He analyzes the context of storytelling in the media, arguing that by telling anecdotes and decontextualized stories of the oppressed, the news media avoid cultural and political analysis and in effect bolster the position of the oppressors. Goodson distinguishes between life stories and life histories and suggests that without providing the cultural contextualization and political analysis that define life history work, educational researchers could be in the same situation as the media.

Leslie Bloom and Petra Munro are the authors of "Conflicts of selves: nonunitary subjectivity in women administrators' life history narratives." This chapter is the report of an analysis of narratives, applying a feminist, postmodern framework. Four women administrators participated as "life historians" in the research, and the analysis of their narratives provides insights into the lived experiences of women in administrative roles and a description of how women's gender identity and nonunitary subjectivities are constructed in everyday life. Three recurrent themes are examined: contradictory gender discourses; resistance to patriarchy; and stories of the body.

In the concluding chapter, "Life history and narrative: questions, issues, and exemplary works," we report findings from a survey of experts in the area of narrative and life history research. Respondents were asked about distinctions between "life history" and "narrative," the relationship of narrative and life history to other qualitative approaches, issues connected with life history or narrative work, and the relationship of life history and narrative to poststructuralism. Respondents also nominated significant works describing life history and narrative methods and important examples of work in which life history or narrative approaches were used. Our findings are discussed in relation to literature in the life history and narrative field, including the chapters in this volume.

We are grateful to the many individuals who helped put this volume together and to Falmer Press (especially Malcolm Clarkson) for giving us the opportunity to turn the *QSE* special issue into a book. Special thanks go to Charlotte Duncan who provided her usual outstanding editorial help with the special issue and the edited volume. Finally, we wish to acknowledge and thank the many *QSE* reviewers who helped with this volume and all of the issues we have been responsible for editing. These reviewers are invisible, but their contributions to the quality of this volume and *QSE* are inestimable.

Narrative configuration in qualitative analysis

DONALD E. POLKINGHORNE
University of Southern California

Narrative inquiry refers to a subset of qualitative research designs in which stories are used to describe human action. The term *narrative* has been employed by qualitative researchers with a variety of meanings. In the context of narrative inquiry, *narrative* refers to a discourse form in which events and happenings are configured into a temporal unity by means of a plot. Bruner (1985) designates two types of cognition: paradigmatic, which operates by recognizing elements as members of a category; and narrative, which operates by combining elements into an emplotted story. Narrative inquiries divide into two distinct groups based on Bruner's types of cognition. Paradigmatic-type narrative inquiry gathers stories for its data and uses paradigmatic analytic procedures to produce taxonomies and categories out of the common elements across the database. Narrative-type narrative inquiry gathers events and happenings as its data and uses narrative analytic procedures to produce explanatory stories.

Narrative configuration in qualitative analysis

There is an increasing interest in narrative inquiry among qualitative researchers. This interest is merited because narrative is the linguistic form uniquely suited for displaying human existence as situated action. Narrative descriptions exhibit human activity as purposeful engagement in the world. Narrative is the type of discourse composition that draws together diverse events, happenings, and actions of human lives into thematically unified goal-directed processes. I am using the phrase *narrative configuration* to refer to the process by which happenings are drawn together and integrated into a temporally organized whole. The configurative process employs a thematic thread to lay out happenings as parts of an unfolding movement that culminates in an outcome. The thematic thread is called the plot, and the plot's integrating operation is called emplotment. When happenings are configured or emplotted, they take on narrative meaning. That is, they are understood from the perspective of their contribution and influence on a specified outcome.

In this discussion of narrative configuration, I am using the term *narrative* to refer specifically to texts that are thematically organized by plots. Qualitative researchers, however, have not limited their use of the term narrative to this meaning. In the qualitative research literature, the term *narrative* is employed to signify a variety of meanings. These multiple uses have caused some ambiguity to be associated with the term and have sometimes led to a lack of clarity and precision in its use. Thus, the first section of the paper is an investigation of the referents of the different meanings of *narrative* and how qualitative researchers employ these referents. In everyday conversation and in the qualitative research literature, the term *narrative* is used equivocally. Although the term has been used to refer to any prose text, in this paper I emphasize its reference to a specific kind of prose text (the story) and to the particular kind of configuration that generates a story (emplotment).

The second section develops Bruner's (1985) distinction between paradigmatic and narrative modes of thought. This distinction is used in the final section to identify two types of narrative inquiry: (a) analysis of narratives, that is, studies whose data consist of narratives or stories, but whose analysis produces paradigmatic typologies or categories; and (b) narrative

0951-8398/95 $10·00 © 1995 Taylor & Francis Ltd.

analysis, that is, studies whose data consist of actions, events, and happenings, but whose analysis produces stories (e.g. biographies, histories, case studies). I place particular emphasis on the second of these two types – narrative analysis – calling attention to the use of emplotment and narrative configuration as its primary analytic tool.

Uses of the term "narrative" in qualitative research

Narrative as prosaic discourse

Among its many uses, *narrative* can denote any prosaic discourse, that is, any text that consists of complete sentences linked into a coherent and integrated statement. In this sense, narrative discourse is differentiated from poetic discourse, that is, text with meter and rhyme. In discussions of data types, narrative as prosaic discourse designates one of the forms of data. Research data can be categorized into three basic forms: short answer, numerical, and narrative. A data-gathering questionnaire illustrates these categories. Respondents can be asked to provide data in a short-answer format (their names, nationality, areas of interest); in a numerical format (choosing a number on a Likert scale indicating their level of interest in a topic); and in a narrative format (a paragraph on why they are interested in a position). Although qualitative research can use all three forms of data, it is primarily characterized by its use of data in narrative form.

The meaning of *narrative* as prosaic text has been extended to refer to any data that are in the form of natural discourse or speech (e.g. interview protocols). For example, Miles and Huberman (1984) write, "We dictated interview and observation notes in *narrative* [emphasis added] form along with any pertinent analytical or methodological notes, and had them transcribed" (p. 19). In this general extension of the term, *narrative* becomes synonymous with the primary linguistic expressions that make up qualitative research projects; it is used to refer to the data form of field notes or original interview data and their written transcriptions. *Narrative* in the sense of any prosaic discourse merely points to the primary kind of data with which qualitative researchers have always worked. In this usage, *narrative* has been employed to signify that qualitative inquiries are concerned essentially with everyday or natural linguistic expressions, not with decontextualized short phrases or with abstracted counts designed for use in computational analysis.

Linked to this usage, qualitative researchers have employed *narrative* to describe the form of the collected body of data they have gathered for analysis. The analytic task of qualitative researchers can involve finding the primary structures and themes in a 1000-page corpus of prosaic text (Kvale, 1989). Miles and Huberman (1984) remonstrate, "The most frequent form of display for qualitative data in the past has been *narrative text* [emphasis in original]" (p. 21). They advocate the use of schematic displays of the collected body of qualitative data as an adjunct (or replacement) for narrative displays to provide more direct access to themes and categories. This usage also has been applied to the form of the final qualitative research report to distinguish it from the form of report used to summarize computationally based research (Carlston, 1987).

Narrative as story

In recent years qualitative researchers have attended to a more limited definition of *narrative* (Connelly & Clandinin, 1990). In this definition, *narrative* refers to a particular type of discourse, the story, not simply to any prosaic discourse. I believe that work with stories holds significant promise for qualitative researchers (Polkinghorne, 1988). Stories are particularly suited as the linguistic form in which human experience as lived can be expressed (Ricoeur, 1986/1991). The focus of this paper is on *narrative* as story and the use of story in qualitative research.

A story is a special type of discourse production. In a story, events and actions are drawn together into an organized whole by means of a plot. A plot is a type of conceptual scheme by which a contextual meaning of individual events can be displayed. To illustrate the operation of emplotment, I will use a simple story. "The king died; the prince cried." In isolation the two events are simply propositions describing two independent happenings. When composed into a story, a new level of relational significance appears. The relational significance is a display of the meaning-producing operation of the plot. Within a storied production, the prince's crying appears as a response to his father's death. The story provides a context for understanding the crying.

I hesitate to use the word *story* to refer to this type of narrative. *Story* carries a connotation of falsehood or misrepresentation, as in the expression, "That is only a story." Narrative has been used in this sense to refer to the story that evinces a culture's world-view or ideology (Fisher, 1989; Lyotard, 1979/1984) and serves to legitimize its relative values and goals. Often, qualitative researchers work with stories that relate events that are alleged to have happened. Instead of using a neologism or an awkward phrase such as *emplotted narrative*, I will use *story*, in its general sense, to signify narratives that combine a succession of incidents into a unified episode. This usage is becoming the accepted practice among qualitative researchers working with life history materials (Josselson, 1993). A storied narrative is the linguistic form that preserves the complexity of human action with its interrelationship of temporal sequence, human motivation, chance happenings, and changing interpersonal and environmental contexts. In this context, *story* refers not only to fictional accounts but also to narratives describing "ideal" life events such as biographies, autobiographies, histories, case studies, and reports of remembered episodes that have occurred.

The subject-matter of stories is human action. Stories are concerned with human attempts to progress to a solution, clarification, or unraveling of an incomplete situation. In Vanhoozer's (1991) words, "Other things exist in time, but only humans possess the capacity to perceive the connectedness of life and to seek its coherence" (p. 43). Stories are linguistic expressions of this uniquely human experience of the connectedness of life (Ricoeur, 1990/1992). The ground of storied expressions is the phenomenon of individual protagonists engaged in an ordered transformation from an initial situation to a terminal situation. The capacity to understand stories derives from the correlation between the unfolding of a story and the temporal character of human experience and the human pre-understanding of human action (Ricoeur, 1983/1984). Although the protagonists of stories can be expanded by drawing analogies to institutions, organizations, or groups of people and by anthropomorphic depictions of animals (as in fairy tales), the story form retains its primary character of an imitation of personal action (Aristotle, 1954).

Bruner (1990) notes that "People do not deal with the world event by event or with text sentence by sentence. They frame events and sentences in larger structures" (p. 64). Plot is the narrative structure through which people understand and describe the relationship among the events and choices of their lives. Plots function to compose or configure events into a story by: (a) delimiting a temporal range which marks the beginning and end of the story, (b) providing criteria for the selection of events to be included in the story, (c) temporally ordering events into an unfolding movement culminating in a conclusion, and (d) clarifying or making explicit the meaning events have as contributors to the story as a unified whole.

Plots mark off a segment of time in which events are linked together as contributors to a particular outcome. The segment of time can range from the boundless (the story of God's creation of the universe), to centuries (the story of the settlement of the United States), to lifetimes (biographies), to daily or hourly episodes (the story of going shopping). In each case, the plot establishes the beginning and end of the storied segment, thereby creating the temporal boundaries for the narrative gestalt.

Plots also function to select from the myriad of happenings those which are direct contributors to the terminal situation of the story (Carr, 1986). For example, if the plot of the story concerns a person's winning a game, those events and actions pertinent to the winning are selected for inclusion in the highlighted figure of the story. Other events such as the clothes worn, the day on which the game was played, or the eating of breakfast, because they are not central to the plot, are included as background.

For meaningfulness and understanding, stories rely on people's presumption that time has a unilinear direction moving from past to present to future and on their sense that events, motives, and interpretations can affect human actions and outcomes. The plot relates events by causally linking a prior choice or happening to a later effect. This causal link differs from the Humean conception of determinate causality and subsumption under laws (Manicas & Secord, 1983) in that it recognizes the effect of choices and planned actions on future consequences. In the narrative story, causal linkage of events is often known only retrospectively (Freeman, 1984) within the context of the outcome of the total episode. The significance and contribution of particular happenings and actions are not finally evident until the denouement of the episode. Events which might have appeared insignificant at the time may turn out to have been a crucial occurrence affecting the outcome. For example, a chance meeting of two people in a grocery store may, in retrospect, turn out to have great significance in that it was the beginning of a romance that led to a lifelong partnership. Plots accomplish these synthesizing functions as a mental construct. Stories exist independently of a particular expressive form. The same plot and its events can be presented through various media, for example, through an oral telling, a ballet, a motion picture, or written document. Recent qualitative researchers have often gathered stories through interviews, later transforming them through transcriptions into written form.

Stories in which a plot is able to unify its diverse elements fully are a normative form most often manifested in fictional tales in which the author is able to shape the elements to conform thoroughly to the design of the plot. Many tales, for example, autobiographies, are only partially integrated into a single plot line. The integrity of some of these tales is maintained by having the same protagonist involved in a series of emplotted episodes, but without an overarching plot that transforms the chronicle of storied episodes into a single, unified story with episodic subplots. Other tellers of tales, for example, Altman (1993) in his film *Short Cuts*, offer a collection of stories concerning a single topic or theme without presenting them as parts of a single plot. Some writers, such as postmodern authors, seek to communicate that experience is fragmented and disorganized. One technique they can employ is based on readers' expectations that when a discourse contains story-like elements, such as a setting and protagonists, a plot will be included that serves to display the elements as meaningful and consequential parts of a single enterprise. By not including a plot in their presentation, these authors call attention to their view that life events lack coherence and causal relationship.

Paradigmatic and narrative cognitions

Narrative as story is of special interest to qualitative researchers as they try to understand the fullness of human existence by including in their inquiries the unique characteristics that differentiate human existence from other kinds of existence (Polkinghorne, 1983). Stories express a kind of knowledge that uniquely describes human experience in which actions and happenings contribute positively and negatively to attaining goals and fulfilling purposes. The knowledge carried by stories differs from that which has been promoted by the Western scientific tradition.

In the Western tradition, with its Classical Greek heritage, the creation and communication of true knowledge has been held to be the province of a logical and formal style of discourse (Olson, 1990). Rationality has been identified with a type of discourse that advanced hypotheses, reported evidence, and systematically inferred conclusions. The notion that there is a distinct type of rational discourse appropriate for producing knowledge was the foundation for the advocacy of a single, unified science for all scholarly disciplines. This kind of discourse is the essence of contemporary scholarly and academic writing. It is the kind of discourse we use when writing a qualitative research report. All other discourse types were understood as unfit to present clear thought and knowledge, and these were lumped together under the term poetic discourse. Poetry, drama, and storied narrative could not provide true knowledge; they were limited to communicating and generating emotional experiences, and, because of this, were seen as having power to lead people dangerously astray.

In recent years, this bifurcation of linguistic forms into cognitive versus emotional (that is, knowledge-generating versus expressive) has received a particularly significant challenge. One of the notable contributors to this challenge is the cognitive psychologist, Jerome Bruner. In his *Actual Minds, Possible Worlds*, Bruner (1985) argued that narrative knowledge is more than mere emotive expression; rather, it is a legitimate form of reasoned knowing. He proposed that there are two distinctive modes of thought or types of cognition or rationality, two ways in which we know about the world. He designated the traditional logical-scientific mode of knowing *paradigmatic cognition* and storied knowing *narrative cognition*:

> There are two modes of cognitive functioning, two modes of thought, each providing distinctive ways of ordering experience, of constructing reality. The two (though complementary) are irreducible to one another. . . . Each of the ways of knowing, moreover, has operating principles of its own and its own criteria of well-formedness. They differ radically in their procedures for verification. (p. 11)

Narrative or storied discourse communicates worthwhile and thoughtful knowledge, although the form of this knowledge differs from that advocated in the received tradition. Paradigmatic cognition has been held as the exclusive cognitive mode for the generation of trustworthy and valid knowledge. The proposal that there is more than one mode of valid rationality is not new. For example, Dilthey and the neo-Kantians at the end of the 19th century argued that knowledge of humans required an understanding (*verstehen*) or reasoning to interpret human expressions and cultural artifacts. The historian Dray, writing in the late 1950s, argued that the deductive-nomological mode of explanation was not as appropriate for understanding human action as is a narrative-like explanation (Polkinghorne, 1988).

Both paradigmatic and narrative cognition generate useful and valid knowledge. They are part of the human cognitive repertoire for reasoning about and making sense of the encounter with self, others, and the material realm (cf. Gardner, 1983). The significance of Bruner's contribution is his expansion of ways of knowing beyond the singular mode advocated by the received tradition to include the narrative mode.

Paradigmatic cognition

The primary operation of paradigmatic cognition is classifying a particular instance as belonging to a category or concept. The concept is defined by a set of common attributes that is shared by its members. General concepts can include subordinate concepts or categories (Strauss & Corbin, 1990). For example, the concept, *furniture*, contains subordinate categories such as *chair*, *table*, or *desk*. Each concept is distinguished from all the others by the possession of some peculiar attribute or group of attributes, called its *specific difference*. Paradigmatic thought attends to the features or attributes that essentially define particular items as instances of a category. This kind of thinking focuses on what makes the item a member of a category. It does not focus on what makes it different from other members of the category. Thus, the actual size, shade of red, or marks on the surface that make a particular item unique are not of primary concern.

The classificatory function of cognition locates or establishes the category of which an item is a member. For example, in a grocery store, a child points to a particular round, red object with a stem and asks, "What is that?" The mother or father responds, "That is an apple." Paradigmatic thought links the particular to the formal. The realm of the particularity of each experienced item differs from the formal realm of concepts. The concept, apple, is not the same as an actual, material piece of fruit. The power of paradigmatic thought is to bring order to experience by seeing individual things as belonging to a category. By understanding that this particular item is an apple, I anticipate and act on the knowledge I have of apples in general (Smith, 1989). Paradigmatic reasoning is common to most quantitative and qualitative research designs.

In the quantitative approach to research, categories often are selected prior to the collection of data. Researchers spell out in advance the operations of measurement and observation that determine whether an event or thing is to be considered an instance of the categories of interest. In most quantitative inquiries, the researcher's concern is not simply a nominal interest in which category an item belongs, but for categories that vary in the extent or amount its instances have of it, they seek to determine this amount. For example, a researcher could be interested in not only determining whether a particular emotional response belongs to the category *anxiety*, but also in how intense is the anxiety of the examined instance. Computational analysis can provide mathematical descriptions of the relations that hold between and among nominal or variable categories. A type of computational analysis, factor analysis, identifies the possibility of common categories underlying combinations of the researcher-identified categories.

In contrast with the preselection of categories of quantitative approaches, qualitative researchers emphasize the construction or discovery of concepts that give categorical identity to the particulars and items in their collected data. Qualitative researchers examine the data items for common themes and ideas. The coding schemes of qualitative analysis are designed to separate the data into groups of like items. The grouped items are inspected to identify the common attributes that define them as members of a category (Strauss, 1987). Most qualitative analytic procedures emphasize a recursive movement between the data and the emerging categorical definitions during the process of producing classifications that will organize the data according to their commonalties. The analysis builds the categorical definitions by continually testing their power to order the data. The categories are revised and retested until they provide the "best fit" of a categorical scheme for the data set. Although the general practice of qualitative analysis follows this description of developing a categorical schematic out of the data, some researchers follow a practice similar to the quantitative approach in which they come to the data to determine whether they fit with a predetermined network. Often these conceptual networks reflect previously developed theoretical systems.

Much qualitative analysis is not content simply to identify a set of categories that provide identity to the particular elements of the database. It seeks a second level of analysis that identifies the relationships that hold between and among the established categories. This analysis seeks to show how the categories link to one another. The kinds of relationships searched for include, for example, causal, correlational, influential, part-whole, or subcategorical.

Paradigmatic reasoning is a primary method by which humans constitute their experience as ordered and consistent. It produces cognitive networks of concepts that allow people to construct experiences as familiar by emphasizing the common elements that appear over and over. The networks are maintained and transported through local languages and are personalized through individual experiences. The networks, however, are abstractions from the flow and flux of experience. By providing a familiar and decontextualized knowledge of the world, they allow us to manage the uniqueness and diversity of each experience as if it were the same as previous experiences. We are able to learn a repertoire of responses to be applied in each conceptually identified situation.

Narrative cognition

Narrative cognition is specifically directed to understanding human action (Bruner, 1985; Mitchell, 1981; Ricoeur, 1983/1984). Human action is the outcome of the interaction of a person's previous learning and experiences, present-situated presses, and proposed goals and purposes. Unlike objects, in which knowledge of one can be substituted for another without loss of information (as in replacing one spark plug with another), human actions are unique and not fully replicable. Whereas paradigmatic knowledge is focused on what is common among actions, narrative knowledge focuses on the particular and special characteristics of each action.

Narrative reasoning operates by noticing the differences and diversity of people's behavior. It attends to the temporal context and complex interaction of the elements that make each situation remarkable. In describing narrative reasoning, Carter (1993) writes that it "captures in a special fashion the richness and the nuances of meaning in human affairs" and that "this richness and nuance cannot be expressed in definitions, statements of fact, or abstract propositions" (p. 6). While paradigmatic knowledge is maintained in individual words that name a concept, narrative knowledge is maintained in emplotted stories. Storied memories retain the complexity of the situation in which an action was undertaken and the emotional and motivational meaning connected with it.

Narrative cognition configures the diverse elements of a particular action into a unified whole in which each element is connected to the central purpose of the action. Hearing a storied description about a person's movement through a life episode touches us in such a way as to evoke emotions such as sympathy, anger, or sadness. Narrative cognition gives us explanatory knowledge of why a person acted as he or she did; it makes another's action, as well as our own, understandable. Narrative cognition produces a series of anecdotal descriptions of particular incidents. Narrative reasoning does not reduce itself to rules and generalities across stories but maintains itself at the level of the specific episode. Nor does it translate its emplotted story into a set of propositions whereby its dramatic and integrative features are forfeited (McGuire, 1990). The cumulative effect of narrative reasoning is a collection of individual cases in which thought moves from case to case instead of from case to generalization.

This collection of storied experiences provides a basis for understanding new action episodes by means of analogy. The collection of stories is searched to find one that is similar in some respects to the new one. The concern is not to identify the new episode as an instance of a general type but as similar to a specific remembered episode. The new episode is noted as similar to, but not the same as, the previously selected episode. Thus, the understanding of the new action can draw upon previous understanding while being open to the specific and unique elements that make the new episode different from all that have gone before. The analogical understanding recognizes the improvisation and change that make up the flexible variability of human behavior (Lave, 1988). The more varied and extensive one's collection of storied explanatory descriptions of previous actions, the more likely that one can draw on a similar remembered episode for an initial understanding of the new situation and the more likely that one will appreciate and search for the elements that make the new different from the recalled instance.

Analysis of narratives and narrative analysis

One purpose of this discussion is to provide a paradigmatic analysis of narrative research, that is, to tease out and present a taxonomy of different kinds of narrative inquiry. I find that there are two primary kinds of narrative inquiry that correspond to the two kinds of cognition – paradigmatic and narrative – described by Bruner (1985). I call the type that employs paradigmatic reasoning in its analysis, *analysis of narratives*, and the type that uses narrative reasoning, *narrative analysis*. In the first type, analysis of narratives, researchers collect stories as data and analyze them with paradigmatic processes. The paradigmatic analysis results in descriptions of themes that hold across the stories or in taxonomies of types of stories, characters, or settings. In the second type, narrative analysis, researchers collect descriptions of events and happenings and synthesize or configure them by means of a plot into a story or stories (for example, a history, case study, or biographic episode). Thus, analysis of narratives moves from stories to common elements, and narrative analysis moves from elements to stories.

In my review of the recent qualitative research identified as narrative inquiry, I find that the research has emphasized the analysis of narratives type of study. By calling attention to the two types, I hope that the particular strengths of the narrative analysis type of research will be apparent and that researchers will engage in more studies of this variety. Both types of narrative inquiry produce valued products; the products, however, are of different cognitive forms. The recognition of the difference in the cognitive form of the results requires that each type of inquiry be judged by specific criteria of validation and trustworthiness. The following sections describe procedures employed in the two types of narrative inquiry.

Paradigmatic analysis of narrative data

Narrative inquiry of the analysis of narrative type contrasts with other qualitative research studies in that its data are in the form of storied narratives. It is similar to other qualitative research in that it employs a paradigmatic analysis of the data.

In regard to temporality, it is possible to classify qualitative data into two kinds – diachronic and synchronic. Diachronic data contain temporal information about the sequential relationship of events. The data describe when events occurred and the effect the events had on subsequent happenings. The data are often autobiographical accounts of personal episodes and include reference as to when and why actions were taken and the intended results of the actions. Synchronic data lack the historical and developmental dimension. They are framed as categorical answers to questions put by an interviewer (Mishler, 1986b) and provide information about the present situation or belief of an informant (e.g. answers to questions about what one feels about his or her neighborhood, tax increases, or the meaning or experience of death of a significant other).

Narrative inquiry of both the analysis of narrative and narrative analysis types requires primarily diachronic data. In this, the two types differ from other qualitative research approaches that often rely on synchronic data. Analysis of narrative research relies on a type of diachronic data, the storied narrative. The storied narrative differs from a mere listing of a sequence of events, that is, from a chronicle. Stories are sustained emplotted accounts with a beginning, middle, and end. The sources of storied narratives are varied, including written documents (personal journals [Berman, 1989], autobiographies, and biographies) and oral statements (from previously recorded oral histories and from interviews). Interviews appear to be the most often used source of storied narratives in contemporary narrative inquiry.

Mishler (1986b) reports that interviewees' responses will often be given as stories. He notes that people frequently understand and recapitulate their experiences in storied form. If the interviewer will not suppress the interviewee's responses by limiting the answers to what is relevant to a narrowly specified question, a storied answer will be provided. The interviewer can solicit stories by simply asking the interviewee to tell how something happened. The stories are generated as reminiscences of how and why something occurred or what led to an action being undertaken. Subjects do not have to be taught how to tell stories; it is part of their cognitive repertoire (Kemper, 1984) and an ordinary way in which they make sense of and communicate life episodes. Nevertheless, the demands on interviewers in the generation of interviewees' personal stories as data are complex and taxing (Young & Tardif, 1992). The orally generated stories need to be transcribed and, thereby, transformed into written texts for analysis. That is, they must be "textualized" for "only in textualized form do data yield to analysis" (Van Maanen, 1988, p. 95).

Analysis of narratives

Much of the literature on doing qualitative research has focused on the techniques of various forms of data gathering: fieldwork, participant-observation, and interviewing. Much less attention has been given to the procedures for analyzing the gathered data. Early ethnographers did not see the analysis of data as problematic once the facts were unearthed. In a comment about the Chicago School that could hold for early ethnographic work in general, Van Maanen (1988) writes, "little need was felt to do much more than gather and arrange the materials, for they would . . . speak for themselves" (p. 19). Although social science concepts and theory influenced and informed the interpretation and analysis of data, little was written about the theory of analysis. More recently, writers on qualitative methods have begun to consider the theoretical concerns that underlie the analytic process (e.g. Polkinghorne, 1991b; Strauss, 1987; Strauss & Corbin, 1990).

Many qualitative research studies employ a paradigmatic type of analysis. As described above, paradigmatic analysis is an examination of the data to identify particulars as instances of general notions or concepts. The paradigmatic analysis of narrative seeks to locate common themes or conceptual manifestations among the stories collected as data. Most often this approach requires a database consisting of several stories (rather than a single story). The researcher inspects the different stories to discover which notions appear across them. Two types of paradigmatic search are possible: (a) one in which the concepts are derived from previous theory or logical possibilities and are applied to the data to determine whether instances of these concepts are to be found; and (b) one in which concepts are inductively derived from the data. An example of the first type of paradigmatic analysis is the use of psychoanalytic theory to locate instances of personality types or uses of defense mechanisms. Another example is categorization of storied data as instances of a logically derived plot typology, such as Aristotle's in which the protagonist achieves the goal (a comedy) or does not achieve the goal (a tragedy). The second type, inductive analysis, is more closely identified with qualitative research (Hammersley, 1992). In this approach, the researcher develops concepts from the data rather than imposing previous theoretically derived concepts. Glaser and Strauss's (1967) grounded theory notion is an instance of this type of paradigmatic analysis. Inductive analysis includes the recursive movement from noted similar instances in the data to researcher-proposed categorical and conceptual definitions. Through these recursions, the proposed definitions are altered until they reach a "best fit" ordering of the data as a collection of particular instances of the derived categories.

The use of these two types of paradigmatic analysis has produced a wide variety of studies. The variety results from the differences in conceptual focus that are of interest to the researcher.

Researchers interested in the cognitive development of children have produced a body of research based on the paradigmatic analysis of children's stories. They have been interested in the form and structure of the stories told by children of different ages (e.g. McCabe & Peterson, 1991). Literary theorists have also focused on the formal attributes of storied narratives, for example, Propp's (1928/1968) classic study of the structure of Russian fairy tales. More often, however, qualitative researchers have been interested in content and meaning exhibited in the storied data they collect (Mishler, 1986a; Sutton-Smith, 1986). They look for various kinds of responses, actions, and understandings that appear across the storied data (Denzin, 1989).

Paradigmatic analysis is employed not simply to discover or describe the categories that identify particular occurrences within the data but also to note relationships among categories. This kind of matrix analysis attempts to detect the covariance among concepts. For example, Gergin and Gergin (1987) asked young adults and older adults to tell their life stories. In analyzing the stories, they noted that, in general, the plots of the young adults' stories depicted a happy childhood followed by a difficult adolescent period and an upward swing in the present (a romantic plot); the older adults' stories described the young adult years as difficult but the period during 50–60 years of age as positive, followed by a time of regression (a tragic plot).

Ruth and Öberg (1992) provide an exemplar of a paradigmatic analysis of storied narratives. Their study was based on the life stories of 23 women between the ages of 75 and 85 living in Helsinki, Finland. The first group of subjects was gathered from respondents to an advertisement asking for people who would tell about their life. Additional subjects were selected in order to include people from different social strata. Extensive interviews were conducted over several settings with each subject. The total amount of time spent interviewing each subject averaged 7 hours and 40 minutes. Subjects were first asked to tell their life stories, then they were asked to provide more detailed information about particular common themes in their life stories that the researchers had decided were important to their project. The interviews were audio recorded and later transcribed. The transcribed text made up the database for the study.

The procedures used in the paradigmatic analysis of the data are described by Ruth and Öberg:

> The data were analyzed using the "Grounded theory" method, that is groups of qualitatively similar life histories were brought together in one category and they were labeled after the dominating qualities in the category. . . . We found six different categories of way of life among the elderly which were named "the bitter life," "the sweet life," "life as a hurdle race," "life as a trapping pit," "the arduous working life," and "the silenced life." All 23 women interviewed could be found represented in the above-mentioned ways of life. The basis of this typification was the way the interviewees started and ended their life stories, what turning points their stories included, how they overcame major changes in their lives, and how they interpreted and evaluated these changes. (p. 135)

The report of the study provides extended descriptions of each of the six ways of life. Further analysis involved examining the place of the categorized stories along a series of dimensions. For example, each category of way of life was inspected for its place on the locus-of-control dimension. The "bitter life" stories displayed an outer-directed locus of control, the "life as a trapping pit" stories displayed the theme of loss of control over life, the "arduous working life" stories displayed an inner-directed locus of control. Other dimensions used by Ruth and Öberg in their analysis include the self-image evinced in the stories of the various ways of life, the evaluation of one's life as a whole, and the evaluation of one's old age.

As the Ruth and Öberg research illustrates, paradigmatic analysis provides a method to uncover the commonalties that exist across the stories that make up a study's database. It functions to generate general knowledge from a set of particular instances. The discussion of the external validity of the paradigmatic findings of commonalities within the database, that is, whether the findings hold for similar, yet unexamined stories, is beyond the scope of this paper. The strength of paradigmatic procedures is their capacity to develop general knowledge about a collection of stories. This kind of knowledge, however, is abstract and formal, and by necessity underplays the unique and particular aspects of each story.

Narrative analysis of eventful data

In research that employs narrative analysis as distinguished from analysis of narratives, the result is an emplotted narrative. The outcome of a narrative analysis is a story – for example, a historical account, a case study, a life story, or a storied episode of a person's life. In this type of analysis, the researcher's task is to configure the data elements into a story that unites and gives meaning to the data as contributors to a goal or purpose. The analytic task requires the researcher to develop or discover a plot that displays the linkage among the data elements as parts of an unfolding temporal development culminating in the denouement.

Events and happenings as data

Unlike narrative inquiry of the paradigmatic type, the data employed in the narrative analytic type are usually not in storied form. The purpose of narrative analysis is to produce stories as the outcome of the research. The data elements required for this production are diachronic descriptions of events and happenings. Narrative analysis composes these elements into a story. The researcher begins with questions such as "How did this happen?" or "Why did this come about?" and searches for pieces of information that contribute to the construction of a story that provides an explanatory answer to the questions. The information can come from various sources, including interviews, journals, public and personal documents, and observations. For example, a biographer wanting to write the life story of a person would seek out personal diaries and letters, interview relatives and friends who knew the person, gather public statements and writings of the person, collect articles and accounts written about the person, and, if the person were living, interview him or her. All of these data need to be integrated and interpreted by an emplotted narrative.

What data are gathered depends on the focus of the research. Narrative analysis requires that the researcher select a bounded system for study. The researcher needs to have "some conception of the unity of totality of a system with some kind of outlines or boundaries" (Stake, 1988, p. 255). The bounded system can be two years in the life of a child with a learning disability, the first years of the development of company, or an academic year for a teacher and his or her pupils. Data which relate to the particular system under study are sought. The search is for data that will reveal uniqueness of the individual case or bounded system and provide an understanding of its idiosyncrasy and particular complexity.

Narrative analysis

Narrative analysis is the procedure through which the researcher organizes the data elements into a coherent developmental account. The process of narrative analysis is actually a synthesizing of the data rather than a separation of it into its constituent parts. Nevertheless, because the meaning of the term *analysis* has been extended in qualitative research to cover any treatment of the data, I retain *analysis* when referring to the configuration of the data into a coherent whole.

Narrative analysis relates events and actions to one another by configuring them as contributors to the advancement of a plot. The story constituted by narrative integration allows for the incorporation of the notions of human purpose and choice as well as chance happenings, dispositions, and environmental presses. The result of a narrative analysis is an explanation that is retrospective, having linked past events together to account for how a final outcome might have come about. In this analysis, the researcher attends to the temporal and unfolding dimension of human experience by organizing the events of the data along a before–after continuum. White's (1975) intensive study of three lives provides an exemplar of the use of narrative analysis in qualitative research.

Narrative analysis synthesizes or configures events into an explanation of, for example, how a successful classroom came to be, how a company came to fail in its campaign, or how an individual made a career choice. Narrative configuration makes use of various kinds of plots as organizing templates. The most basic plot types are the "tragic," in which the protagonist does not achieve the goal, and the "comedy," in which the protagonist does achieve the goal. Within these two basic types are many variations dealing with different movements within the narrative toward the goal (satisfaction) and away from it (disappointment) before the final outcome.

The analytic development of a story from the gathered data involves recursive movement from the data to an emerging thematic plot. Evolving a plot that serves to configure the data elements into a coherent story requires testing the beginning attempts at emplotment with the database. If major events or actions described in the data conflict with or contradict the emerging plot idea, then the idea needs to be adapted to better fit or make sense of the elements and their relationships. The development of a plot follows the same principles of understanding that are described by the notion of the hermenuetic circle. The creation of a text involves the to-and-fro movement from parts to whole that is involved in comprehending a finished text.

As the plot begins to take form, the events and happenings that are crucial to the story's denouement become apparent. The emerging plot informs the researcher about which items from the gathered data should be included in the final storied account. Not all data elements will be needed for the telling of the story. Elements which do not contradict the plot, but which are not pertinent to its development, do not become part of the research result, the storied narrative. This process has been called *narrative smoothing* (Spence, 1986). Human experience does not match a carefully crafted, congruent story. It consists of extraneous happenings and everyday chores as well as simultaneous multiple projects (Carr, 1986). The very act of bringing these happenings into language imposes a higher level of order on them than they have in the flux of everyday experience. The move to narrative configuration extracts a still higher order from the fullness of lived experiences (Kerby, 1991). The configuration, however, cannot impose just any emplotted order on the data. The final story must fit the data while at the same time bringing an order and meaningfulness that is not apparent in the data themselves.

Dollard (1935) proposed seven criteria for judging a life history. Although written almost 60 years ago, the criteria are still applicable and can be used by the researcher as guides in generating a storied history or case study from the gathered data. The following is my statement of Dollard's criteria in the form of guidelines for developing a narrative.

(1) The researcher must include descriptions of the cultural context in which the storied case study takes place. The protagonist has incorporated, to some extent, the values, social rules, meaning systems, and languaged conceptual networks of the culture in which he or she developed (Bourdieu, 1980/1990). Particular meanings of happenings and actions are provided by the cultural heritage; assumptions about acceptable and expected personal goals are maintained by the social environment; and normal strategies for achieving these goals are sustained by the milieu. In generating the story, the researcher needs to attend to the contextual features that give specific meanings to events so that their contributions to the plot can be understood.

(2) In gathering and configuring the data into a story, the researcher also needs to attend to the embodied nature of the protagonist. The incarnate nature of human existence locates the person spatially and temporally. The bodily dimensions (such as height and physique) and genetic-given propensities (such as academic intelligence and probabilities of illnesses) affect personal goals and produce life concerns. The body undergoes continuous change throughout life, and its developmental stages provide an essential context for actions; for example, the physical and cognitive development of a 3-year-old and a 73-year-old are fundamentally different. People's emotional responses to events and others are not merely cognitive but also bodily (Lazarus, 1991). Illness and bodily incapacity affect a person's self-identity as well as influencing one's productivity. The body places temporal limits on life, and the recognition of approaching death influences goals and actions. It is important that researchers include the bodily dimension in their storied explanation of a given topic.

(3) In developing the story's setting, the researcher needs to be mindful not only of the general cultural environment and the person as embodied, but also of the importance of significant other people in affecting the actions and goals of the protagonist. An explanation of the relationships between the main character and other people – parents, siblings, spouse, children, friends, and personal antagonists – is required in the development of the plot. The reasons for undertaking actions are often related to concern for another's happiness, not simply to fulfill a personal agenda. Carr (1986) uses the term "we-subject" (p. 134) when referring to narratives in which the purpose of the person's actions is the achievement of the well-being of others.

(4) Although the cultural setting, the body, and other people provide the context and limits in which the protagonist acts, he or she makes choices to pursue particular goals, decides on a series of activities designed to accomplish these goals, and undertakes the selected actions. The story is about the central character and movement toward an outcome. The researcher needs to concentrate on the choices and actions of this central person. To understand the person, we must grasp the person's meanings and understandings; the agent's vision of the world; and his or her plans, purposes, motivations, and interests. Attention to the inner struggles, emotional states, and valuing of the protagonist provides important data. The protagonist is not merely a pawn buffeted by the setting, but an actor who alters the scene. Different people respond differently to the same events. The story needs to describe the interaction between this particular protagonist and the setting.

(5) In constructing the story, the researcher needs to consider the historical continuity of the characters. People are historical beings retaining as part of themselves their previous experiences. Past experiences manifest themselves in the present as habits and are partially available through recollection. Embedded habits present themselves not only as motor skills and body movements but also as patterns of thought. In considering the person as a biographical being, attention needs to be given to social events that the protagonist and his or her historical cohorts have experienced. For example, in developing life stories of older Americans, it is important to understand the impact of the Depression on their goals and strategies. In making the protagonist's decisions and actions understandable and sensible, the researcher needs to present them as consistent with previous experience. Although a person's past experiences persevere into the present, they do not necessarily determine future actions. The plot of many case histories is about a person's struggle to change habitual behaviors and to act differently.

(6) The outcome of a narrative analysis is the generation of a story. A story requires a bounded temporal period; that is, it needs a beginning, middle, and end. The researcher must mark the beginning point of the story and the point of denouement. A story needs to focus on a specific context in which the plot takes place. The researcher should present the characters with enough detail that they appear as unique individuals in a particular situation. The researcher

should not overlook details that differentiate this story from similar ones. The power of a storied outcome is derived from its presentation of a distinctive individual, in a unique situation, dealing with issues in a personal manner; this power is contrasted with research findings which present *l'homme moyen*, the abstracted, statistically average person (Gigerenzer *et al.*, 1989).

(7) The final guideline for judging the adequacy of a narrative analysis is whether it makes the generation of the researched occurrence plausible and understandable. The previous guidelines refer to dimensions that need to be considered in generating a story from the data. This final guideline concerns the need for the researcher to provide a story line or plot that serves to configure or compose the disparate data elements into a meaningful explanation of the protagonist's responses and actions. Although the configuration process cannot be accomplished by following an algorithmic recipe, certain steps are commonly used in the production of storied narratives. The story is a reconstruction of a series of events and actions that produced a particular outcome. The configuration process often begins with the story's ending or denouement. By specifying the outcome, the researcher locates a viewing point from which to select data events necessary for producing the conclusion. The researcher asks, "How is it that this outcome came about; what events and actions contributed to this solution?" Examples of outcomes include the achievement of a high reading score, overcoming performance fears, and overcoming an addiction to drugs. From its conclusion, the researcher retrospectively views the data elements in order to link them into a series of happenings that led to the outcome.

After the denouement is identified, the researcher can work directly with the data elements. A first step in configuring the data into a story is to arrange the data elements chronologically. The next step is to identify which elements are contributors to the outcome. Then the researcher looks for connections of cause and influence among the events and begins to identify action elements by providing the "because of" and "in order to" reasons (Schutz & Luckmann, 1973) for which they were undertaken. Often these connections are not simply one to one but are combinations and accumulations of events that influence a response or provide sufficient reason for an action.

The final step is the writing of the story. The storied product is a temporal gestalt in which the meaning of each part is given through its reciprocal relationships with the plotted whole and other parts. The researcher cannot simply compile or aggregate the happenings; they must be drawn together into a systemic whole. As Vanhoozer (1991) summarizes, "Just as painting is a *visual* representation which shapes or configures *space*, so narrative is a *verbal* representation of reality which shapes or configures *time*" (p. 37). The problem confronting the researcher is to construct a display of the complex, interwoven character of human experience as it unfolds through time and as it stands out at any present moment through recollection and imagination (Heidegger, 1927/1962). The plot provides the systemic unity to the story; it is the glue that connects the parts together. Thus, the final writing begins with the construction of the plot outline. The outline is an intellectual construction (Stake, 1988) or temporally patterned whole that the researcher develops from working with the sequentially ordered data.

With the outline in mind, the researcher fills in and links the data elements to other data elements and to the plotted whole story. Filling in the outline with detail often has the effect of displaying weaknesses in the plot's capacity to unite the data. This requires adjustments to the outline so that it better fits the data. During the process of linking the elements together and identifying their contribution to the plotted outline, it sometimes becomes apparent that there are gaps in the data. When possible, the researcher gathers additional data to fill in the missing links in order to produce a full and explanatory story. The interdependence of story and data is described by Bruner (1986):

> It is not that we initially have a body of data, the facts, and we then must construct a story or theory to account for them. . . . Instead . . . the narrative structures we construct are not

secondary narratives about data but primary narratives that establish what is to count as data. (pp. 142–143)

In the decades since Dollard developed his criteria, changes have occurred in the philosophy of science that call attention to the constructive processes that underlie the production of knowledge (Rosenau, 1992). The storied finding of a narrative analytic inquiry is not a third-person "objective" representation or mirrored reflection of a protagonist's or subject's life as it "actually" occurred; rather, the finding is the outcome of a series of constructions. Researchers engaged in narrative analysis need to be attuned to their contributions to the constructive aspects of their research and to acknowledge these in their write-ups. The data used in narrative inquiries are not simple descriptions of sense-impressions. They are dialogical productions resulting from interactions between subjects and the researchers (Tierney, 1993). The write-up itself is not a neutral representation of the research finding; it is a composition that molds the story to fit the current grammatical conventions and conceptual framework of the language in which the story is expressed (Clifford, 1986). In addition to Dollard's seven criteria, a life history produced by a narrative analysis can be expected to include a recognition of the role the researcher had in constructing the presented life story and the effect the researcher's views might have had in shaping the finding.

The function of narrative analysis is to answer how and why a particular outcome came about. The storied analysis is an attempt to understand individual persons, including their spontaneity and responsibility, as they have acted in the concrete social world. The storied production that is the outcome of the research is the retrospective or narrative explanation of the happening that is the topic of the inquiry (Polkinghorne, 1988). The plausibility of the produced story is in its clarification of the uncertainty implied in the research question of why the happening occurred. The explanation needs to satisfy the subjective needs of the reader of the report to understand how the occurrence could have come about. The story has to appeal to the reader's experienced general sense of how and why humans respond and act (Ricoeur, 1983/1984). It needs to be compatible with the reader's background knowledge or beliefs in characteristic behavior of people or nature in order for the reader to accept the explanation as possible (McGuire, 1990).

The configurative analysis is produced after the storied events have occurred. Although the collection of the data may occur while the episode is in process, the analysis occurs afterward. The researcher is not simply producing a description of action but is writing a history. Although elements of the data may reflect the thoughts and plans of the protagonist at the time they happened, in the analysis these elements are transformed into historical data. From the point of view of the narrative analyzer, the nonintentional as well as the intentional effects of the actions are included (Carr et al., 1991). A narrative configuration is not merely a transcription of the thoughts and actions of the protagonist; it is a means of making sense and showing the significance of them in the context of the denouement. In the storied outcome of narrative inquiry, the researcher is the narrator of the story, and often the story is told in his or her voice.

In producing the story, the researcher draws on disciplinary expertise to interpret and make sense of responses and actions. Because the story is offered as a scholarly explanation and realistic depiction of a human episode, the researcher needs to include evidence and argument in support of the plausibility of the offered story. Manicas and Secord (1983) summarize the analytic process of the kind of research I have termed *narrative analysis*:

> It is engaged in understanding the concrete person and his or her life history and particular patterns of behavior, including as reflexively applied, self-understanding. . . . As a scientific effort it requires also that the inquirer use whatever special knowledge is available regarding implicated psychological structures and mechanism as these operated in the

individual biography. And since the person is born and matures in a social world, this understanding inevitably also includes references to what is known about social structures pertinent to that biography. Finally, in contrast to our prescientific mode of understanding, hermeneutic inquiry as a science would be constrained by the systematic, public demands of establishing the evidential credibility of its accounts. (p. 407)

In judging the credibility of a story, a distinction can be made between the accuracy of the data and the plausibility of the plot. It is the researcher's responsibility to assure that the reported events and happenings actually occurred. The use of triangulation methods in which several independent reports of an event are sought can help in producing confidence that the event occurred. Although respondents may agree that an event happened, their interpretations of the meaning of the event may vary. Researchers need to treat interview-based data with care. Recollection of past events is selective and produced from the present perspective of the respondent. The significance and meaning of the event in the present may differ from its effect at the time of the original experience. Also, respondents do not have full access to those aspects of the experience that did not achieve awareness or to the complexity of their motives in undertaking an action (Lyons, 1986).

The question of the accuracy of the configurative plot is of greater complexity. Some writers, for example White (1973, 1981), hold that narrative configuration is a culturally derived literary imposition on what otherwise is a fragmented and disorganized reality. Other writers (e.g., Carr, 1986; Carr et al., 1991; Kerby, 1991) hold that a primitive form of narrative configuration is inherent in people's understanding of their own and others' actions. My position is similar to that of Carr and Kerby (Polkinghorne, 1991a). The storied narrative form is not an imposition on data of an alien type but a tightening and ordering of experience by explicating an intrinsically meaningful form. Because of the gap between experienced actions and the emplotted explication of them, it is possible that the same data elements can be configured by more than one plot (Stake, 1988). Thus, a sociological or psychological plot can be used to configure the data. The seven guidelines given earlier advance the ideal of an integrated plot that synthesizes the cultural, biological, historical, and individual aspects of the person into a unified story. Nevertheless, because configurative analysis is the researcher's construction, it is inappropriate to ask if it is the "real" or "true" story.

The purpose of narrative analysis is not simply to produce a reproduction of observations; rather, it is to provide a dynamic framework in which the range of disconnected data elements are made to cohere in an interesting and explanatory way (du Preez, 1991). Van Maanen (1988) states, "The criteria put forth for truth claims in the literary tale seem more similar to the fieldworker's 'personal experience' standard than the reporter's 'two people told me so' standard" (p. 143). The evaluation of the configurative analytic work of the researcher is based on the generated story's production of coherence among the situated, contextual, and particular elements of the data, that is, on its explanatory power (Connelly & Clandinin, 1990) and plausibility. The evaluation of the story has a pragmatic dimension in the sense that its value depends on its capacity to provide the reader with insight and understanding. The pragmatic dimension of the evaluation of researcher-generated stories is not to be confused with the pragmatic evaluation of therapeutic stories (Spence, 1984). The researcher's story should not only be useful; it should also be faithful to the actual historical happenings (Sass, 1992).

The classic examples of narrative analysis are Freud's case studies (see Brooks, 1984; Hillman, 1983) and studies by the symbolic interactionists of the Chicago School (Hammersley, 1989; Manis & Meltzer, 1978). Recent writers have called attention to the storied structure of the reports of anthropological field studies (Bruner, 1986; Van Maanen, 1988). Although the basic model of the story is the action of a single person (Ricoeur, 1983/1984), the notion of the protagonist has been expanded by analogy to social groups and organizations; for example, corporate case studies have served as the basic teaching tool in the Harvard Business School.

Narrative inquiries often include a set of case studies related to the same topic. Seidman (1991) discusses the method of creating a set of profiles or vignettes that, alongside each other, provide greater insight and understanding of the topic than any single vignette. His study of community college teaching (Seidman, 1985) includes a collection of storied vignettes of faculty experiences based on extensive interviews. Forrester's (1993) study of depressed children consists of comprehensive case studies of six children with depressive symptoms. The six stories were based on a variety of sources: She interviewed the children's parents and therapists; she interviewed the children and observed their play and interactions with other children; her data also contained treatment process notes from the clinic where the children received therapy. The six stories of the children's experiences with depression depict the diverse effects depression had on the individual lives of these children. Often, a set of case studies is followed by a commentary chapter in which the differences and similarities among the cases is highlighted. Forrester's study has such a commentary in which she notes the variety of depression in the lives of the children and the limits of the single diagnostic category of childhood depression. The commentary chapter normally does not consist of a paradigmatic analysis because the stories are not those produced by subjects but those produced by the researcher him- or herself.

Conclusion

Narrative inquiry is one of the many kinds of research that are part of the research approaches that have been gathered under the umbrella of qualitative research. I have advocated the importance of identifying two types of narrative inquiry. Both share the general principles of qualitative research such as working with data in the form of natural language and the use of noncomputational analytic procedures. Although both types of narrative inquiry are concerned with stories, they have significant differences. The paradigmatic type collects storied accounts for its data; the narrative type collects descriptions of events, happenings, and actions. The paradigmatic type uses an analytic process that identifies aspects of the data as instances of categories; the narrative type uses an analytic process that produces storied accounts. The paradigmatic type is based on what Bruner has termed paradigmatic reasoning; the narrative type is based in narrative reasoning. Narrative inquiry of the paradigmatic type produces knowledge of concepts; the narrative type produces knowledge of particular situations. Both types of narrative inquiry can make important contributions to the body of social science knowledge.

References

Altman, R. (Director) & Brokaw, C. (Producer) (1993). *Short cuts* [Film]. New York: Fine Line Features.

Aristotle (1954). *The rhetoric and poetics of Aristotle* (W.R. Roberts & I. Bywater, Trans.). New York: Random House.

Berman, H.J. (1989). May Sarton's journals: attachment and separateness in later life. In L.E. Thomas (Ed.), *Research on adulthood and aging: a human science approach* (pp. 11–26). Albany: State University of New York Press.

Bourdieu, P. (1990). *The logic of practice* (R. Nice, Trans.). Stanford: Stanford University Press (Original work published 1980).

Brooks, P. (1984). *Reading for the plot: design and intention in narrative*. New York: Alfred A. Knopf.

Bruner, E.M. (1986). Ethnography as narrative. In V.W. Turner & E.M. Bruner (Eds), *The anthropology of experience* (pp. 139–155). Urbana: University of Illinois Press.

Bruner, J. (1985). *Actual minds, possible worlds*. Cambridge: Harvard University Press.

Bruner, J. (1990). *Acts of meaning*. Cambridge: Harvard University Press.

Carlston, D.E. (1987). Turning psychology on itself: the rhetoric of psychology and the psychology of rhetoric. In J.S. Nelson, A. Megill & D.N. McCloskey (Eds), *The rhetoric of the human sciences: language and argument in scholarship and public affairs* (pp. 145–162). Madison: University of Wisconsin Press.

Carr, D. (1986). *Time, narrative, and history*. Bloomington: University of Indiana Press.

Carr, D., Taylor, C. & Ricoeur, P. (1991). Discussion: Ricoeur on narrative. In D. Wood (Ed.), *On Paul Ricoeur: narrative and interpretation* (pp. 160–187). London: Routledge.

Carter, K. (1993). The place of story in the study of teaching and teacher education. *Educational Researcher, 22,* 5–12.

Clifford, J. (1986). Introduction: partial truths. In J. Clifford & G.E. Marcus (Eds), *Writing culture: the poetics and politics of ethnography* (pp. 1–26). Berkeley: University of California Press.

Connelly, F.M. & Clandinin, D.J. (1990). Stories of experience and narrative inquiry. *Educational Researcher, 19*(4), 2–14.

Denzin, N.K. (1989). *Interpretative interactionism.* Newbury Park: Sage.

Dollard, J. (1935). *Criteria for the life history.* New Haven: Yale University Press.

du Preez, P. (1991). *A science of mind: the quest for psychological reality.* London: Academic.

Fisher, W.R. (1989). *Human communication as narration: toward a philosophy of reason, value, and action.* Columbia: University of South Carolina Press.

Forrester, M. (1993). *Childhood depression.* Unpublished doctoral dissertation, University of Southern California, Los Angeles.

Freeman, M. (1984). History, narrative, and life-span developmental knowledge. *Human Development, 27,* 1–19.

Gardner, H. (1983). *Frames of mind: the theory of multiple intelligence.* New York: Basic.

Gergin, M.M. & Gergin, K.J. (1987). The self in temporal perspective. In R. Abeles (Ed.), *Life-span perspectives and social psychology,* pp. 121–137. Hillsdale: Erlbaum.

Gigerenzer, G., Swijtink, Z., Porter, T., Daston, L., Beatty, J. & Krüger, L. (1989). *The empire of chance: how probability changed science and everyday life.* Cambridge: Cambridge University Press.

Glaser, B.G. & Strauss, A.L. (1967). *The discovery of grounded theory: strategies for qualitative research.* New York: Aldine de Gruyter.

Hammersley, M. (1989). *The dilemma of qualitative method: Herbert Blumer and the Chicago tradition.* London: Routledge.

Hammersley, M. (1992). *What's wrong with ethnography? Methodological explorations.* London: Routledge.

Heidegger, M. (1962). *Being and time* (J. Macquarrie & E. Robinson, Trans.). New York: Harper & Bros (Original work published 1927).

Hillman, J. (1983). *Healing fiction.* Barrytown: Station Hill.

Josselson, R. (1993). A narrative introduction. In R. Josselson & A. Lieblich (Eds), *The narrative study of lives* (pp. ix–xv). Newbury Park: Sage.

Kemper, S. (1984). The development of narrative skills: explanations and entertainments. In S.A. Kuczaj II (Ed.), *Discourse development: progress in cognitive development research* (pp. 99–124). New York: Springer.

Kerby, A.T. (1991). *Narrative and the self.* Bloomington: Indiana University Press.

Kvale, S. (1989). The primacy of the interview. *Methods, 3,* 3–37.

Lave, J. (1988). *Cognition in practice: mind, mathematics and culture in everyday life.* Cambridge: Cambridge University Press.

Lazarus, R.S. (1991). *Emotion and adaptation.* New York: Oxford University Press.

Lyons, W. (1986). *The disappearance of introspection.* Cambridge: MIT Press.

Lyotard, J.-F. (1984). *The postmodern condition: a report on knowledge* (G. Bennington & B. Massumi, Trans.). Minneapolis: University of Minnesota Press (Original work published 1979).

Manicas, P.T. & Secord, P.F. (1983). Implications for psychology of the new philosophy of science. *American Psychologist, 33,* 399–413.

Manis, J.G. & Meltzer, B.N. (1978). *Symbolic interaction* (3rd edn). Boston: Allyn and Bacon.

McCabe, A. & Peterson, C. (Ed.). (1991). *Developing narrative structure.* Hillsdale: Erlbaum.

McGuire, M. (1990). The rhetoric of narrative: a hermeneutic, critical theory. In B.K. Britton & A.D. Pellegrini (Eds), *Narrative thought and narrative language* (pp. 219–236). Hillsdale: Erlbaum.

Miles, M.B. & Huberman, A.M. (1984). *Qualitative data analysis.* Beverly Hills: Sage.

Mishler, E.G. (1986a). The analysis of interview-narrative. In T.R. Sarbin (Ed.), *Narrative psychology: the storied nature of human conduct* (pp. 233–255). New York: Praeger.

Mishler, E.G. (1986b). *Research interviewing: context and narrative.* Cambridge: Harvard University Press.

Mitchell, W.J.T. (1981). Foreword. In W.J.T. Mitchell (Ed.), *On narrative* (pp. vii–x). Chicago: University of Chicago Press.

Olson, D.R. (1990). Thinking about narrative. In B.K. Britton & A.D. Pellegrini (Eds), *Narrative thought and narrative language* (pp. 99–111). Hillsdale: Erlbaum.

Polkinghorne, D.E. (1983). *Methodology for the human sciences: systems of inquiry.* Albany: State University of New York Press.

Polkinghorne, D.E. (1988). *Narrative knowing and the human sciences.* Albany: State University of New York Press.

Polkinghorne, D.E. (1991a). Narrative and self-concept. *Journal of Narrative and Life History, 1*(2&3), 135–153.

Polkinghorne, D.E. (1991b). Qualitative procedures for counseling research. In C.E. Watkins & L.J. Schneider (Eds), *Researching in counseling* (pp. 163–207). Hillsdale: Erlbaum.

Propp, V. (1968). *The morphology of the folktale* (L. Scott, Trans.; 2nd ed.). Austin: University of Texas Press (Original work published 1928).

Ricoeur, P. (1984). *Time and narrative, vol. 1* (K. McLaughlin & D. Pellauer, Trans.). Chicago: University of Chicago Press (original work published 1983).

Ricoeur, P. (1991). *From text to action: essays in hermeneutics. II* (K. Blamey & J.B. Thompson, Trans.). Evanston: Northwestern University Press (Original work published 1986).

Ricoeur, P. (1992). *Oneself as another* (K. Blamey, trans.). Chicago: Chicago University Press (Original work published 1990).

Rosenau, P.M. (1992). *Post-modernism and the social sciences: insights, inroads, and intrusions.* Princeton: Princeton University Press.

Ruth, J.-E. & Öberg, P. (1992). Expressions of aggression in the life stories of aged women. In K. Bjorkqvist & P. Niemela (Eds), *Of mice and women: aspects of female aggression* (pp. 133–146). San Diego: Academic.

Sass, L.A. (1992). The epic of disbelief: the postmodernist turn in contemporary psychoanalysis. In S. Kvale (Ed.), *Psychology and postmodernism* (pp. 166–182). London: Sage.

Schutz, A. & Luckmann, T. (1973). *The structures of the life-world* (R.M. Zaner & H.T. Engelhardt, Jr, Trans.). Evanston: Northwestern University Press (translated from an unpublished manuscript).

Seidman, I.E. (1985). *In the words of the faculty: perspectives on improving teaching and educational quality in community colleges.* San Francisco: Jossey-Bass.

Seidman, I.E. (1991). *Interviewing as qualitative research.* New York: Teachers College Press.

Smith, E.E. (1989). Concepts and indication. In M.I. Posner (Ed.), *Foundations of cognitive science* (pp. 501–526). Cambridge: MIT Press.

Spence, D. (1984). *Narrative truth and historical truth.* New York: Norton.

Spence, D.P. (1986). Narrative smoothing and clinical wisdom. In T.R. Sarbin (Ed.), *Narrative psychology: the storied nature of human conduct* (pp. 211–232). New York: Praeger.

Stake, R.E. (1988). Case study methods in educational research: seeking sweet water. In R.M. Jaeger (Ed.), *Complementary methods for research in education* (pp. 253–300). Washington: American Educational Research Association.

Strauss, A. (1987). *Qualitative analysis for social scientists.* Cambridge: Cambridge University Press.

Strauss, A. & Corbin, J. (1990). *Basics of qualitative research: grounded theory procedures and techniques.* Newbury Park: Sage.

Sutton-Smith, B. (1986). Children's fiction making. In T.R. Sarbin (Ed.), *Narrative psychology: the storied nature of human conduct* (pp. 67–90). New York: Praeger.

Tierney, W.G. (1993). Self and identity in a postmodern world: a life story. In D. McLaughlin & W.G. Tierney (Eds), *Naming silenced lives: personal narratives and processes of educational change* (pp. 119–134). New York: Routledge.

Van Maanen, J. (1988). *Tales of the field: on writing ethnography.* Chicago: University of Chicago Press.

Vanhoozer, K.J. (1991). Philosophical antecedents to Ricoeur's Time and Narrative. In D. Wood (Ed.), *On Paul Ricoeur: narrative and interpretation* (pp. 34–54). London: Routledge.

White, H. (1973). *Metahistory: the historical imagination in nineteenth-century Europe.* Baltimore: Johns Hopkins University Press.

White, H. (1981). The value of narrativity in the representation of reality. In W.J.T. Mitchell (Ed.), *On narrative* (pp. 1–23). Chicago: University of Chicago Press.

White, R.W. (1975). *Lives in progress* (3rd ed.). New York: Holt, Rinehart & Winston.

Young, B. & Tardif, C. (1992). Interviewing: two sides of the story. *International Journal of Qualitative Studies in Education, 5,* 135–145.

Fidelity as a criterion for practicing and evaluating narrative inquiry

DONALD BLUMENFELD-JONES
Arizona State University

"Fidelity" is presented as a criterion for practicing and evaluating narrative inquiry, linking narrative inquiry to both social science and art. "Fidelity" is contrasted with "truth" and characterized as moral in character. "Fidelity" is further characterized as a "betweenness," construed as both intersubjective (obligations between teller and receiver) and as a resonance between the story told and the social and cultural context of a story. Storytelling as an arena of purposeful reconstruction of events on the part of both the teller and the narrative inquirer links narrative inquiry to art making. Using Ricoeur's work on emplotment and Langer's work in aesthetic philosophy, a criterion of "believability" is established. The narrative is believable when it can be credited with conveying, convincingly, that the events occurred and were felt in ways the narrator is asserting. Dilemmas with achieving "fidelity" and aesthetics in narrative inquiry are investigated.

Introduction

Narrative inquiry has become an accepted mode of qualitative research. While it has gained acceptance, its practitioners have not focused upon explicating criteria whereby its quality can be evaluated. This essay is an attempt to develop such criteria. To begin, issues of definition and general qualitative research evaluation need addressing.

A useful definition of narrative inquiry comes from the work of Connelly and Clandinin (1990). They state that narrative inquirers "describe ... lives, collect and tell stories of them, and write narratives of experience" (p. 2). This definition, while sufficiently broad to include many kinds of inquirers (who would differ substantially regarding methods and perspectives while not necessarily subscribing to Clandinin's and Connelly's particular approach), needs more specificity. We can distinguish between "analysis of narratives" and "narrative analysis." The former represents those who analyze the narratives in order to generate themes for further analysis. The latter represents those who focus upon the stories of individuals as story with meaning. It is to this form that this essay is addressed.

The criteria for narrative inquiry cannot be taken wholly from general visions of qualitative research. As Eisenhart and Howe (1992) put it: "The subareas [of a tradition] share some general orientations ... [but] within subareas, researchers make different decisions about the topics of major importance, the primary assumptions, and methodological preferences" (p. 665). Narrative inquiry may be taken as one subarea of qualitative research which, therefore, ought to identify criteria consonant with its purposes.

A special characteristic of narrative inquiry is that it appears to inhabit both social science and artistic spaces. This can be seen by examining ideas from, again, Connelly and Clandinin (1990). They write, "Narrative names the structured quality of experience to be studied, and it names the patterns of inquiry for its study" (p. 2). The elucidation of structures and patterns is a common purpose of interpretive social science practice (i.e. hermeneutic research, phenomenological method, grounded theory, heuristic research). On the other hand, Connelly and Clandinin refer to researchers and the subjects of research as storytellers and characters.

0951-8398/95 $10·00 © 1995 Taylor & Francis Ltd.

These are not accidental metaphors and suggest that narrative researchers might see their inquiry as an aesthetic reconstruction of a person's life with the inquirer acting in a fashion similar to the artist who takes a situation and reconstructs it in order to convey something about it.[1]

The science/art conjunction distinguishes narrative inquiry from other qualitative research types. This can be seen in criteria proposed by Lincoln and Guba (1986) and Eisenhart and Howe (1992). Lincoln and Guba (1986) present two sets of evaluative criteria: trustworthiness and authenticity. Trustworthiness and its subcriteria are characterized as "parallel" to the "conventional paradigm ... using the conventional criteria as analogs or metaphoric counter-parts" (p. 76). They assert that parallelism is a problem in that "[the criteria] deal only with issues that loom important from a positivist construction ... [and] ignore the influence of context" (p. 78). They counterpose this to "authenticity" as a term subsuming a set of "new, embedded, intrinsic naturalistic criteria" (p. 78). Their notion of context appears to be grounded in the "constructions and value structures" (p. 78) of participants, dealing with these through a "fairness" criterion dedicated to "improvement of the individual's (and group's) conscious experiencing of the world" (p. 81) and whether the individual or group is empowered or impoverished by the research. These criteria "are addressed largely to ethical and ideological problems ... confluent with an increasing awareness of the ideology-boundedness of public life and the enculturation processes that serve to empower some social groups and classes and to impoverish others" (p. 83). While the criterion to be explored in this paper will be bound strongly to ethical relationships and be concerned with contextual issues, it will not be bound to issues of individual or group improvement or empowerment. While these may be part of a narrative inquirer's agenda, they are not an absolute necessity for valuing narrative inquiry.

Eisenhart and Howe (1992) promote sets of criteria for establishing the validity of a specific piece of research. "Validity" is a difficulty for narrative inquiry – we might ask what validity has to do with a piece of art. Issues of validity might inhibit the aesthetic reconstruction of a particular life by calling (as Eisenhart and Howe do) for consonance with a particular research tradition. Some art "succeeds" by breaking with tradition, not continuing it. In all fairness, they also note that the question to be addressed determines questions of methodology. This allows us, therefore, to consider that narrative inquiry, by setting out its appropriate questions, will establish particularized criteria, one of which will have to allow for such breakage. But this runs ahead of the development of the criterion.

The positivist dilemma pointed to by Lincoln and Guba (1986) may be avoided by developing a criterion that dialectically[2] conjoins notions of objective truth (conventionally a positivist science value) and subjective interpretation (both part of qualitative inquiry and an aesthetic value). I call this criterion "fidelity." Fidelity itself will be described followed by ideas about artistic practice in relation to fidelity. The discussion concludes by identifying particular issues of a social science character.

Fidelity

I take the concept of fidelity from a statement by Madeleine Grumet (1988) regarding autobiographical research (a form of narrative inquiry): "Fidelity rather than truth is the measure of these tales" (p. 66). In this distinction I take truth to be "what happened in a situation" (the truth of the matter) and fidelity to be "what it means to the teller of the tale" (fidelity to what happened for that person). Truth treats a situation as an object while fidelity is subjective. The object/subject distinction can become a test for the presence of fidelity and a warning for when fidelity is slipping over into truth.

Narrative inquiry may be construed as being, in part, moral in perspective; when the tale teller entrusts his or her tale to a receiver, the worth and dignity of the teller will be preserved. This suggests that fidelity will need moral connections and this appears evident in an examination of the term itself. Dictionary definitions relate fidelity to faithfulness. In one dictionary, fidelity is defined as (a) "faithfulness to duties, obligations, vows, etc." (b) "adherence to truth or fact" and (c) "exactness of reproductive detail" (*Reader's Digest Encyclopedic Dictionary*, 1966, p. 494). In *Webster's*, fidelity is defined as "careful observance of duty, or discharge of obligations" and suggests "fealty" as a prime synonym. *Webster's* asserts that "fidelity implies strict adherence to that which is a matter of faith or of keeping faith, such as one's word, one's friends, one's mate, or the like" (*Webster's New Collegiate Dictionary*, 1956, p. 308). Further, the obligation to keep faith is "a compelling one" (p. 308). One is compelled to act with fidelity by fulfilling a promise or completing an agreement. One feels duty-bound to care for ailing parents, to care for one's children, to help a friend in distress. Duty and obligation are not necessarily onerous as they preserve a relationship sufficiently valuable so that one wishes to fulfill such obligations and duties. This is fidelity in the strong, positive sense.

The other side of fidelity speaks to an "exactness of reproductive detail" (*Reader's Digest Encyclopedic Dictionary*, 1966, p. 494). This suggests an attempt to create a match between the "real" object and the reproduction of the object. This makes of fidelity a form of truth seeking in keeping with positivist science. Positivist scientists understand themselves as attempting to match their models or symbols of a phenomenon with the situation described. The match ought to exist outside the constraints of particular contexts or be a priori. Bohm (Bohm & Peat, 1987), a theoretical physicist, disagrees with this perspective and writes of his experience with physics, "The general spirit was that the main aim of physics is to produce formulae that will correctly predict the results of experiments" (p. 5). Bohm was disturbed by this spirit in which formulae appeared to be the phenomena rather than Bohm's idea that "the thing ... is never exhausted by our concepts" (p. 8). While some contemporary theoretical physicists and chemists have taken up more postmodern concepts which eschew stable truth (Bohm & Peat, 1987; Capra, 1977; Doll, 1988; Einstein & Infeld, 1938), hard, stable truth appears to remain the dominant belief. Given Grumet's (1988) distinction between fidelity and truth, we must be careful to locate the reproductive aspect of fidelity so that it does not slip into such truth.

Grumet (1988) provides one way to avoid such slippage when she quotes William Earle: "Is not one's fidelity to objects really a fidelity to others and oneself about objects?" (p. 199, note 18). In this triangular relationship, a situation attains meaning through interactions between (a) the teller of the narrative, (b) the narrative and its objects, and (c) the receiver of the narrative. This relationship focuses upon the tale and its objects and its personal significance as the object is invested with importance and meaning by both the teller and the receiver. The exactness of reproduction aids in maintaining the relationship as both the teller and the receiver of the narrative and its objects can agree to the quality of fidelity in the new image: "Yes, you seem to have captured what I see in it."[3] This notion of reproduction is both faithful to the object (the narrative and its objects) as it stands and adds to our understanding in that the maker of the image reveals and enables a "subjectivity that is always open to new possibilities of expression and realization" (p. 67). Thus, truth for fidelity is simultaneously factual (that is, reasonably accurate) and a function of perspective (meaningful).

I wish to maintain the notion of "factual," even though "perspective" would seem to displace it; and we will often mistake interpretation for fact. Without a factual base, narrative inquiry would run the danger of wild speculation. To agree to an interpretation, there must be some consensual validation as to the pertinent facts. If an audience member at a concert speaks of "red cars" while the concert contained neither the color red nor cars, then the viewer's response is only minimally based upon the concert and his or her interpretations of specific concerts appear to be weak. For fidelity to be of value, some factual agreement must obtain. On the other hand, while some adults take it as factual that watching violent television nurtures violence in the behavior of children, it is actually interpretive. The child may report that television has no affect on his or her behavior, that his or her violence is due to some other factor. The "fact" that violent television breeds violent children becomes the adult's interpretation by noting similarities between a child's behaviors and what he or she has been watching. The only facts in the case are that the child watches violent television and acts violently. We make sense of the situation through our own imaginative structuring of a set of not necessarily correlated events.

In sum, fidelity in this context becomes: an obligation towards preserving the bonds between the teller and receiver by honoring the self-report of the teller and the obligation of the original teller to be as honest as possible in the telling. The judgment of fidelity depends on at least two people and is established through the perspectives of at least these parties, referenced by "vows," "obligations," or "duties." I characterize this bond as the "betweenness" of the situation.

"Betweenness," like fidelity, has two aspects. It refers not only to the intersubjective bond between original teller and narrative inquirer but also to the perceived interaction of the original teller and the context of the narrative.[4] Here the narrative inquirer must act with fidelity by being true to the situation of the teller by recognizing, constructing, and establishing linkages between events, small and large, immediate and distant, immediate and historical. An attempt at fidelity illuminates the way the world is a web within which actions are performed and motivated and understandings are directed. This is fidelity in a weak sense; if we are attempting to distinguish fidelity from truth, linking individual events to larger social and historical contexts runs the risk of losing the original teller's perspective, thus losing the intersubjective quality of fidelity. This weak sense of fidelity can be subverted only by persevering in the initial betweenness of fidelity – that of "between two individuals" or "parties." This latter bond predicates all others. The fidelity to a situation and its context turns into conventional truth without it.

There are several difficulties here. First, the narrative inquirer must maintain fidelity both toward the story of a person (and what the person makes of his or her story) and toward what that person is unable to articulate about the story and its meanings (the context in which the story exists). Second, what the original teller makes of her or his own story is bounded by her or his purposes in telling that story. This reminds us that even the original teller is also reconstructing the narrative. To make the situation still more complex, the narrative inquirer must remember that she or he has intentions and is reconstructing as well. Narrative inquiry is an artificial endeavor existing within layers of intention and reconstruction. This artificiality brings fidelity and narrative inquiry into the arena of artistic process.

Fidelity and art

Both narrative inquirers and narrative artists attempt to reconceive the world through story. Paul Ricoeur (1975/1977, 1983/1984a, 1983/1984b, 1983/1984c), in elaborating his theory of the relation between time and narrative, provides a perspective on the process of reconception. Ricoeur (1983/1984a) develops the Aristotelian ideas of *muthos* and *mimesis* as central to the creation of stories. A story re-presents reality in the form of a symbol that encapsulates human experience:

> Mimesis establishes precisely the "metaphorical" transposition of the practical field [reality] by the muthos [emplotment] … [and is] a reference to this prior side [reality] of poetic composition. … The meaning of mimetic activity … draws its intelligibility from its mediating function, which leads us from one side of the text [reality] to the other through the power of refiguration. (p. 46)

Mimesis has three aspects. Mimesis$_1$ is prefiguration or the reality which is referenced in the work. Mimesis$_2$ is the creation of the symbol or the configuration of reality via mimesis and muthos [emplotment]. Mimesis$_3$ is refiguration or the act of reading which transforms the symbol or refigured reality into meaning. Muthos may be roughly translated as "emplotment" and the mimesis of mimesis$_2$ may be roughly translated as "imitation." Ricoeur (1983/1984a) understands these two ideas as active "operations the artists uses" (p. 33) and he identifies "narrative in the broad sense … as the 'what' [the emplotment] of mimetic activity" (p. 36). Ricoeur makes emplotment synonymous with narrative. Emplotment is "the active sense of organizing the events into a system" and mimesis is "mimetic activity … in the dynamic sense of making a representation, of a transposition into representative works" (p. 33).

What specifically is emplotment? When we have a "real experience," it has a particular chronological sequencing. The artist's work is to ignore this chronological order so as to invent an order which is true to the mimesis, to the making of a representation. The artist is not being true to the real but to the emplotment of the narrative. Reality does not carry meaning with it. Meaning is derived from reality by this act of ordering. This organization of events does not focus on the temporal character of reality but on its "logical character" (Ricoeur, 1983/1984a, p. 38). In this, Ricoeur points us toward the extreme artificiality of art or at least the profoundly human activity of meaning making.

Logic is central to narrative. Ricoeur (1983/1984a) points out that Aristotle is sharply critical of the notion of "plot" as a series of episodes:

> What [Aristotle] condemns is disconnected episodes. … The key opposition is here: one thing after another [episodic] and one thing because of another [plot]. … One after the other is merely episodic and therefore improbable, one because of the other is a causal sequence and therefore probable. (p. 41)

That the plot is intelligible in a narrative derives from "the connection as such established between the events" (p. 41). "To make up a plot is already to make the intelligible spring from the accidental, the universal from the singular, the necessary or the probable from the episodic" (p. 41). It is this that is meant by "logic."

Ricoeur (1983/1984a) describes the "poetic act … [as being] the triumph of concordance over discordance" (p. 31). By discordance, Ricoeur means the accidental in life and the occurrence of chance within a narrative reflecting the accidental. In art, discordance cannot reign. What is needed in art is "the fusion of the 'paradoxical' and the 'causal' sequence, of surprise and necessity" (p. 43). Emplotment is "concordant discordance" which "constitutes the mediating function of the plot" (p. 66).

> By mediating between the two poles of event [reality] and story [art, narrative], emplotment brings to the paradox [reality] a solution that is the poetic act itself … the story's capacity to be followed. To follow a story is to move forward … under the guidance of an expectation that finds its fulfillment in the "conclusion" of the story. … To understand the story is to understand how and why the successive episodes led to this conclusion, which, far from being foreseeable, must finally be acceptable, as congruent with the episodes brought together by the story. (pp. 66–67)

While we may demur that congruence is the ultimate end of all stories, there is some congruence which must be made between events in order for us to credit a story with the rubric "narrative."

Ricoeur (1983/1984a) claims that the ability of story to be experienced as such is grounded in experience itself. "Experience … [has] an inchoate narrativity … that constitutes a genuine demand for narrative. … I shall not hesitate to speak of a prenarrative quality of experience" (p. 74). Earlier I wrote of "betweenness" in part as the narrative inquirer "recognizing, constructing, and establishing linkages between events, both small and large, immediate and distant, immediate and historical." These contextual events are the prenarrative which lies outside the immediate narrative being told. Ricoeur is worth quoting at length on this point. He writes:

> A judge undertakes to understand a course of actions, a character, by unraveling the tangle of plots the subject is caught up in. The accent here is on "being entangled" ... a verb whose passive voice emphasizes that the story "happens to" someone before anyone tells it. The entanglement seems like the "prehistory" of the told story, whose beginning has to be chosen by the narrator. This "prehistory" of the story is what binds it to a larger whole and gives it a "background." The background is made up of the "living imbrication" of every lived story with every other lived story. Told stories therefore have to "emerge" ... from this background. With this emergence also emerges the implied subject. We may thus say, "the story stands for the person". ... The principal consequence of this existential analysis of human beings as "entangled in stories" is that narrating is a secondary process, that of "the story's becoming known". ... Telling, following, understanding stories is simply the *continuation* of these untold stories. (p. 75)

These "untold stories" which underlie the present story are "always already articulated by signs, rules, and norms" (Ricoeur, 1983/1984a, p. 57). Neither reality nor story lie outside the symbols whereby we represent experience to ourselves. These symbols are culturally based, and so we must understand artistic work as not being the production of a unique, free-willed individual but as a cultural being living in specific ways within cultural bounds. This is not to say that the artist does not turn particularized attention based on specific experience and an individual making of sense but, rather, that sense-making does not float free. I discuss issues of context (prenarrative) after further detailing of the aesthetics of narrative.

Ricoeur asserts that through emplotment reality is redescribed and that this is the power of fictional art. (Ricoeur, 1975/1977) Emplotment requires that the artist intelligently select details of life for re-presentation (mimesis$_2$). Re-presentation does not simply mean reorganizing the details but having in place certain values through which the details are filtered and selected: beliefs about what is important and what is not and ideas about how the juxtaposition of one particular detail with another will produce new understandings. To accomplish the latter, the artist will employ an array of formal operations to produce effects. This intention to produce effects may range from those artists who only hope to stimulate the audience in some way to those who believe that they can plan their art so as to deliver a nearly univocal "reading" of the art.[5] What binds artists together is the employment of common formalistic values that can be seen through a comparison of artistic and scientific activity.

Susanne Langer (1967) has contrasted this activity through a comparison of what is meant in both art and science by the concept of abstraction. She asserts: "Scientific concepts are abstracted from concretely described facts by a sequence of widening generalizations; progressive generalizations systematically pursued can yield all the powerful and rarified abstractions of physics, mathematics, logic" (p. 153). She calls such abstraction "generalizing abstraction" (p. 155). In contrast with science, she notes that art deals with what she terms "presentational abstraction" in which "the artist's most elementary problem is the symbolic transformation of subjectively known realities into objective semblances that are immediately recognized as their expression in sensory appearances" (p. 157). Abstraction in science is the exclusion of particularities for the purposes of prediction and regularity. A general case is presented which subsumes particular cases. Abstraction in art is just the opposite: the inclusion of particularized sensory experience which achieves the status of symbol (as opposed to what Langer calls "ordinary perceptual datum" [p. 179]).

Both scientists and artists produce objects which represent the findings of their investigations. Scientists produce formulae, laws, generalized principles or the like that can be validated by empirical means rather than crediting the belief of the scientists. These objects can be "right" or "wrong." Artists, on the other hand, produce particular, carefully detailed objects which the artist hopes will convey subjective apprehensions through concrete forms. Art objects are neither right nor wrong. They only either do or do not successfully convey some subjective reality that animates the making of the object. For many contemporary artists, it is not important whether or not audiences "get" the particular meaning of a piece. The artist hopes to stimulate in a direction rather than dictate exact interpretations. This, too, distinguishes artists from scientists; scientists prefer more exactness in the meaning of their work.[6] In order for artists to enable audiences to derive meaning from a given work, they must create a piece that appears lifelike. Langer writes about the "as-if" quality of a piece whereby audiences believe that the piece actually contains the subjective apprehensions of the artist rather than being merely a form. The form is transcended in favor of what Langer (1967) terms "physiognomic self-expression" (p. 176): the art symbol appears to be actually feeling the emotion of which the form speaks. Physiognomic self-expression and fidelity are related in that both require the achievement of an empirical exactness of real detail in order to develop the feeling within the form. Exactness and feeling lead toward what I term "believability." Audiences believe that the form conveys, convincingly, that this event occurred and was felt in the way that the artist is asserting. In a similar fashion, Bruner asserts that narrative "would convince us of its lifelikeness, 'rather than its truth,' as argument would" (cited in Willinsky, 1989, p. 259).

To assign believability, audiences must experience a congruence with their own experiences of similar, parallel, or analogous situations. They do not have to derive the same meaning as the artist's original meaning. This is what provides art (and narrative inquiry) with its power of redescription of reality. Beyond such believability, the audience must be able to find that the artist's (or narrative inquirer's) version of reality can usefully or meaningfully redescribe their situations. The audience members may think that the artist (narrative inquirer) is out of touch with reality or simply cannot see other contingencies in the situation. Believability and fidelity ("This situation seems to have happened") need not be damaged by such a judgment ("I would have made a very different interpretation of it").

Achieving fidelity and believability

I develop next some criteria whereby we may judge the adequacy of particular efforts.[7] These criteria are mostly pointed toward the creating of narrative inquiry; they include ideas about the analysis of inquiry data and the presentation of those data. The issues at hand are several: the aesthetic process of selecting salient data from the original data; the way the inquirer's ideas and values recode the data; accounting for how the reader of the research also recodes the data; and, finally, how the inquiry relates to the original story.

Selecting salient data is, of course, both central to the inquiry and difficult to operationalize. In art, the artist must be selective in presenting the characteristics that he or she believes embody the situation in order to convey a specific perspective. These extracts should speak to it richly, functioning, to borrow Clifford Geertz's phrase, as *thick description*. Thick description in art, however, does not necessitate a wealth of words or details (although that may be the case). Rather it is the particularity both of parts and of the relation between parts that is important. Jerome Stolnitz (1960) described this well when he wrote on imitation theories of art:

> Given an object which is a wholly literal recording of some "real life" happenings, or a straightforward pictorial representation of some natural scene: would we be prepared to call

it a "work of fine art"? It is doubtful that we would, unless the object has some reason for being other than its literalness. An exact recording of a prosaic conversation, or a flat, literal photograph taken by an amateur photographer, does not epitomize "fine arts." The "model" must somehow be organized and made significant, and there must be some enhancement of its interest, if the created object is to be one of "fine art." (p. 112)

Narrative inquirers, no less than artists, need to attend to the enhancement of interest if their work is to "speak" of the world which they would portray. Saliency for enhancement may be a predicative criterion for selection.

Selection is not merely a technical issue. The primacy of the inquirer's ideas and values which structure the narrative alter it as well. Willinsky (1989) writes that the inquirer must ask "to what degree the represented is invented, the decoded inevitably recorded" (p. 253). It is not possible to avoid such recoding. Even when the inquirer and the subject are one and the same person, the issue of recoding would still exist. Willinsky (1989) quotes Grumet as saying "telling is an alienation ... telling diminishes the teller" (p. 260). Even to tell your own story is to invent yourself, to select what you will tell, to suppress what you will not tell, to forget altogether what might be of most importance to your listener or even to yourself. How much more so is the alienation when the narrative inquiry is about another. The alienation is twofold: as the subject is diminished by his or her telling, and the narrator further diminishes as she or he selects material.

Recoding, inventing, and diminishing conjoin narrative inquiry and art. As the inquirer builds a picture of the narrative subject's circumstances, he or she invents the situation in order to set the story within a context or against a background from which the narrative may stand out. Returning to Langer (1967), she describes the "gestalt principle" of abstraction in art as "... [the organization of] the impinging sensations spontaneously into large units: the tendency to closure of form, to simplification" (p. 164). The chaos of sensory experience becomes organized into patterns which foreground some moments of an art piece and background others. Artists may attempt to guide the viewer to more narrow interpretations of the art. It would be far too broad to say that all artists utilize this principle (there are innumerable examples of artists who attempt to decenter interpretation so that the meaning possibilities of a work are opened, not narrowed). It is reasonable to assert that audience members simplify by placing accessible parts of a piece into their existing framework in order to assimilate that piece of art. Concern for fidelity in narrative inquiry would need to account for such receiver response.

Artists and narrative inquirers also seek to fashion a work that has "resonance" with the situation under scrutiny. Resonance, like the other terms, has two senses: the sense of a commonality existing between an audience member's life-experience and the art aspect of narrative inquiry being experienced and the sense that the situation depicted resonates with its own context. I discussed this earlier in Ricoeur's (1983/1984a) notion of the "prenarrative quality of experience" (p. 74) in which every lived story is "imbricated ... with every other lived story" (p. 75). This second form of resonance suggests that should an audience member not feel resonance of the first kind, they may find fidelity in (although not necessarily agreement with) the narrative through its contextualization. As Willinsky (1989) puts it, whatever account is made of a situation by the subject has a place in:

> ... a larger, inherited script ... [an effort is needed] to include a theoretical component with a strong dimension, such as Goffman's framing ... [to situate] the individual within the social formations that sustain and give meaning to these personal and practical ways of knowing." (p. 250)

It should be understood that in all cases neither narrative inquiry nor art can capture the "wholeness of the person" or completely account for "a larger, inherited script." Nevertheless, an account must be made of the social embeddedness of the subject and the narrator. This context is not readily apparent. It may only appear in the forms, languages, and absences within the texts of the documents as read by the inquirer or as read by both subject and inquirer (if the subject of the study has access to and takes part in deciphering the meanings of the texts).

Conclusion

Fidelity as a set of emerging criteria for evaluating the quality of a piece of narrative inquiry has a twofold character. First, the inquiry should address a sense of "betweenness," acknowledging and making explicit the bond between the inquirer and the subject *and* between the story and the story's context (with all the complexities the term "context" suggests). Second, there should be "believability" of the work in the story as both a reasonable portrayal of the specific story and as the story "resonates" with the audience's experiences. In addition, the process of both decoding and recoding of the narrative must be included in the account.

I call these "emerging" criteria as opposed to set criteria or firm criteria. Like narrative inquiry itself, they are interpretive criteria. There may be much variation in how the criteria are understood and this could manifest itself in the way a reviewer of a piece of narrative inquiry communicates to the inquirer. Perhaps he or she would be forced to define these terms freshly and speak to the inquirer in terms of rationales and explicated criteria. This would encourage an evaluation situation in which both the reviewer and inquirer would develop new understandings and not merely stand in judgment over one another.

I am arguing for a fluid set of criteria that reflects the fluidity of that which the criteria elucidate, which is rigorous in being well thought-out but which still accounts for individual readings and understandings of both texts and the consciousness of an individual. In short, if narrative inquiry is a type of hermeneutic act, then the criteria which we apply to it also ought to be hermeneutic in character.

There is one last possible criterion that has not been addressed thus far. Considering that there is a possible relationship between narrative inquiry and art, it is reasonable to ask of narrative inquiry whether or not aesthetics ought to be required of, at least, the presentation of such inquiry. Ricoeur (1975/1977) writes of metaphor as a redescription of reality. Donmoyer (1985) writes of inquiry which develops a language. Clandinin (1986) and Ricoeur (1975/1977) write of narrative inquiry and metaphor as heuristic. Narrative art often features a great evocative beauty of language and image (a beauty which draws us in as it transforms our imagination). Focusing upon highly particularized images enables us to imagine the situatedness of the lives being experienced. Art is exemplary of such re-imagining by finding new languages through which to think. These new languages enable the reader to transcend the specificity of the story at hand. For example, in *Death of a Salesman* (Miller, 1957), Willy Loman is an Everyman figure so that others who are not traveling salesmen of a certain era can understand his story. In a more poetic vein, in Tennessee Williams' (1945/1970) *The Glass Menagerie*, Amanda Wingfield is not just a Southern mother of a certain sort, although she is realized in great detail; she becomes a mother in whom many can discover some form of "motherness" with which to relate. Toni Morrison (1970) in *The Bluest Eye* allows us to enter in mysterious ways into the consciousness of Black children in Ohio of a certain era, and yet those children in some ways also become Everychildren. There is a fidelity to these characters that simultaneously focuses upon their situatedness in great detail (exact replication) and delivers them into aspects of our own lives, despite our having not known a traveling salesman or a Southern mother. In one example from the visual arts, Picasso's *Guernica* is a "truth" about war delivered through a collage referencing Spanish themes; yet it is possible, while not being Spanish and not having lived through that war, to gain some understanding of war as an experience. In two examples from dance, Murray Louis's dance, *Calligraph for Martyrs*, tells us something about the fear of nuclear holocaust and also the fear of destruction in general. Phyllis Lamhut's dance, *Passing*, also deals with nuclear death, but in a way that brings us to the numbness of the pain of any dying.

In scholarly writing there also exist possibilities for fidelity couched in aesthetic language. As one example, Julia Kristeva (1986) in "Stabat mater" writes of her experience of motherhood through a novel use, graphically and lexically, of language that is, at least, suggestive of art. The quality of Madeleine Grumet's (1988) writing in *Bitter Milk* may be taken to be extremely artful and not just in the sense of being intellectually masterful.

All of these examples point towards the possibility of a fidelity in both the process and in the presentation of a narrative inquiry which is not bound to standard social science language. Achieving the use of aesthetic language is not a necessary criterion for valuing narrative inquiry, however. My greater concern is with the notion of fidelity rather than particular manifestations of it. I present aesthetics as only one way to achieve fidelity. I would hope that the door can be opened to aesthetic language and other forms of presentation as valued forms of narrative inquiry.

Notes

1. It is the case that many inquirers, both social scientists and artists, engage in a reconstructive process for the purpose of conveying something about a situation. While this might suggest that I have perpetuated an artificial distinction between social science and art, the point here is that the mode of processing and redescribing is sufficiently different to allow such a distinction to stand. The distinction is not artificial even though we might also talk about how scientists and artists are alike (Ghiselin, 1952). Difference and sameness are dialectically related.

2. "Dialectic" is here defined as the binding together of seeming opposites so that they do not have meaning unless so joined. This form of "dialectic" is non-Hegelian in that no resolution of the opposites, in the form of a new synthesis, is offered. Rather, the terms of the dialectic remain both joined and separate. If there is a resolution, it is found only in this paradox.

3. "Receiver," here, means both the researcher and the reader of the research. Thus, agreement as to fidelity refers both to the original telling of the tale by the subject and also to the publishing of the tale by the researcher.

4. An early understanding in the importance of context to story in life-history research was forwarded by John Dollard (1935/1949), especially in the relation between context and individual. As he puts it:

> The culture forms a continuous and connected wrap for the organic life. ... In pure cultural studies ... the organic man [*sic*] has disappeared and only that abstracted portion of him remains that is isolated and identified by the culture pattern. ... The formal view of culture provides an indispensable backdrop ... but via it we do not arrive at meaningful action. (pp. 4–5)

This presents a complex relation between culture and person.

5. In bringing art and narrative inquiry together, I am aware that, conventionally, art is often taken to be abstract (either in the form of the Impressionists, Futurists, Dadaists, Abstract Expressionists, and even the wildly colored Pop Art of the 1960s and 1970s). Narrative inquiry usually appears to be nonabstract, almost representational, as it presents itself as a particularized description of what is there. At the same time, both art and narrative inquiry are associated with being decidedly subjective. The difference between them appears to come down to the level of abstract versus concrete. Is there validity in this distinction? I want to show that even the most "abstract" of art has great kinship with narrative inquiry, so that discussing using art-making creates a valid relationship. Conversely, narrative inquiry is a practice of progressive abstraction rather than a transparent presentation of reality.

6. Today it does appear as if these distinctions are on the wane. The appearance in science of such concepts as "fuzzy logic" and chaos theory indicates the possibility that exactitude is less important than it once was. Nevertheless, there remains a culturally dominant distinction between scientists and artists by virtue of their relative attitudes toward the value of diffuse interpretations. In this sense, it is still valid, generally, to characterize scientists as objectivists and artists as subjectivists.

7. It is not my purpose, however, to delineate highly specific techniques for achieving fidelity and believability. Actual narrative inquiries might, like prose fiction and poetry, take many forms and be created by many different processes. To posit highly particular approaches would suggest that there is only one legitimate form and process and this is not my intent.

References

Bohm, D. & Peat, F.D. (1987). *Science, order, and creativity*. Toronto: Bantam.

Capra, F. (1977). *The Tao of physics*. New York: Bantam.

Clandinin, D.J. (1986). *Classroom practice: teacher images in action*. London: Falmer.

Connelly, F.M. & Clandinin, D.J. (1990). Stories of experience and narrative inquiry. *Educational Researcher, 19(5)*, 2–14.

Doll, W.E. (1988). Curriculum beyond stability: Schon, Prigogine, Piaget. In W.F. Pinar (Ed.), *Contemporary curriculum discourses* (pp. 114–133). Scottsdale, AZ: Gorsuch Scarisbrick.

Dollard, J. (1935/1949). *Criteria for the life history with analyses of six notable documents*. New York: Peter Smith.

Donmoyer, R. (1985, April). *Distinguishing between scientific and humanities-based approaches to qualitative research: a matter of purpose*. Paper presented at annual meeting of the American Educational Research Association, Chicago, Illinois.

Einstein, A. & Infeld, L. (1938). *The evolution of physics from early concepts to relativity and quanta*. New York: Simon & Schuster.

Eisenhart, M.A. & Howe, K.R. (1992). Validity in educational research. In M.D. Lecompte, W.L. Millroy & J. Preissle (Eds.), *The handbook of qualitative research in education* (pp. 643–680). New York: Academic.

Ghiselin, B. (Ed.). (1952). *The creative process, a symposium*. Berkeley: University of California Press.

Grumet, M. (1988). *Bitter milk: women and teaching*. Amherst: University of Massachusetts Press.

Kristeva, J. (1986). Stabat mater. In T. Moi (Ed.), *The Kristeva reader* (pp. 160–186). New York: Columbia University Press.

Langer, S. (1967). *Mind: an essay on human feeling, Vol. 1*. Baltimore: Johns Hopkins University Press.

Lincoln, Y. & Guba, E. (1986). But is it rigorous? Trustworthiness and authenticity in naturalistic evaluation. In D.D. Williams (Ed.), *Naturalistic evaluation* (pp. 73–84). San Francisco: Jossey-Bass.

Miller, A. (1957). Death of a salesman. In Arthur Miller (Ed.), *Arthur Miller's collected plays*, (pp. **??–??**). New York: Viking.

Morrison, T. (1970). *The bluest eye*. New York: Washington Square.

Reader's Digest great encyclopedic dictionary. (1966). Pleasantville, NY: Reader's Digest Association.

Ricoeur, P. (1977). *The rule of metaphor*. (R. Czerny with K. McLaughlin & J. Costello, trans.). Toronto: University of Toronto Press (original work published 1975).

Ricoeur, P. (1984a). *Time and narrative: Vol. 1* (K. McLaughlin & D. Pellauer, trans.). Chicago: University of Chicago Press (original work published 1983).

Ricoeur, P. (1984b). *Time and narrative: Vol. 2* (K. McLaughlin & D. Pellauer, trans.). Chicago: University of Chicago Press (original work published 1983).

Ricoeur, P. (1984c). *Time and narrative: Vol. 3* (K. McLaughlin & D. Pellauer, trans.). Chicago: University of Chicago Press (original work published 1983).

Stolnitz, J. (1960). *Aesthetics and philosophy of art criticism: a critical introduction*. Boston: Houghton Mifflin.

Webster's new collegiate dictionary (1956). Springfield, MA: G. & C. Merriam.

Williams, T. (1945/1970). *The glass menagerie*. New York: Directions.

Willinsky, J. (1989). Getting personal and practical with personal practical knowledge. *Curriculum Inquiry, 19*, 247–264.

Distancing passion: narratives in social science

CATHERINE EMIHOVICH
University at Buffalo, State University of New York

How knowledge is framed determines its importance. This essay explores the use of narratives in social science writing and posits that the way in which academics choose to display their meaning shapes their identity as scholars. The argument that emotion and reason can be linked through narratives is discussed in relation to issues of textual organization, narrative voice, and the politics of metaphor. By using narratives, scholars become storytellers, and the implications of this role with regard to truth value and authenticity of narrative accounts is examined. Becoming comfortable with narrative accounts means accepting the idea that the world has no fixed *rules* for assigning meaning to behavior. The answer to this existential dilemma lies in collaborating with others to build consensus around shared meaning and to ensure the inclusion of multiple voices.

Creating conventions

How shall the social scientist write? James Clifford posed this question in a *New York Times Book Review* (cited in Randall, 1984), and it is not an idle question. How we frame knowledge determines its importance. Writing is one of the primary means by which educated people display their competence in a realm perceived by persons of action to be primarily cerebral. As Vygotsky described it, "Thought undergoes many changes as it turns into speech. It does not merely find expression in speech; it finds its reality and form" (1962, p. 126). For Vygotsky, speech refers not only to talk; Wertsch (1985) noted that his concept of speech refers to the sense we have of language, both oral and written. In a Vygotskian sense, for academicians, writing is one way (some would argue the primary way) we communicate meaning, and meaning itself takes form through language. Social interaction is key, as writer Carlos Fuentes observed, "Nothing is shared in the abstract. Like bread and love, language and ideas are shared with human beings" (1988, p. 100).

The way in which social science writers construct their meaning and then choose a form in which to display it shapes their identity as scholars. Part of the socialization process for novices into a discipline is to understand the conventions of form, to develop a sense of what is appropriate. At the same time, novices struggle to accommodate it to their own personal identities. The tension many initiates experience in the profession revolves around this struggle. I explore here how narratives can help free social scientists from the conventional rhetorical forms that alienate many students, especially disenfranchised students, from their own traditions.[1]

The use of certain rhetorical devices within the narrative tradition can also become a new way of excluding marginalized groups. This issue is especially critical in higher education since we can expect to see more and more students who lack an understanding of the traditions that have shaped the canons of scholarly knowledge. How do we involve our students and restore passion and feeling to scholarship, recognizing the power of subjectivity, without changing the nature of social science knowledge? Or is it the case that the canons should be transformed to incorporate these new perspectives? Others pose different questions: Does subjectivity distort the meaning of what scientific knowledge is?

One way of thinking about this issue is to consider how the writing of scientific results has changed over time. For example, around the turn of this century scientists not only described their results, they also wrote of their false starts and unproductive investigations into phenomena. According to Warman (1910), these writings were transformed by the secretarial staff who edited them to make the scientists appear more omniscient by eliminating errors. The musings of scientific imagination disappeared, to be replaced by an all-knowing sense of purpose and outcome where mistakes were glossed over or hidden from the public's view but with a corresponding loss of style and beauty of expression.

This notion of scientists as omniscient, whose writings are not subject to the same type of literary analysis as are texts produced by humanists and ethnographers, has received sharp criticism from critical theorists such as Stanley Aronowitz (1988). He argues that "science is not free of historical and discursive presuppositions" and that it has "constituted itself as an autonomous power precisely through its convincing demonstration that it is free of such preconditions" (p. 8). He suggests that "our culture requires belief in discourse that it takes outside the universe of social determination" (p. 8). But if we accept Vygotsky's (1962) contention that word meanings are acquired through social interaction, that language and thought are inextricably linked, then it can never be the case that science can stand apart from the discourse structure it uses to communicate results.

The philosophical arguments upon which Aronowitz bases his analysis are drawn primarily from the works of Hagel (Kojève, 1969) and Habermas (1971/1968). These authors posit that there can be no objectivity of thought apart from the language used to create meaning, and that use of a particular discourse structure is always subjectively bound within "webs of meaning," to use Clifford Geertz's (1973, p. 5) apt phrase. How then, do we prevent ourselves from being snared in our own webs, by being forever caught in an endless self-reflectivity of what is being said? How do we give shape to meaning? One way, and I acknowledge it is only one of many possible ways, is to tell stories or create narratives where the purpose is not to relate the *truth* but to come to a sense of shared understanding as to what is *known* (since the word *narrative* is derived from the Latin, *narros*, meaning *to know*). To give shape to this narrative, before moving into the more formal academic arguments about writer subjectivity, a story about a story is presented to illustrate the power of narratives to shape meaning and which challenges the academic conventions of social science writing.

Breaking conventions

The story concerns a talk that was given by Peggy Sanday (1991) at the Ethnography in Education Research Forum at the University of Pennsylvania. To have the story make sense, I need to give some background information about the main character and foreshadow the plot. Professor Sanday is a noted anthropologist most widely known for research on cannibals reported in her book, *Divine hunger: cannibalism as a cultural system* (1986). She had been invited as one of the keynote speakers. Many in the audience knew that the subject of her recent research, which would form the basis of her talk, was on the sensitive issue of a gang rape that had recently taken place in a fraternity at a well-known Eastern university. We filed into the hall after lunch, eagerly anticipating Professor Sanday's "cutting edge" analysis of this issue, using, we assumed, the postmodern rhetorical strategies with which we were all familiar.

Professor Sanday began her talk with her own story of an event that happened when she was a girl of about 14 years of age. She described how much she enjoyed playing basketball with a group of young men in the neighborhood and revealed her pleasure in both observing their physical prowess and feeling her body move to the rhythms of the game. As the hot summer afternoon wore on and the shadows lengthened, she gradually became aware of a subtle shift in the dynamics of the game. As she graphically put it, she was "becoming the ball," and the bumping, pushing, and shoving that are a natural part of the game were no longer random actions but calculated, intended to drive her literally up against the wall where she was then surrounded by all the boys.

At this point in her narrative, as she recounted her terror at being trapped by the boys, the rising tension felt among the audience was palpable. We held our collective breath, each one of us thinking privately "My God, what is she going to say next"? Listening to Peggy talk, I wondered then how many people sat listening as I did – dry mouthed, heart jumping, wondering if we were to be silent witnesses to a wrenching story of the emotional pain of her own gang rape that none of us felt ready to deal with, dismayed that we were even being asked to do so. After all, she was breaking the rules for academic discourse where the mention of highly charged material is not sanctioned, especially not in conference presentations. Fortunately, for her and for us, she broke free from the boys and ran away, with only the searing memory of being prey to mark the experience.

As already noted, Professor Sanday is known for her work among cannibalistic tribes, a topic she has written about in a coolly dispassionate, scientific manner. She even treats it as a dichotomous variable – tribes who eat others vs. those who do not – the ultimate scientific objectivity. Yet, her detached treatment of one form of ritualistic behavior (cannibalism) could not be sustained in the discussion of what could be described by an outsider to this culture as essentially another ritualistic form of behavior among certain groups of young men – gang rape in a fraternity. Her own emotional involvement precluded this and led to a more passionate denunciation of the practice than one would expect from an *objective* social scientist who studies cultural behavior. From this perspective, her story disconcerts us because it presumes scientific objectivity is possible only in cases where one's emotions are not involved.

Ironically, her publisher would not allow her to use this story of her own experience in her book on gang rape, arguing that to do so would render her analysis suspect in the eyes of her colleagues. But Sanday's (1981) gender research in another book suggests one way of understanding violence against women in American culture is that "a focus on the body sometimes reflects a ritual response to physically threatened social boundaries" (p. 91). My initial dismayed reaction to Sanday's story was precisely because it was a painful reminder of every woman's continued vulnerability in a patriarchal culture, a too-imaginative retelling of the vulnerability that women who live in an intellectual, nonphysically threatening environment quite often forget. In this sense, Sanday followed the classic storytelling dictum: "The storyteller takes what she tells from experience – her own or that reported by others. And she in turn makes it the experience of those who are listening to her tale" (Benjamin, 1968, p. 87).[2]

To be an intellectual in a modern university culture is to trade in the value of information; yet, as Benjamin (1968) reminds us:

> The value of information does not survive the moment in which it was new. It lives only at that moment; it has to surrender to it completely and explain itself without losing any time. A story is different. It does not expend itself. It preserves and concentrates its strength and is capable of releasing it even after a long time. (p. 90)

The truth of his assertion is validated in my experience. Sanday's story remains vivid in my memory after the passage of several years; it was the driving force which led to the writing of this essay.

Her talk made a powerful impression on me because of her story. Stories do not pretend to be objective because they deal with emotions, the irrational part of behavior; they tap into the qualities of imagination and fantasy. Maxine Greene (1988) has suggested that "it takes imagination to bring people together in these times in speech and in action, to provoke them to try and understand each other's perspectives, to tap into other's desires, even other's dreams" (p. 55). A literary critic, Benjamin DeMott (1969) described imagination as the ability to construct "the innerness of others' lives" (p. 98). But that ability is precisely what the discourse of scientific objectivity was intended to prevent. The social science world is about distancing passion, of pursuing knowledge without being involved, of holding imagination at bay. The academy is suspicious of the language of the heart because it implies the restoration of feeling in the absence of reason. Yet by distancing passion, academicians become desiccated intellectuals as they master the trick of becoming "self-referential without intimacy – the use of the intellect to divorce self from experience" (Mairs, 1993, p. 26).

I am convinced that emotion and reason can be linked through narratives, and I am not alone in this assertion. Mary Catherine Bateson (1991) offered a succinct comment: "There's no need to drain intelligence out of situations where emotions are important." By using narratives, scholars become storytellers; and in the social sciences, most notably in history and anthropology, there is a pronounced shift to an interpretive perspective. In the field of psychology, Jerome Bruner (1986) and Robert Coles (1989) have paid serious attention to how adults' and children's constructions of narratives reveal the workings of the inner mind. The anthropologist, Clifford Geertz, noted that "analogies drawn from the humanities are coming to play the kind of role in sociological understanding that analogies drawn from the crafts and technologies have played in understanding the physical sciences" (cited in Randall, 1984, p. 31).

In education, Egan (1988) suggested that stories can be used as curriculum content. His book raised the question of whether certain abstract concepts are only accessible through a decontextualized language. Can the same meaning be conveyed through stories where the meaning is implicit and contextualized? Egan suggested that children could acquire the deep meaning of abstract concepts like death, love, honor, and courage (to name a few of the virtues encountered in stories), noting that stories are a timeless human endeavor that have been used by virtually every culture to make sense out of experience and to preserve its meaning for future generations. Shuman (1986) noted that "stories are a way of packaging experience" (p. 20). McKenna (1990) studied returning women's stories of their graduate school experience and found that the women often used a story or metaphor as a way to help themselves make a difficult change in their lives.

McKenna's observation is related to Stantostefano's (1985) assertion that people use metaphors as a way to understand and integrate developmental processes. Lakoff and Johnson (1980) noted that people:

> . . . seek out *personal* metaphors to highlight and make coherent our own pasts, our present activities, and our dreams, hopes, and goals as well. A large part of self-understanding in the search for appropriate personal metaphors that make sense of our lives. (pp. 232–233)

The metaphor as a rhetorical device is as old as the Greeks: Aristotle noted that "midway between the unintelligible and the commonplace, it is a metaphor that produces knowledge" (1946). By using her metaphor of "becoming the ball," Sanday illustrated Geertz's (1973) comment that the "whole point of a semiotic approach to culture is to aid us in gaining access to the conceptual world in which our subjects live so that we can, in some extended sense of the term, converse with them" (p. 24). Better knowledge of how people use stories and metaphors to understand their lives and handle stress would enable social scientists to create meanings that reach people on a more personal level.

Reframing conventions

The issue of using narratives is considerably more complex than just saying scholars should become storytellers. Embedded in Sanday's narrative is the central issue raised in this article: If social scientists choose not to distance passion, what implications does this choice have for their being recognized as scientists? As Van Maanen (1988) states, "Culture is not strictly speaking a scientific object, but is created, as the reader's view of it, by the active construction of a text" (p. 7). Hess (1989) suggested three issues that form the core of ethnographic criticism literature: (a) textual organization, (b) voice, and (c) the politics of metaphor. Using his framework, I question whether social scientists are free to treat empirically derived data from real peoples' lives as *text*, to use emotion in the service of science, and to create narratives that can serve as a means of establishing valid accounts of social reality to inform moral action. I argue that reason and emotion can be fused in narrative inquiry, but it cannot be done without reconsideration of several critical assumptions.

Textual organization

Of the three issues, textual organization is least contested and most easily acquired by novices. According to Van Maanen (1988), ethnographers have three choices: realist tales, confessional tales, and impressionist tales. Realist tales are the ones most familiar in the ethnographic literature. They are the least likely to disconcert positivistically oriented colleagues since the interpretive authority of the researcher is preserved. These tales have four conventions: the absence of the author's voice; a documentary style of reporting with a focus on the minute, mundane details of everyday life; presentation of the natives' point of view with heavy use of quotes and verbatim transcripts; and interpretive omnipotence where the final construction of meaning is left to the author. All of these conventions embody what Hammersley (1991) strongly disputed as the "ethnographic reproduction of reality" (p. 23), a view shared by scholars advocating the postmodern approach.[3]

A second type, the confessional tale, centers on how the fieldworker came to acquire knowledge, built rapport, or encountered hardships. One classic example, *Doing fieldwork* by Rosalie Wax (1971), contains harrowing tales of the travails that she and her husband faced in their various studies that could be used quite easily to discourage novices from pursuing ethnography as a field of study. Another classic example is the book by Powdermaker (1966) who wrote freely of the dilemmas she encountered in four different field sites.[4]

The third type, the impressionist tale, takes the most dramatic license with ethnographic descriptions. (Warning! Since it involves risk, this form is not for novices. It is the form you experiment with when you have tenure.) This form is characterized by a heavy use of stylized rhetoric and literary conventions such as using allegories; writing scripts, including poetry; or using multiple perspectives. Gregory Bateson's (1936) classic study, *Naven*, was ahead of its time for its experimentation with multiple perspectives; a more recent example of interpretive ethnography is Shostak's (1981) study of a !Kung woman. Despite breaking with conventional academic forms in these studies, one device remained constant and unchallenged: the writer's authority to speak for the participants being studied.[5] It is the authority that must be interrogated if narratives are to be used in interpretive research.

Narrative voice and power relations

Brodkey (1987) noted that a distinction needs to be drawn between a narrative point of view, the aspect Van Maanen referred to in describing the different kinds of tales, and narrative voice, which is a central concern in the work of rising scholars from previously marginalized feminist and ethnic groups. The question of whose authority takes precedence in the retelling of stories and the kinds of stories that will be told can be framed from multiple perspectives that range from the simple to the complex. Since it comes down to a question of syntactical forms in the difference between passive and active voice and the use of "I," the simplest perspective can be dealt with easily. Ask yourself why the passive voice and the taboo on the "I" has been so pervasive in academic social science writing. Why did we resort to the clumsy device of saying "one says" or "the author says" instead of "I"? Why wasn't the author's voice acknowledged? Why did we create a fictional persona to state our claim to adding to the knowledge base? One possibility was that the lack of directness allowed the writer to evade responsibility for his or her statements or opinions. If you did not say it, then you could not have been held accountable for the beliefs being expressed. Your disembodied voice as author was no longer connected to your research. Given this model, no wonder many in Sanday's audience were made so uncomfortable by an author's voice where pain and anguish were clearly evident.

A lack of directness has other implications. Academe adheres to the tenet that if meaning becomes too accessible, profundity disappears.[6] In high-stakes academic politics, people judge academic competence in inverse relation to their ability to understand what is said. Graduate school is the means by which students are socialized into using the right jargon, "acquiring the cant" to use Phillips' (1982, p. 176) phrase. Students learn how to embark on programmed writing (first an assertion, then a reference). Students from the underclass[7] are especially vulnerable; the vibrancy and life expressed in their prose is replaced by the sterile prose of academe. Mike Rose (1989), the director of the UCLA writing program for many years, said it well in describing the effect of blind adherence to grammatical rules on marginalized students' writing: "literacy is severed from imagination" (p. 212). In effect, these students experience what Michaels (1991) has called the "dismantling of narrative abilities" (p. 326).

Hymes and Cazden (1980) directly confronted the issue of "storytelling rights" (p. 126) and the use of narratives within the classroom. In their ongoing dialogue, Hymes suggested that students from marginalized social and ethnic groups receive the clear message that their stories do not count, even though:

> Students may come from homes in which narrative is an important way of communicating knowledge. . . . A classroom that excludes narratives may be attempting to teach them both new subject matter and a new mode of learning, perhaps without fully realizing it. (p. 132)

While Sanday's *passion* can be contested from different perspectives, the fact remains that she was a distinguished speaker who had *earned the right* to tell her story by demonstrating mastery of the more distanced forms of social science rhetoric in other contexts. Her story illuminated the complexity of privilege and academic status; could another woman, less well known, have attempted this tale without being negatively perceived as one whose gender-related emotions clouded her objectivity?

An even more complex issue for writers of ethnographic texts is how writing narratives can become a political act since narratives are embedded in a system of social power relations. As E. M. Bruner (1986) noted, "Narrative structures are not only structures of meaning but structures of power as well" (p. 144). The fact that a researcher chooses to do interpretive research plays a central role in the detailing of findings does not preclude problems with narrative voice. Just because people are called informants or participants and not subjects does not mean the researcher has given them voice in the research process. Michelle Fine (1990) described academic research as "ventriloquy – we use others' voices to speak our message." And despite Henry Trueba's assertion that "ethnographers are the conscience of social science" (personal communication, 1993), we too are not free of issues of power and exploitation. The simple fact that we can leave the scene and tell the story places us in a privileged position vis-à-vis our informants.

How much voice do we accord participants, and in what form? Many choices confront the ethnographer. There is a problem of data selection: Who chooses the stories to tell (and the ones to omit); who frames the quotes; and who challenges the researcher's conclusions? Employing the strategy of multiple authorship, of using polyphony, addresses the problem but also raises a new one: Who now is the *true* author of the text; who gets the academic credit? It is not an idle question when the granting of a PhD degree is at stake. While multiple authors have always been present in science, the convention requires that with two or more authors, there should be a seamless presentation with no discernable shift in voice. Even so, during tenure decisions, being first author is better than second; being sole author is best of all. If the informants help shape the text in substantive ways, then how are the boundaries preserved as to who created the knowledge?[8]

The politics of metaphor

Once we decide to take narrative seriously as a means of representing knowledge, the most pressing issue is that of authenticity and, ultimately, of truth value in narratives and in science. What Hess (1989) called the "politics of metaphor" (p. 174) is the key issue in determining how we evaluate the validity of knowledge. For example, does Sanday's metaphor of "becoming the ball" interfere with her ability to write and speak on an issue that affected her so personally; and how will her writing be evaluated by the social science community?

One obstacle that must be confronted is whether social scientists can lay claim to *truth* in the sense that it is interpreted in the natural sciences. Diesing (1991) undertook a comprehensive review of philosophies of science that serve as the epistemological basis for modern social science and concluded that:

> Social science produces a multiple, contradictory truth for our time – that is, a set of diversified perspectives and diagnoses of our changing, tangled, and contradictory society. These truths live on in the practices and understandings of a research community, not in particular laws, and when that community peters out, its truth passes into history along with the society it tried to understand. (p. 364)

If Diesing's assertion is accepted, all that is left is the willingness of a research community to monitor its own practices to ensure authenticity.

Mishler (1990) advocated a similar position, that validation be reformulated as the social construction of knowledge among a community of researchers who use exemplars to establish trustworthiness. From this perspective, the question can be raised as to how far the ethnographic community can stretch ethnographic writing conventions and still accommodate current academic social science standards. Brodkey (1987) suggests that:

> . . . in the course of examining narratives and narrative practices researchers will learn that all narratives, including those deeply embedded in academic discourse, are deeply entailed by disciplinary commitments, their validity limited therefore by other disciplinary interpretations of an experience, and by other experiences. (p. 47)

Her point was echoed by Marshall and Barritt (1990) who argued that the rhetorical choices of social scientists cannot mimic those of the natural sciences since the social world is constituted by human interaction and language that is always grounded in specific cultural contexts. From their perspective, adhering to conventional forms (the politics of citation, the careful use of prior research, the use of statistical rather than narrative data to buttress arguments) loses sight of the fact that all researchers become rhetoricians, whose claims are no more substantive than those who use other rhetorical strategies.

The level on which standards will be maintained is still contested ground. Moving from the passive to the active voice is a relatively simple change in rhetorical level, one that even the American Psychological Association has already sanctioned. An infinitely more complex level concerns the truth value of the research as it is told in narrative format. I am reminded of an anthropology maxim attributed to Sir Edmond Leach, the British anthropologist who lost his field notes during the Second World War in Southeast Asia. Nonetheless, he wrote the classic ethnography, *The Political Systems of Highland Burma*: "The best way to write a compelling ethnography is to lose your field notes" (cited in Shweder, 1986, p. 38). Such a statement casts doubt on the place of narratives in ethnographic scholarship; how do we distinguish ourselves from the novelists who also write compelling tales of others' lives, albeit imagined? Postman (1992) holds the radical view that we cannot, in that:

> Both a social scientist and a novelist give unique interpretations to a set of human events and support their interpretations with examples in various forms. Their interpretations cannot be proved or disproved but will draw their appeal from the power of their language, the depth of their explanations, the relevance of their examples, and the credibility of their themes. And all this has, in both cases, an identifiable moral purpose. (p. 154)

The key, I believe, lies in Postman's last three words, "identifiable moral purpose." In view of this assertion, Clifford's (1986) point concerning truth value that "all constructed truths are made possible by powerful lies of exclusion and rhetoric" becomes relevant (p. 7). In short, the truth exists either because we have excluded the evidence that contradicts our argument, or the truth exists because the style in which we have claimed the truth blinds people to the content that is missing.[9] Ethnographers do have to justify claims of adequacy and plausibility from the perspective that "a plausible account is one that tends to ring true" (Connelly & Clandidin, 1990, p. 8). But who decides that it rings true; even more importantly, in the world of meaning and perception where there are no tangible physical referents to guide us, can the *truth* ever be established? My contention is that while truth cannot be definitively established, social scientists must act as if the world is *real*, or more importantly, as if "the world is more than a text" (Hawkesworth, 1989, p. 555). This position suggests that we need to reflect self-critically on our actions, to examine whether they are consistent with the meaning of theories we have constructed.

The "second coming" of social science narratives

One criticism of the postmodern ethnographic approach is that it is nihilistic and relativistic (Mascia-Lees, Sharpe & Ballerino-Cohen, 1989; Megill, 1985). As Hawkesworth (1989) cogently noted:

> There is an unmistakable escapist tendency in the shift to intertextuality, in the movement from fact to fiction. The abandonment of reason(s) is accompanied by a profound sense of resignation, a nihilistic recognition that there is nothing to do because nothing can be done. (p. 557)

If the position advocated by some writers that all narrative constructions are equally valid is *not* challenged, then new scholars can only compete for the privilege of being recognized as the new authority, replacing the old, but leaving intact structures of power and domination. This prospect is truly nihilistic and bleak since it precludes the possibility that social science can lead to any transformation or revitalization of human behavior or society.

The key for transformation through narrative lies in collaboration, of constantly testing our meaning against that of others, building consensus around shared meaning, and ensuring that as many voices as possible are included. In effect, we need to create what Zagarell (1988) called the "narrative of community" whereby "embracing increasingly heterogeneous visions of the collective path, narrative of community is expanding the story of human connection and [...]"[10] Becoming comfortable with narrative accounts means accepting the idea [...] assigning meaning to behavior. While the rational laws of [...] transcended, the laws governing human interaction are [...] consensus as to what constitutes reality is always in effect. As Maturana (1988) stated:

> We human beings are not rational animals; we are emotional, languaging animals that use the operational coherences of language, through the constitution of rational systems, to explain and justify our actions, while in the process, and without realizing it, we blind ourselves to the emotional grounding of all the rational domains we bring forth. (p. 78)

To end at the point where this essay began, social scientists cannot be discoverers of *true* knowledge like other scientists; as Postman (1992) noted: "Unlike science, social research never discovers anything. It only rediscovers what people once were told and need to be told again" (p. 151). All we have are the stories we write using the methodological tools at our disposal. As scientists, we feel threatened by passion and use our rhetoric to distance it because it reminds us of W. B. Yeats' poem, "The Second Coming": "Things fall apart; the centre cannot hold; mere anarchy is loosed upon the world. . . . The best lack all conviction, while the worst are full of passionate intensity" (Finneran, 1989, p. 187). Sanday's talk was disconcerting because she openly and passionately revealed her emotions and refused to distance her experience in the language of objectivity. She used her passion to frame a sophisticated analysis of how women are devalued by a set of cultural practices she would not, and could not, discount by the prevailing social ethos of "boys will be boys." Strathern (1991) described this technique well: "This is another ethnography for our times, then, simultaneously situating itself within the discourses to which it is a party and retaining the participant's right to passionate criticism" (p. 32).

We need to hear more "passionate criticism," to privilege more writers on the margins to use emotion in the service of rational action, and become a community of writer/scientists to share our insights, where "knowledge and art and caring are intertwined" (Bateson, 1984, p. 216). In Rabinow's (1986) words, we need to become "critical cosmopolitan intellectuals where the ethical is the guiding value" (p. 256). In doing so, we will invert Yeats' lines to reflect the idea that the best are full of passionate conviction, while the worst lack rational intensity. The center of social science will then hold true, and the "rough beast" of uncaring humanity will be kept at bay.

How, then, shall the social scientist write? The following statement is a guide to our existential dilemma of self-producing knowledge in narrative forms to inform our actions:

> How will your work help alter these conditions? . . . The question is this: how will you refuse to let the academy separate the dead from the living, and then, yourselves, declare allegiance to life? As teachers, scholars, and students, how available will you make your own knowledge to others as tools for their liberation? (Russell, 1981, p. 107)

Bateson (1991) concluded that "change can happen if we keep recirculating the visions." If we collaborate in the work of making real to ourselves the "innerness of others' lives" and find ways to restore passion and genuine commitment, the texts we create today will become the blueprints for tomorrow, guiding us to the most critical narrative construction of all, becoming human.

Acknowledgements

This paper is a revised version of a talk presented at the Language, Literacy and Learning Seminar Series, Florida State University, Tallahassee, Florida, November 1991. I wish to acknowledge the comments of Gail Weinstein-Shr and anonymous reviewers of an earlier draft, although the final opinions rendered are my own.

Endnotes

1. The focus here is primarily on elaborated narratives (written accounts that use stories from personal experience) and not on the production of oral narratives. I confine my remarks to social science research where narratives constitute a central role in the analysis.

2. This quote appears verbatim except for the change in pronouns to underscore the point being made.

3. The works by Marcus and Fischer (1986), Clifford and Marcus (1986), and Sanjek (1990) are good sources of postmodern criticism.

4. A burgeoning literature has developed around this issue since the time these authors wrote. A useful source can be found in Smith and Kornblum (1989).

5. A notable and recent exception to this genre is Ruth Behar's (1993) study, *Translated Woman*. Her informant, Esperanza, has full voice in the text and because of her understanding of the shifting boundaries between historical and fictional truth, her "historias" blur the boundaries between fact and fiction in a way that Westerners find difficult to comprehend.

6. Rather surprisingly, what Giroux (1992) has called the "politics of clarity" (p. 219) has generated an acrimonious debate among critical pedagogists. I suggest that Giroux has confused clarity of expression with simplicity of thought. Complex ideas can be presented in clear, compelling prose that empowers people to take action. As an example, Postman and Weingartner (1969) in *Teaching as a Subversive Activity* have a chapter whose pithy title says it all about the purpose of education – "crap detecting" (p. 19).

7. I base this argument on class and not ethnicity because I believe Basil Bernstein (1974) was right in seeing language use as a function of class.

8. The fact that the winner of the 1992 AERA Division D Outstanding Dissertation Award in qualitative research (White, 1991) allowed her informants' voices to speak through separate chapters written by them without further editing suggests that academe is beginning to recognize that multiple voices can indeed shape scholarship.

9. Clifford's statement applies to all forms of social science research, including the one that prides itself most on maintaining standards of scientific objectivity, psychology. I remind readers of the lies of exclusion told by Sir Cyril Burt in his work on purported racial differences in intelligence. Only when Leon Kamin (1975) went to England to see his files was the *truth* revealed that the data did not exist.

10. Although narrative of community was a genre developed in 19th-century literature primarily by women, it did not focus only on the concerns of women nor did it preclude the possibility that male writers could create these narratives as well. By centering narratives within a community, I want to avoid the essentialist argument that "the deployment of a uniquely female knowledge – a knowledge that is intuitive, emotional, engaged, and caring – could save humanity from the dangers of unrestrained masculinity" (Hawkesworth, 1989, p. 543). Both Whyte's (1943) *Street Corner Society* and Peshkin's (1978) *Growing Up American* are good examples of the narrative of community.

References

Aristotle (1946). *Rhetoric, III, 1401b* (R. Roberts, trans.). Oxford: Oxford University Press.
Aronowitz, S. (1988). *Science as power: discourse and ideology in modern society.* Minneapolis: University of Minnesota Press.
Bateson, G. (1936). *Naven.* Cambridge: Cambridge University Press.
Bateson, M.C. (1984). *With a daughter's eye.* New York: Washington Square.
Bateson, M.C. (1991, January). *Keynote address.* Qualitative Research in Education Conference, University of Georgia, Athens.
Behar, R. (1993). *Translated woman.* Boston: Beacon.
Benjamin, W. (1968). *Illuminations.* New York: Harcourt, Brace & World.
Bernstein, B. (1974). *Class, codes and control.* New York: Schocken.
Brodkey, L. (1987). Writing ethnographic narratives. *Written Communication, 4,* 25–50.
Bruner, E.M. (1986). Ethnography as narrative. In V.W. Turner & E.M. Bruner (Eds), *The anthropology of experience* (pp. 139–155). Chicago: University of Illinois Press.
Bruner, J. (1986). *Actual minds, possible worlds.* Cambridge, MA: Harvard University Press.
Clifford, J. (1986). Introduction. In J. Clifford & G.E. Marcus (Eds), *Writing culture: the poetics and politics of ethnography* (pp. 1–26). Berkeley: University of California Press.
Clifford, J. & Marcus, G.E. (Eds). (1986). *Writing culture: the poetics and politics of ethnography.* Berkeley: University of California Press.

Coles, R. (1989). *The call of stories: teaching and the moral imagination.* Boston: Houghton Mifflin.

Connelly, M. & Clandidin, J. (1990). Stories of experience and narrative inquiry. *Educational Researcher, 19(5),* 2–14.

DeMott, B. (1969). *Supergrow: essays and reports on imagining in America.* New York: Dutton.

Diesing, P. (1991). *How does social science work?* Pittsburgh: University of Pittsburgh Press.

Egan, K. (1988). *Primary understanding.* New York: Routledge.

Fine, M. (1990, March). *Ventriloquy, voices, or activism: positioning the politics in our research.* Invited address at the eleventh annual meeting of the Ethnography in Education Research Forum, University of Pennsylvania, Philadelphia.

Finneran, R. (Ed.). (1989). *The collected works of W.B. Yeats.* New York: Macmillan.

Fuentes, C. (1988). How I started to write. In R. Simonson & S. Walker (Eds), *The graywolf annual five: multicultural literacy* (pp. 83–111). St Paul: Graywolf.

Geertz, C. (1973). *The interpretation of cultures.* New York: Basic.

Giroux, H.A. (1992). Language, difference, and curriculum theory: beyond the politics of clarity. *Theory Into Practice, 31,* 219–227.

Greene, M. (1988). What happened to imagination? In K. Egan & D. Nadener (Eds), *Imagination and education* (pp. 45–55). New York: Teachers College Press.

Habermas, J. *Knowledge and human interests* (Shapiro, trans.). Boston: Beacon (original work published 1968).

Hammersley, M. (1991). *What's wrong with ethnography?* London: Routledge.

Hawkesworth, M.E. (1989). Knowers, knowing, known: feminist theory and claims of truth. *Signs: Journal of Women in Culture and Society, 14,* 533–557.

Hess, D.J. (1989). Teaching ethnographic writing: a review essay. *Anthropology and Education Quarterly, 20,* 163–176.

Hymes, D. & Cazden, C. (1980). Narrative thinking and storytelling rights: a folklorist's clue to a critique of education. In D. Hymes (Ed.), *Language in education: ethnolinguistic essays* (pp. 126–138). Washington: Center for Applied Linguistics.

Kojève, A. (1969). *Introduction to the reading of Hegel* (Nichols, trans.). New York: Basic.

Kamin, L.J. (1975). *The science and politics of IQ.* New York: Wiley.

Lakoff, G. & Johnson, M. (1980). *Metaphors we live by.* Chicago: University of Chicago Press.

Mairs, N. (1993, February 25). On depression. *The New York Times Book Review,* 1, 26.

Marcus, G.E. & Fischer, M.J. (1986). *Anthropology as cultural critique.* Chicago: University of Chicago Press.

Marshall, M.J. & Barritt, L.S. (1990). Choices made, worlds created: the rhetoric of *AERJ. American Educational Research Journal, 27,* 589–609.

Mascia-Lees, F.E., Sharpe, P. & Ballerino-Cohen, C. (1989). The postmodern turn in anthropology: cautions from a feminist perspective. *Signs: Journal of Women in Culture and Society, 15,* 7–33.

Maturana, H.R. (1988). Reality: the search for objectivity or the quest for a more compelling argument. *Irish Journal of Psychology, 9,* 25–82.

McKenna, A. (1990). The "talk" of returning women graduate students: an ethnographic study of reality construction. Unpublished doctoral dissertation, Florida State University, Tallahassee.

Megill, A. (1985). *Prophets of extremity: Nietzsche, Heidegger, Foucault, Derrida.* Berkeley: University of California Press.

Michaels, S. (1991). The dismantling of narrative. In A. McCabe & C. Peterson (Eds), *Developing narrative structure* (pp. 303–351). Hillsdale: Erlbaum.

Mishler, E.G. (1990). Validation in inquiry-guided research: the role of exemplars in narrative research. *Harvard Education Review, 60,* 415–442.

Peshkin, A. (1978). *Growing up American.* Chicago: University of Chicago Press.

Phillips, S. (1982). The language socialization of lawyers: acquiring the "cant." In George Spindler (Ed.), *Doing the ethnography of schooling* (pp. 176–209). New York: Holt, Rinehart & Winston.

Postman, N. (1992). *Technopoly: the surrender of culture to technology.* New York: Knopf.

Postman, N. & Weingartner, C. (1969). *Teaching as a subversive activity.* New York: Delacorte.

Powdermaker, H. (1966). *Stranger and friend.* New York: W.W. Norton.

Rabinow, P. (1986). Representations are social facts. In J. Clifford & G.E. Marcus (Eds), *Writing culture* (pp. 234–261). Berkeley: University of California Press.

Randall, F. (1984, January 29). Why scholars become storytellers. *The New York Times Book Review,* 1, 31.

Rose, M. (1989). *Lives on the boundary.* New York: Penguin.

Russell, M. (1981). An open letter to the academy. In *Building theory: essays from Quest, a feminist quarterly* (pp. 101–110). New York: Longman.

Sanday, P. (1981). *Female power and male dominance: on the origins of sexual inequality.* Cambridge: Cambridge University Press.

Sanday, P. (1986). *Divine hunger: cannibalism as a cultural system.* Cambridge: Cambridge University Press.

Sanday, P. (1991). *Invited address.* Twelfth annual meeting of the Ethnography in Education Research Forum, University of Pennsylvania, Philadelphia.

Sanjek, R. (Ed.). (1990). *Fieldnotes: the making of anthropology.* Ithaca: Cornell University Press.

Shostak, M. (1981). *Nisa: the life and words of a !Kung woman.* Cambridge: Harvard University Press.

Shuman, A. (1986). *Story telling rights.* Cambridge: Cambridge University Press.

Shweder, R.A. (1986, September 21). Storytelling among the anthropologists. *The New York Times Book Review,* 1, 38.

Smith, C.D. & Kornblum, W. (Ed.). (1989). *In the field: readings on the field research experience.* New York: Praeger.

Stantostefano, S. (1985). Metaphor: integrating action, fantasy, and language in development. *Imagination, Cognition, & Personality, 4,* 127–146.

Strathern, M. (1991). *Partial connections.* Savage: Rowman & Littlefield.

Trueba, H. (1993) Personal communication. April 13.

Van Maanen, J. (1988). *Tales of the field*. Chicago: University of Chicago Press.

Vygotsky, L.S. (1962). *Thought and language*. Cambridge: MIT Press.

Warman, P.C. (1910). *A plea for better English in science*. Washington: McQueen Press.

Wax, R. (1971). *Doing fieldwork: warnings and advice*. Chicago: University of Chicago Press.

Wertsch, J.V. (1985). *The social formation of mind: a Vygotskian approach*. Cambridge: Cambridge University Press.

White, C.J. (1991). Experiencing upward bound: an interrogation of cultural landscapes. Unpublished doctoral dissertation, University of Illinois, Urbana-Champaign.

Whyte, W.F. (1943). *Street corner society: the social structure of an Italian slum*. Chicago: University of Chicago Press.

Zagarell, S.A. (1988). Narrative of community: the identification of a genre. *Signs: Journal of Women in Culture and Society, 13*, 498–527.

Audience and the politics of narrative

JAN NESPOR
Virginia Tech
LIZ BARBER
Lynchburg College

This paper explores how definitions of audience shape and are shaped by the politics of writing, in particular how the use of narrative in collaboratively constructed texts situates the texts politically. The paper describes the writing of a book of "resistance narratives," jointly co-authored by university-based writers and parents of children with disabilities. The paper is not about the parents' struggles per se, but it is about how those struggles shaped the book and about how audience assumptions shape the collaborative production of a text into a political act within a local setting.

A text's unity lies not in its origin but in its destination. (Roland Barthes, 1977, p. 18)

Composing *with* the people who are part of your research – seeing them as co-authors and part of the audience for the text – is different than writing *about* them for other audiences. The difference is not just in the process of composition – how we talk and write and put the words together in a text – it is in how the practice of composing collaboratively redefines the potential audiences of the work to be produced and positions us in the local setting where we live and where the people we compose with live. Writing with and for people extends and complicates our connections to them; writing about them encapsulates and closes off relationships.

We explore here how the definition of audience shapes the politics of writing, in particular how the use of narrative in collaboratively constructed texts situates the texts politically. With the Popular Memory Group (1982), we think the critical question in writing narrative and oral history is "for whom then, to guide whose practice, is this knowledge intended?" (p. 250). The answer hinges upon "the extent to which such knowledge returns to its originating constituency":

> More commonly the reading constituencies are similar to those for this book: not the popular constituencies themselves but those particular social groupings to which the author now belongs, the more academic or intellectual elements in the professional middle class. (Popular Memory Group, 1982, p. 250)

Academic writing binds together networks of professional power. The question is whether oral history and narrative accounts are simply a different kind of thread or whether they imply a reconfiguration of the traditional networks, a reconfiguration in which social groups previously marginalized and treated as sources of data become central audiences and co-constructors of accounts. We agree in general with the assertion that "an adequate politics of popular memory" must "involve, as one moment, the production and circulation of first accounts with a direct popular authorship" (Popular Memory Group, 1982, p. 251). We think, however, that there are complexities in this process, in the idea of "popular memory" itself.

Our aim is to examine these complexities by looking at our experience composing a text with a group of parents of children with disabilities. When we met them in 1989, their children were segregated from the rest of the school population. We had been drawn into the situation initially to evaluate a technical assistance effort that had been requested by the district administrators who were under state pressure to integrate some of the children into "normal" schools.

What we at first thought would be a short, well-defined effort to document the various stakeholders' perceptions of the inclusion process evolved into a five-year and ongoing relationship with the parents. As soon as we began the work, we discovered ourselves in the middle of an intense struggle between parents and school administrators over special education practices. We were pulled in several directions: the parents and the administrators wanted our work to support their conflicting efforts, while the technical assistance providers wanted us to generate "neutral" data about the other two groups. In the end, for reasons we will touch on later, we devoted much of our time to trying to articulate our ideas about special education in dialog with the parents. One result is a book of "resistance narratives" (Harlow, 1987) we co-authored with them. This paper is not about the parents' struggle per se, but about how that book fits into those struggles; it is about the collaborative production of a text as a political act within a local setting. We need to review first the workings and politics of non-narrative research practices.

Tactics of representation in non-narrative texts

Narratives have always flowed out of research activities. There is, however, an elaborate disciplinary apparatus for condensing and reconstituting those narratives. This apparatus is premised on a particular kind of spatial relationship between researchers and the people and things studied. Research is a way of imposing order on an external world. Researchers go outside their own setting and craft representations that reduce parts of the world to mobile forms (notes, tapes, pictures, numbers) by means of which "information [can be] captured and made to flow from outside to inside" (Rose, 1987, p. 167). Once mobilized, pieces of the world can be carried back to centers (such as universities or corporations), distilled into "coded" categories (Smith, 1987, p. 182), and combined into authoritative statements that allow one to speak *for* and *act upon* the represented portions of the world (Latour, 1987).

All of this results in what Latour (1987) calls a "cascade of re-representation" (p. 241) in which accounts undergo successive simplifications and reductions to progressively more mobile and combinable forms. Interactions and events become transcripts and fieldnotes; these are coded with discursive categories and combined with other accounts and ultimately structured into articles or other texts that move through circuits of presentation and publication. The articles that result then continue along the cascade (in citations and summative quotations) as mobilizations of entire projects (as well as of their authors, who now become citable entities that can be appropriated in support of any number of arguments).

Each cascade takes the work further from the originating site, the people who participated in its production there, and the local sphere of political activity. Narrative accounts are reduced and inserted into the stream of representation and are transformed, within that network, into objects in a debate between researchers from which the producers of the narrative are excluded. The place of publication, the disciplinary lexicon within which narratives are subsumed, and, perhaps less obviously, the use of pseudonyms[1] frames the possible audiences for the text as distant in time and space and thus subverts uses of the account in the site from which it was derived.

Our point is that the network of circulation defines the politics of the text: there are no politics outside the networks. The definition of "audience," the network for which the text is constructed and into which it is introduced, is crucial. There is force in the arguments of literary theorists that the meanings of texts are constructed in the activities of reading and that readers can appropriate unintended meanings or "read against the grain of the text's dominant voice" (Clifford, 1988, p. 53). But there is a risk in such arguments of treating texts as autonomous, free-floating objects and ignoring what Said (1983) calls their "worldliness," the network of "affiliation" (p. 175) that connects texts to the world. Academic texts are always written for specific audiences and circulated through limited-access channels to those audiences.

An increase in the use of "narrative" within a discipline does not, by itself, change this. Reconstructing academic networks to accumulate narratives (instead of, say, counting the distribution of variables) may merely replace one academic élite with another.[2] The point, we would assert, is *not* simply to shift power within academic networks by reconstructing the kinds of representation that flow through them. As Said (1993) argues in a different context, narratives can serve as the tools of both the dominant and the subordinated: "Stories are at the heart of what explorers and novelists say about strange regions of the world; they also become the method colonized people use to assert their own identity and the existence of their own history" (p. xii). One goal of narrative analysis, then, should be to reshape the networks through which knowledge is constructed so that groups previously marginalized and represented by others can become representers of their own experience. This implies a simultaneous redefinition both of authorship and of audience.

Attempting to compose a collaborative text

It follows that collaborative writing does not mean simply training the people with whom one works to do traditional research or getting them to buy into a particular research agenda (or turning oneself into a selected or self-appointed scribe). It means having a dialog about pressing issues. If we want the people with whom we do research to take an interest and active role in it as co-constructors and readers, we have to work with them to acquire shared reasons to *need* the research. Clifford (1988), for example, argues that the goal of "plural authorship that accords to collaborators not merely the status of independent enunciators but that of writers" (p. 51) is Utopian in part because:

> The few recent experiments with multiple-author works appear to require, as an instigating force, the research interest of an ethnographer who in the end assumes an executive, editorial position. The authoritative stance of "giving voice" is not fully transcended. (Clifford, 1988, p. 51)

To the extent that our collaboration with the parents of children with disabilities worked, it was because we were not the lone instigators. The parents had organized themselves in opposition to school district policy the year before we met them. They claimed a stake in our activity from the beginning; they explicitly saw it as a way to strengthen and extend their political voice. Several of them spoke to us of having tried to write about their experiences. We wanted to support their efforts to build a public voice and at the same time explore issues we saw from our standpoint as "outsiders."

Initially those issues revolved around the question of parental attitudes towards inclusion. When we first became involved, we were told by district administrators that the problem was that a number of the parents were strongly opposed to the district's efforts to include their children in regular education classrooms. Such parental opposition would not have been unusual (Taylor & Searl, 1987), but from our first encounter in the setting, a meeting of the district's special education advisory board, we began to see a more complicated scenario. Parents seemed to hold a wide range of opinions on inclusion, some deeply antagonistic, some tentatively supportive; on some issues (such as integrating students with severe and profound disabling conditions), administrators were as resistant to inclusion as any parent.

As we began to interview parents, we saw that to make sense of the situation we needed to understand the recent history of special education in the county. We realized, belatedly, that there were deep tensions underlying the relations between parents and school administrators. The debate over inclusion was not a self-contained event; it was one issue in a long-running struggle over the ends and meanings of special education in the county. The core of disagreement was not about "inclusion" issues per se. Indeed, by 1991, the parents had become the strongest proponents of inclusion and were prodding the now-reluctant administrators for the right to speak about and for students with disabilities.

The issues that came to be central for us were the roles of expertise, language, and knowledge use in political encounters between parents and educational and medical personnel. In particular, we became interested in how the categorization of students' (and parents') competencies were shaped in those encounters. We became participants in a parent support group and witnesses and advisors at IEP (individualized education program) meetings, due process hearings, and meetings between parents and school administrators. This shift in engagement complicated how we thought of our own roles. We did not want to become yet another pair of "experts" reducing parents' experiences to the academic categories of our disciplines (Nespor & Barber, 1991).

Instead, we wanted to frame the situation as an opportunity to help produce a critical analysis of special education from a previously silenced standpoint. Serres (1982) has suggested that there is an essential agonistic quality to dialogue:

> [Dialogue] is a sort of game played by two interlocutors considered as united against the phenomena of interference and confusion, or against individuals with some stake in interrupting communication. . . . *To hold a dialogue is to suppose a third man and to seek to exclude him*; a successful communication is the exclusion of the third man. (Serres, 1982, pp. 66–67)

Teachers, parents, and students have all been "third men" of educational research. They will continue to be so, regardless of how we talk *about* them, until they are allowed into the discussion, not just as "voices" added to the academic debate, but as speakers choosing their audiences, and as powerful audiences themselves to whom other voices are addressed. Again, we make no pretense of having "empowered" the parents. It was precisely because they had already initiated action against administrative policy – and hence had a *need* for knowledge and documentation – that we were able to collaborate with them in studying special education practice in the district. Producing a text out of that study, however, generated special problems that serve as the focus of the remainder of our paper.

Narrative as analysis

We had been invited to attend monthly meetings of a group of activist parents and had been struck with the role that storytelling played in these events, in particular, stories of resistance in which parents dealt with the problems put in front of them, not by their children, but by various professionals. We developed a proposal in which we asked the parents if they would like to collaborate on a book with us. We were trying to write with a group of people, most of whom were not practiced writers. Short of asking the parents to actually write the text, we tried to outline a procedure for composing the book that would give them maximum control over what went into it.[3] The core of the book would be selections from transcripts of interviews that we would conduct with them. We promised to give parents the opportunity to review and revise interview transcripts before we used them, to negotiate the book's chapters before writing, and to revise and edit drafts before they were made public.

Most of the data for the book were taken from some 30 long, open-ended interviews that we conducted with parents, teachers, and school administrators. Instead of following a standardized questioning procedure,[4] we encouraged parents to talk about their experiences dealing with doctors, schools, and other professionals. If they needed more of a frame, we suggested that they talk about their experiences chronologically from the birth of the child or begin with the present situation and move back and forth across the child's life. We asked questions only when we needed to clarify something. Since "interviews" place constraints on how people talk (Briggs, 1986), we also drew on transcripts of several dozen meetings that we attended, participated in, and audiotaped over a two-year period (county special education advisory committee meetings in which several of the parents participated, PTA meetings, "inservices" conducted by the school district for parents and teachers, and notes and audiotapes from parent support group meetings).

We did not try to channel what people said in the interviews into neat categories by asking tightly focused questions, nor did we then "code" their narratives by category or type. Listening to the parents talk about the political and technical intricacies of special education practice convinced us that their narratives should be treated as "perspectives, philosophies, and systems of logic" rather than "unrefined data for the omniscient, powerful stranger [researcher] to interpret" (Gwaltney, 1980, p. xxx). As Rosaldo (1989) puts it: "Rather than being merely ornamental, a dab of local color, protagonists' narratives about their own conduct merit serious attention of social analysis" (p. 142).

We will later qualify this line of argument, suggesting that such narratives have an illocutionary political force. When we first worked through them, however, these ideas brought about a major shift in our thinking. Once we understand ourselves to be members of the same world as our "protagonists," engaged in kindred reflections and analysis of that world, we begin to think of ourselves not so much as "researchers" studying parents but as their co-investigators studying practices of concern to us both. In particular, we shared interests in understanding the origins and dynamics of the conflict between parents and administrators, in how the assessment and categorization of children functioned simultaneously as a medium and a stake in that conflict, and in the question of how change could be brought about in the situation.

This statement may trouble readers who believe that researchers should be detached and uninvolved in the lives of those they study,[5] but that belief was never more than a myth designed to make one "voice" (that of professionals) more authoritative than that of others in society (Latour, 1987; Rosaldo, 1989; Stoller, 1990). To say that parents' remarks are inherently as "analytical" as anything psychologists, researchers, or administrators might say does not privilege parents' voices over others, it simply incorporates them as full members of the conversation. All of the voices – ours, parents', school psychologists', administrators' – animate partial, politicized perspectives. No one is detached or "neutral."

> We begin from where we are. The ethnographic process of inquiry is one of exploring further into those social, political, and economic processes that organize and determine the actual bases of experience of those whose side we have taken. Taking sides, beginning from some position with some concern, does not destroy the "scientific" character of the enterprise. Detachment is not a condition of science. Indeed, in sociology there is no possibility of detachment. We must begin from some position in the world. (Smith, 1987, p. 177)

This is not a mere methodological point (unless we understand "methodology" as a continuation of politics by other means). When school officials or researchers assert that their decisions are grounded in purely "scientific," clinical, technical considerations, they deny that other considerations – which they label political or moral – should be allowed to influence decisions. The argument that "scientific" or "technical" issues can be separated from political or moral issues is one tool special education practitioners (and other bureaucrats and researchers) use to justify and maintain their power over teachers, parents, and students (Biklen, 1988, p. 137).

To dismiss parents' views of their children as intrinsically less analytical or valid than those of school psychologists, or ethnographers for that matter, is an attack on their political rights, an attempt to suppress their vision of the world. As Rosaldo (1989) suggests, the perspectives of members of such groups, no matter how apolitical people like parents might consider themselves, are generally subversive of administrative and bureaucratic definitions of reality:

> Both the content and the idioms of "their" [in this case, the parents'] moral and political assertions will be more subversive than supportive of business as usual. They will neither reinforce nor map onto the terrain of inquiry as "we" [researchers and practitioners] have known it. Narrative analysis told or written from divergent perspectives . . . will not fit together into a unified master summation. . . . [This] makes it imperative to attend with care to what other people are saying, especially if they use unfamiliar idioms and speak to us from socially subordinate positions [which tends to be the position of parents in most school districts]. (Rosaldo, 1989, pp. 147–148)

The parents themselves saw the issue of legitimizing their voice as a key stake in composing the book. The following exchange took place at a dinner meeting to discuss the second draft of the book:

Renata: What I'd like to see this do is really to overcome that barrier between parents and administration. Because we've all encountered a tremendous *wall* between parents and administration. Especially female parents. We're "hysterical," you know, we "don't know what we're talking about," we're just hysterical. Men are taken more seriously, and I don't think that's right.

Kay: Well, to have the assistant superintendent call you up and tell you "you can't get emotional." Well, heck, it's only my child. . . . Just for them to even say something like that to you.

Renata: Or just to dismiss you before you ever walk in the door.

Vivian: Yeah.

Renata: . . . On the bulletin board[6] I put down, if you even mention mainstreaming, much less inclusion, administrators roll their eyes toward the ceiling and it's like, "oh God, here we go again." And this fellow from Texas wrote back and said, yeah, this is because *they* are threatened. We're *not* trying to threaten them. . . . If this book can help to break down some of those barriers and open some of those doors, then my God, it's worth more than its weight in gold.

The problem the two of us from the university faced in assembling the book was how to mobilize the parents' voices without subsuming them within *ours* (or the discursive categories or our disciplines). The crux of this, we discovered, was not just *how* we wrote but who we saw as our *audiences* and how we understood our relation to those audiences. In our discussions, at least three basic audiences had been mentioned: the parents who were involved in composing the book; the professional audience of administrators, teachers, and researchers to whom we were helping parents articulate their analyses; and other parents who might also be involved in the special education system.

Writing for those being written

We had been struck by how, at social occasions and support group meetings, parents shared experiences, established identities, fashioned analyses of events, and suggested strategies of action by telling stories. They clearly saw the book as grounded in these stories – often telling us, when we interviewed them, to collect a particular story from a particular parent. We began to see a major goal of collaboration as the creation of a body of stories to help preserve the collective memory of the parents and reinforce the sense of shared experience uniting them as storytellers.

As parents responded to early drafts of the text, this set of assumptions began to seem more than a little problematic. It became clear that we were ignoring the emotional force of the stories and the storytelling process. We were also interpreting the politics of storytelling too narrowly. We quoted, for example, Milan Kundera's (1980) aphorism that "the struggle of man against power is the struggle of memory against forgetting" (p. 3). But memory – especially of powerlessness and oppression – can be dispiriting and disabling. Commenting on the first draft of the book, Kay Clarke said it was:

> . . . hard for me to go back and read because I realize how there were three years there that were really, really crummy rotten years where I knew something was wrong, but I couldn't say what it was, and I had no idea what to do about it.

Later, at a dinner where we were discussing the book's second draft, other parents made similar points:

> Robin: I think the scary part is actually sitting down and reading [pause] what you've been through. That was scary for me [pause] when I actually sat down and read it [pause] on paper. And trying to articulate to you all what it meant and how I felt. It was really hard. And then to read it was even more difficult for me.
>
> Renata: Well, you relive it.
>
> Vivian: Mm hmm.

No one suggested that painful accounts be excluded from the book, but the discussion reveals some of the complex negotiation of audience involved in the writing. For the two of us, the knowledge that the parents were deeply involved in the construction of the text made us think constantly about how they would judge it. But as we came to realize, the parents did not see *themselves* as a primary audience for the book. They were *still* engaged in ongoing struggles flowing out of the events they spoke of in the book. The past it described was a painful place they continued to fight against. They held on to it to work against it, to separate it from their present experience. Although there was some pleasure for them in seeing their perspectives on past events articulated in a public fashion, for them the main value of reliving those events seemed to lie in what *others* might learn from reading about them. How we and the parents conceptualized those "others" became a key issue in producing the book.

Writing for external audiences

From the start, we all saw administrators, teachers, and researchers in special education as major audiences for the book. We saw the book as a corrective to the literature on parents designed to help school personnel categorize and control them. Those kinds of texts, filled with summary descriptions of faceless, nameless parents reduced to exemplars of attitudinal or psychodynamic categories, flow into a cascade of re-representation designed to allow experts to make decisions about students and parents from a distance. Simply changing the form and dynamics of the text, however, does not necessarily disrupt these power dynamics. Crafting an account with people using their own words and narratives does not automatically get around the problem of writing from a standpoint outside their experience. It is easier than we think to turn narrative analysis into a bureaucratic, academic style that exposes narrators to greater public scrutiny without increasing their public voice.

Although these points may seem obvious to some, we came to understand them only after we had completed two drafts of the book. No one had criticized the first version of the book as being too "academic," but many suggested concrete changes in portions of their narratives we had quoted. For example, this was the response to the second version, which had been significantly altered by the parents' comments:

Vivian: I liked it a lot better than the first draft.
Renata: Yeah, I did too.
Vivian: My feeling was people *would* pick this up and go for it, whereas the other one was sort of more [pause] I'm probably coming at it from the wrong angle, but the other was more clinical. I thought this was a nice combination, I don't know the right word, educationally oriented stuff, research stuff, references to that, a compilation of that. The other seemed to be, I don't know, a little more stilted.
Renata: A little bit slow.
Vivian: Didn't flow as well, yeah.

In fact, we had removed relatively little of the text they had contributed. What had changed between the two versions was the deletion of some quoted material from parents (at their request)[7] and a thorough "cleaning up" of the remaining quotations to render them in a more standard written English prose. While some authors (e.g., Blauner, 1987) worry that such editing distorts what people said, we have come to think the opposite. We originally used quotes that included hesitations, pauses, false starts, and so forth. We now think that far from being markers of "authentic" speech, these are artifacts of interview practices. We were forcing people to talk extensively about complex issues (about which they may not have spoken previously), treating *what* they said as if it somehow represented a trace of some stable internal set of "beliefs,"[8] and treating *how* they said things as reflections of underlying rules and interactional competencies. But it is an arrogance that harks back to the idea of research as an extractive enterprise to act as if only researchers should have rights of revision. The parents edited their texts (adding or deleting portions and, in one case, retyping and revising all of their quoted speech) or asked us to. For example, here is a paragraph transcribed from tape (the words in italics were edited out of the first draft by us):

Then when Annette was born and I was home and had more time, I picked it up again and re-read it. But then so much crap started happening, *you know*. The homebound. When I started off with my book I really wanted it to be a self-help, sort of a how-to, *you know*. But a self-help how-to. But then so much crap started hitting that *it* – my perspective changed. And I couldn't, I just couldn't get back into that mode at all. And it's like R – said, "how do you write it?"

Here is the version rewritten by the parent-author, with complete sentences and clarifying information provided:

Then when Annette was born and I was home and had more time, I picked it up again and re-read it. But by then so much started happening. Karla was on homebound instruction. When I started off with my book I wanted it to be a self-help, sort of a how-to. I really wanted to help other parents of special needs children. I guess I felt I could help smooth out some of those rough spots for them. That in some way it would prevent some of the pain you have to deal with. I don't know. But then so much crap started hitting that my perspective changed. I realized that I didn't have all the answers for myself, much less for anyone else. And I couldn't, I just couldn't get back into that mode at all. And it's like R – said, "how do you write it?"

By privileging versions like the first example above – freezing the parents' narratives in written analogs of spoken forms while writing *our* comments in standard written discourse – we unwittingly recreated the very divisions between ourselves and the parents we had been trying to overcome through collaboration. It is not that we wrote less "academically" in the second version,[9] it is that the parents revised and shaped *their* analyses as *written* texts that flowed more smoothly for the reader and made their analytic points more explicitly. We researcher-writers say of "faithful" transcriptions that "that's the way people really speak" (cf. DeVault, 1990), but that is never completely true. People do not speak on paper. Transcripts are written forms, and when we freeze interview speech into print, we construct those we have talked to as subordinate writers: We make them look ignorant. The parents, commenting on the text, saw this very clearly:

Renata: The only thing, I wish I had spoken more clearly. [Everybody makes noises of assent].

Kay: We said all these "uhs" and "duhs."

Vivian: I have no idea how any of you ever got through a conversation!

Kay: "You know," "you know," "you know."

Renata: You get half-way through a sentence and then you get to this totally opposite subject. It's like "I talk like that??!!" What did I have in that coffee! [laughter] It was embarrassing to read!

. . .

Vivian: Mine was the pits! They couldn't even edit out half of the stuff [laughter]. They tried.

To look "intelligent" to an audience distant in space and time was important to parents because they saw little likelihood of the book having an impact on local special educational practice. The exchange below is from a meeting to discuss the second draft:

Vivian: Well, I think that the other problem is that the people who need to read this book are educators, and we're not just talking this county, we're talking the college teachers of future teachers need to be educated.

Robin: Yeah, I can't see anyone in this county picking this up and looking at it.

Vivian: Yeah, we may never be found out! With their record on not being current on what's out there. [laughter]

. . .

Renata: You don't *want* to introduce it here, because you're *not* going to be successful here with it. You're going to want to take it to another area, where they're going to go "My God, you mean this stuff happens? Read this, you've got to see this." That's when it will filter down.

At the same time, most of the parents still had children in the school district that we were studying. We all had to think through how the book might be read at the local level – not just by administrators but by other parents. This concern raised a variety of issues for us and the parents, issues from the inclusion of specific material to the question of whether parents should mask themselves with pseudonyms or use their names.

Writing for a local audience

The third audience for the book was the teachers and administrators in the local setting. It was not the case, however, that the parents simply wanted to "make their voices heard": they had been making their voices heard often enough in their running battles with administrators over inclusion, testing, and the provision of physical and occupational therapy. Instead, this was a case of attention to a potentially hostile audience. We were all wary of what the political consequences of participating in the book and using real names might be. A fragment of our discussion over dinner about the second draft of the book illustrates this point:

Vivian: We keep waiting for the other shoe to drop. And right now we just got what we'd really like to have, and then the next thing I know I've got to be at a meeting about the book and I mean, oh shit, maybe I shouldn't put my name in the book. And I think, well, that isn't the way I like to do things. So I don't know, but I feel . . .

Joyce: Give it a week, things will be going wrong.

Vivian: Yeah, that's probably good advice.

Joyce: We went through that period when we didn't want to rock the boat, and it didn't last.

Jan: What do you think would bother them [administrators], other than the existence of the book?

Renata: The truth.

Bridget: The truth.

Vivian: The truth.

Kay: The truth, period.

. . .

Jan: We tried to edit out anything that might look out-and-out offensive. [laughter]

Robin: That's why I wasn't in much of it! [laughter]

Jan: . . . Is it possible to publish any of this?

Vivian: Without irritating them? Ahh, I venture to say not. . . . The fact that we may make other people upset should not – I keep *telling* myself – should not [laughing] be the determining force in whether I have my name in the book.

Robin: We have to live with this, I mean, we have to live with these people. We have to continue to work with them. [long pause]

. . .

Liz: Do you think it would do any good to anybody? Let's put it that way, 'cause we're pretty much aware of what some of the risks are. Are there any benefits?

Renata: I think this book is going to do a lot more good than harm, especially on a broader scale. I think we're looking too much at what impact it's going to have on this local area. Forget that. I mean, they can continue to do to us what they've done to us for years, if we allow them to do that. . . . They certainly don't seem to give a flying fig if they upset *me* – why should I care if I upset them? . . .

Bridget: You guys have sat in the room.

Renata: Yeah, you have seen it for yourselves. And they can deny it till they all turn purple and turn over dead, but the facts are there. . . . And it's just like at the school board meeting where Kathleen got up and was totally blasted out of the water,[10] and they [school board members] said, "Oh, no, we don't believe that parents are afraid to speak out." Yes they are! And we're a prime example of this right now. We have spoken out and yet at the same time we are still afraid to speak out and give our names. And I'm really tired of that! So, my own personal opinion is yes, I want my name in there, and let the rocks or chips fall where they may. Probably be rocks, I don't care.

Robin: Boulders is what I was thinking.[11]

It is clear from this conversation that the book and the narratives need to be examined as political acts. These are not just stories *about* politics but "political stories" intended to have effects on real audiences. In part, this is because parents saw themselves *from the beginning* as participants in the composition of the book. "Interviewing" practices usually distort audience definitions. When the people being interviewed do not have any clear idea about what is going to be done with what they say, the interviewer becomes a prime, perhaps *the* primary, audience. The parents we worked with, however, knew as much as we did about the outline of the book and knew they were going to be involved in its writing and editing. As far as they were concerned, their narratives were not neutral recitations of what had happened in the past – *stories about politics* – they were simultaneously *political stories* meant to enroll other parents in activism. Renata Dobbins said:

> The schools are a political game, you know. A dear friend of mine and I had a conversation one day. I was so frustrated about the way things were at [the segregated school] and at the "bull" I seemed to *continually* encounter any time I asked a question, especially if the question was "why?" My friend go so ticked off at me when I told her "it's all politics." "How can the schools be political? I don't understand what you're saying Renata, I mean, that's the dumbest thing I've ever heard."
>
> So then, we had an issue that we wanted to take before the regional board, but I couldn't do it because my child's not covered under the regional umbrella, but my friend's was. I told her, "You need to get on top of this thing, because if you don't, it's going to blow up in your face." So of course, we go down and we talk with [the special education administrators] and we take a tape recorder and of course [they don't] want anything on tape. They convinced my friend to cut it off, which she did. And [the administrator] convinced my friend that no, the regional board was nowhere to take your gripes to. He thought really that this issue could be resolved. He never did diddly-squat. . . . Now my friend calls and says, "I can't believe that I fell for [the special education administrator's] line of crap. He just talked us out of going and that's all he did." And I said, "Didn't I sort of say that? I hate to say it, but didn't I say that when it happened?" . . . You know, you just sort of get bought off enough, and it's just a game; and now she understands that, yes, the school system is political.

Narratives like this one are not referential traces of inner feelings, "beliefs," personal knowledge, or the like. Neither are they mere "analyses," as Rosaldo (1989, p. 142) suggests. (Why should we presume that the people we work with want to be "analysts," like us?) Renata Dobbins' story is about talking to other parents about politics, but it is also a *political* story *addressed* to other parents. It is a narrative to move others in the parents' position towards activism. The emphasis is on illustrating the necessity and possibility of activism. Portrayals that would generate sympathy, pity, or outrage were to be avoided. Kay Clarke, whose son Adam was in an elementary-aged TMH (trainable mentally handicapped) class at the segregated school, articulated this clearly at the beginning of our interview with her:

> There are things that I really wouldn't want somebody else to know – I might sit and tell you, but I wouldn't want everybody to know. I mean, I feel like people would go "oh, poor woman, poor pitiful thing." You know, and I wouldn't want that. . . . We have had literally people who would not have more children because of Adam – they were afraid that they would be faced with something like that. . . . I wouldn't want some new parent reading what I had to say and going, "Well, we might as well throw in the towel now." I just wouldn't want anybody to read anything or hear anything that would make them feel like that.

At issue here is not just an aversion to being pitied by others. If academic writing generally depoliticizes issues by forcing experience into categories or stages of a theory, pathos-generating stories run the risk of depoliticization by making a situation seem so overwhelming that the reader feels helpless to effect change. If there is any consistent theme in our interviews, it is the parents' insistence, exemplified below in comments by George Kent (the father of Susan, an adolescent girl with Down's syndrome) on the necessity of becoming active and fighting for one's child:

> And I went to a few of the meetings, the board meetings, that we attended, and saw how they talked themselves our of some things, talked around some things. It's all politics, or a lot of it, you know, in the upper administrative environment. It's tax dollars and politics is what it is. And we decided that whatever Susan gets we're just going to have to personally make sure that we're there to see that it's put in writing and that it's carried out. You know, it's terrible to mistrust your public school system, but I see no way around it. You can't let them put her on a bus, say, "You're off to school," and let it go at that.

These kinds of comments were not just descriptions; they were prods to get other parents involved in school politics. Our collaboration in the composition of the book was not just a matter of using narrative, allowing spaces for different voices, or writing in a more accessible vocabulary. It was also a matter of engaging with political positions and defining relationships between ourselves, the parents, and the other participants in the local setting.

The problem of conclusions

Those political engagements and relationships are not static. Writing a book grounded in narratives written from the standpoint of the parents helped them construct an identity – "parents of children with disabilities" – that has political consequences. Many of the parents and *their* situations – their children, the district, its problems – were unique and unlike those of others elsewhere.[12] They later saw themselves as belonging to much larger, national and regional communities of parents of children with disabilities. Several joined a major national organization, The Association for Persons with Severe Handicaps; others belong to a facilitated communication support group, started by Bridget, with ties to a major center of innovation, Syracuse University; several formed the core of a parent activist group, now disbanded, that had a major impact on local politics; and Renata, as we saw, explores special education issues on an electronic communication network. From positions of isolation in their confrontations with the school system, the parents came to see themselves as parts of larger, collective actors engaging special education issues on regional, state, and national levels.

These transformations in association, outlook, and activity among the parents cannot be attributed to the book project, though it played a role. They raise a critical problem by reminding us that the lives we describe keep moving beyond the events in the texts. It is possible to forget this point in extractive research where we distance ourselves from the places and people we study. As researchers, our ways of telling stories and putting them together into articles and books seem to push towards endings and conclusions that resolve narratives. Embracing the ideas of dialog and "returning research to its originating constituency" (Popular Memory Group, 1982, p. 250), however, make it difficult to bring collaborative texts to resolutions.

The narratives people tell do not necessarily have clear resolutions. Endings or "conclusions" that resolve problems or complications are standard components of Western narrative, but they are not necessarily characteristic of stories meant to evoke emotion and spur political commitment and action. Instead of having end points, such narratives describe situations as portions of complex journeys that continue to unfold. Their incompleteness and contingency is critical to their meaning. The parent-authors responded to the first draft of the book, for which we had written a short, final, cadenced chapter to frame what we saw as implications of the book for external audiences, with surprise. Vivian told us, "I never expected it to have a conclusion."

The temporal nature of writing differs from the temporality of ongoing political experience. In the time it takes to create a draft of a book, the meaning of the stories that compose it, the lives of its authors, and the stories they would tell to make sense of themselves, change. Written documents segment out strips of experience and freeze them into completed moments. This is a commonplace of non-narrative research; cascades of reduction and re-representation are designed to detach and distance tales from the situations of their telling. A sense of distance allows the analyst to impose resolutions on the events described. Conclusion and resolutions are expected and required by readers who wish to draw implications for policy and practice from the texts. In narrative writing where the narrators are engaged as co-authors, where the texts stay in the contexts of their production, and where the aim is to draw others into collective action in the local setting, the datedness of texts is jarring to those whose experiences they describe. The political relevance of the texts becomes increasingly problematic as their authors' lives flow beyond the boundaries of the settings the texts have described.

In short, texts, authors, and audiences are linked through varying spatial and temporal relationships. To engage politically with all of our relevant audiences, we need to see texts as multiples, not *monographs*, but clusters of many texts. Such texts would be written at different tempos with different participants, some resolving, some contingent, circulating through different networks to different audiences.

Notes

1. Anonymity textually disconnects those described or quoted from their specific positions in the social world. It depoliticizes the research from the point of view of the person(s) masked. Anonymity allows the ethnographers to disengage from the particular struggles described. If you dislodge someone from an identifiable setting, the implication is that they could be anyone, anywhere. Pseudonyms in this sense play a curious counterpoint to the specificity and detail of a narrative case study: They function as membership categorization devices that define the person described as an interchangeable "unit of analysis" of a larger class. Authors treat their pseudonymous characters as specific unique individuals in order to constitute a class of objects (e.g., teachers, parents, students) endowed with specific attributes (e.g., beliefs). Pseudonyms, in this sense, allow a form of bootleg generalization by disconnecting the words quoted from the political struggles of the speakers and position the writer outside those struggles. We do not mean to suggest that pseudonyms should not ever be used. Pseudonyms can be useful for protecting privacy, making it difficult for other people to identify, interact with, or take action against them. The point is that they are neutral devices for protecting privacy; they intersect with fundamental methodological, political, and theoretical concerns (Lincoln, 1990, pp. 279–280).

2. Gates (1992) suggests that critics conflate "what a text *could* mean . . . and . . . what a text *does* mean (the issue of its actual political effectivity). Political criticism usually works by demonstrating the former and insinuating the latter" (p. 183). Similarly, when speaking of writing we often conflate the possible politics of a text (assuming that it would be read by all relevant audiences) with its political uses (its uses by the audiences for whom and to whom it is actually mobilized). Narrative has played a key role in the reappraisal of "research" within academic communities, but any possible role it might have in our relations with nonacademic audiences remains to be constructed.

3. We gave them the option of literally writing portions of the book, and three parents did so.

4. Asking each person a standardized set of questions forces them to fit their experiences into the categories that you have defined prior to the interview (Briggs, 1986; Rose, 1987; Smith, 1987). Needless to say, the interviewer runs the risk of producing a fundamentally distorted view of what life is like for the people being interviewed.

5. Even Rosaldo (1989) qualifies himself by saying that "social thinkers must take other people's narrative analysis *nearly* as seriously as 'we' take our own" (emphasis added). Why only "nearly"? This hesitation seems to undercut the basic argument Rosaldo makes regarding "narrative analysis" (p. 142).

6. Renata is referring to the electronic network "Prodigy."

7. Most of the deletions were of "uhs" and "ahs," ellipses, and so forth. One parent, however, asked us to remove large sections of her narratives because the institutional placement of her child within the local special education setting had changed radically for the better since our interviews. She was afraid of jeopardizing the child's situation.

8. Our recordings of conversations at meetings, at dinner, and so forth, sound nothing like our recordings of interviews. Interviews, even for people who understand them as recognizable speech events, are not proxies for other kinds of speech and do not produce discourse that resembles how people talk outside interviews (cf. Briggs, 1986). To insist on rigorous transcriptions reifies the speech and denies the speakers' rights to revision and reconsideration that we allow ourselves (researchers) as composers of texts.

9. The only reason we try to write "academically" is for the audience of researchers and administrators. Even so, we also try to write in a way that will be accessible to as wide an audience as possible.

10. Over the course of our work with them, the parents became the nucleus of an activist group of parents and children with disabilities (we are also members of the group). The leader of the group, Kathleen, asked for time to make a presentation in the group's name to the school board about special education services in the county. The presentation had a positive tone, emphasizing the values of inclusion, but it also included a critique of the district's methods of writing IEPs. When we arrived at the meeting, we discovered that the usual procedures for getting a place on the agenda had been changed. Instead of having to call in advance, people were allowed to sign up on the spot. Parents of children labeled "learning disabled" had been mobilized, exactly by whom we are not sure. They spoke in great number and at length of the virtues of the school administration and its practice of segregating children with disabilities from the regular population (cf. Coles, 1987, for suggestions why parents might favor having their children labeled "LD"). Some of the LD parents' comments took the form of veiled personal attacks on Kathleen.

11. In the end, about half of the group wanted to use their real names, and half wanted pseudonyms. The obvious problem is that by naming one half we pretty much give away who the other half are. As the quoted conversation makes clear, there was a deeply felt disagreement among parents on this issue. The fact that these parents consciously aligned themselves in a single group did not mean they agreed on all issues. By satisfying one group we undercut the intentions of the other. After going through many drafts using some real names and some pseudonyms, we decided to take the safest course of action to protecting parents, giving all of them pseudonyms.

12. "Our SPH [severely and profoundly handicapped] children are not like other SPH kids" was a typical comment.

References

Barthes, R. (1977). *Image, music, text*. New York: Hill and Wang.

Biklen, D. (1988). The myth of clinical judgment. *Journal of Social Issues, 44*, 127–140.

Blauner, R. (1987). Problems of editing "first-person" sociology. *Qualitative Sociology, 10*, 46–64.

Briggs, C. (1986). *Learning how to ask*. Cambridge: Cambridge University Press.

Clifford, J. (1988). *The predicament of culture*. Cambridge, MA: Harvard University Press.

Coles, G. (1987). *The learning of mystique*. New York: Fawcett Columbine.

DeVault, M. (1990). Talking and listening from women's standpoint: feminist strategies for interviewing and analysis. *Social Problems, 17*, 96–116.

Gates, H.L. (1992). *Loose canons*. New York: Oxford University Press.

Gwaltney, J. (1987). *Drylongso*. New York: Vintage.

Harlow, B. (1980). *Resistance literature*. New York: Methuen.

Kundera, M. (1980). *The book of laughter and forgetting*. Harmondsworth: Penguin.

Latour, B. (1987). *Science in action*. Cambridge, MA: Harvard University Press.

Lincoln, Y. (1990). Toward a categorical imperative for qualitative research. In E. Eisner & A. Peshkin (Eds.), *Qualitative inquiry in education: the continuing debate* (pp. 277–295). New York: Teachers College Press.

Nespor, J., & Barber, L. (1991). The rhetorical construction of the "teacher." *Harvard Educational Review, 61*, 417–433.

Popular Memory Group. (1982). Popular memory: theory, politics, method. In R. Johnson, G. McLennan, B. Schwarz, & D. Sutton (Eds.), *Making histories* (pp. 205–252). Minneapolis: University of Minnesota Press.

Rosaldo, R. (1989). *Culture and truth: the remaking of social analysis*. Boston: Beacon.

Rose, D. (1987). *Black American street life*. Philadelphia: University of Pennsylvania Press.

Said, E. (1983). *The world, the text, and the critic*. Cambridge, MA: Harvard University Press.

Said, E. (1993). *Culture and imperialism*. New York: Knopf.

Serres, M. (1982). *Hermes: literature, science, philosophy*. Baltimore: Johns Hopkins University Press.

Smith, D. (1987). *The everyday world as problematic*. Boston: Northeastern University Press.

Stoller, P. (1990). *The taste of ethnographic things*. Philadelphia: University of Pennsylvania Press.

Taylor, S., & Searl, S. (1987). The disabled in America: history, policy, and trends. In P. Knoblock (Ed.), *Introduction to special education* (pp. 5–64). Boston: Little, Brown.

Persuasive writings, vigilant readings, and reconstructed characters: the paradox of trust in educational storysharing

THOMAS BARONE
Arizona State University

This paper addresses the issue of trust/mistrust in relation to the discourses of educational storytelling. Poststructuralists have highlighted the power relationships embedded within these kinds of discourse. Their recommended attitude is one of suspicion. But the author insists that, like discursive forms of critical science, story genres can sometimes achieve critical significance. That is, stories addressing educational phenomena can promote emancipatory moments within readers and thereby earn their trust. Examples of such moments in the life of the author-as-reader are provided. The author suggests that the integrity of such trustworthy stories be honored by publication in education journals.

> I really am looking for new narratives to replace the old ones. I distrust words and stories
> and yet probably they are what I value most. Paradox rules. (Lynne Tillman, 1991)

Can educational stories[1] be trusted? This may appear to be a curious question in an essay within a volume thematically devoted to stories as forms of educational research. Is this collection itself one signal among many that the educational research community has advanced beyond positivistic anxieties regarding the distorting tendencies within personal accounts? Certainly. Nonetheless, several prominent narrative researchers have suggested caution in trusting stories for reasons that have not occurred to more traditional educational research methodologists. What are they?

The first is that an account may not be phenomenologically truthful. Grumet (1988), for example, described stories as "masks through which we can be seen," and asks about trustworthiness when "every telling is a potential prevarication" (p. 69). Nespor and Barylske (1991) contended that a portrait of oneself will vary with the "specific situation within fields of power, history, and culture" (p. 811).

A second reason cited for not fully trusting story accounts is that they tend to record unmediated experienced phenomena in a superficial manner. For some critics, the superficiality of stories composed in the vernacular bespeaks a lack of penetrating scholarship. Narrative accounts unaccompanied by scholarly analysis are viewed as incapable of advancing knowledge about educational matters. A session at the 1993 Annual Meeting of the American Educational Research Association explored the question of whether case studies of teaching need to be surrounded by theoretical discourse before they are deemed publishable.[2] Indeed, the prevailing vision of what constitutes legitimate scholarship may partially explain the relative scarcity of published examples of autobiographies, biographies, and other fictional and nonfictional stories about schoolpeople written entirely in the vernacular (Barone, 1992). Stories by and about teachers and students in professional journals are nearly always folded within didactic material aimed at extracting scholarly meaning from the accounts.

For other narrativists, a life story unaccompanied by textual analysis exhibits a second deficiency. Stories, this argument goes, may recreate life experiences, but they cannot critically examine the political, cultural, and ideological systems engendering experience. Thus, the story

0951-8398/95 $10·00 © 1995 Taylor & Francis Ltd.

may contain a record of constrained consciousness (Goodson, 1992). For Goodson, life stories are less than "critical" because (unlike many "life histories") they cannot be trusted to challenge stereotypical, taken-for-granted ideas and beliefs or to shed light on the cultural forces conspiring to constrain the awareness of the "self" being described. Some scholars have provided examples of how this perceived failure can be corrected by focusing theoretical lenses on the lived experiences of schoolpeople, lenses crafted within various schools of emancipatory-minded social science, including poststructural literary criticism, neo-Marxism, and feminism. For example, Britzman (1991) presented and analyzed the stories of two student teachers from feminist, deconstructivist, and critical ethnographic perspectives. McLaren (1989) brought Marxist/critical theory to bear on a literary-style journal of his own teaching experiences.

In this essay, I revisit the issue of trust/mistrust of storytelling forms of discourse. I concede that a story never tells the absolute truth. Since the onset of deconstructivism, who can believe that any text does? Life stories are now suspect because of the power relationships discovered hidden in their authorial baggage. However, I contend that stories about schoolpeople can achieve a degree of critical significance. Just as discourse partaking of a critical science format and patois can promote emancipatory moments, so can story genres (biography, autobiography, literary journalism, and the novel) that are derived from literary forms and that honor the norms of everyday speech. I further argue that if educational stories are to reach maturity as a form of educational research, some of the most insightful among them must be left, at least momentarily, unaccompanied by critique or theory. To that end, I identify examples of literary style with emancipatory potential. My goal is to generate dialogue on what I term *emancipatory educational storysharing.*

I begin with an important reminder from the schools of literary criticism known as *reader-response* and *poststructuralism.* Critics in these fields have taught us no longer to view the literary text, the story, as a noun, a thing, whether a reified textual object or a piece of ghostly "mental furniture" (Ryle, 1949) in the mind of the writer or reader. They have persuaded us to regard it, instead, as a verb, as an activity, a literary experience characterized by a process of construction (by the writer) and of deconstruction and reconstruction (by the reader). The reality of the text, therefore, resides within the interaction between the writer and the reader, who, Polkinghorne (1988) noted, "function as parts in a whole communication event that occurs when the created narrative text is taken to be understood by different individuals" (p. 99).

Many deconstructivists view authoring and reading, in one sense, as identical activities. Writers, for example, must continuously read what they have written in order to proceed; we know that writing is silent dialogue. Readers become writers, as Agger (1990) has expressed it, when they read "strongly . . . engag[ing] dialogically with texts and thus remak[ing] them and the world to which they are an address" (p. 178). Furthermore, Bakhtin (1981) has introduced a third set of agents into the dialogue. These are the characters constructed by the author and reconstructed by the readers. For Bakhtin, many literary texts are a dialogue exchange between a multiplicity of voices speaking simultaneously (Holquist, 1990).

Each utterance within a dialogic exchange, moreover, should not be viewed as the exertion of the private will of an existential isolate operating within a cultural vacuum. It is an action that is historically contingent, never impervious to social conditions within a specific culture and time. To inquire, therefore, into the nature of particular stories about schooling is not to examine the qualities of textual objects but to consider attributes, including the power relationships, that adhere to the engagements within which stories are written and read. Indeed, I would like to distinguish between the activities of composing stories and of reading them in terms of the *primary attitudes* adopted by writers and readers, and the stances they take vis-à-vis the persons or characters portrayed in the stories.

Specifically, I propose that inevitably associated with the act of writing is the attitude of *persuasiveness*. When the act is a literary one, the form of persuasion can be identified as not argumentative or declarative but artistic. Moreover, since an important intention of the writer is indeed the intention to persuade, then the corresponding stance of the storyreader is understandably one of *vigilance* against abuse of authorial power. Writers and readers of narrative can also occasionally share a mutual aim in their textual activity. This is the aim of securing power for the characters whose stories they choose to craft and remake. Pursuance of this common goal can lead to dialogue in which mistrustful, writer-versus-reader antagonisms are temporarily suspended, as all agents conspire within an emancipatory moment.

Artfully persuasive storytellers

Within modern western culture, authors of texts have traditionally assumed a position of privilege, with special access to supposedly objective (and therefore politically neutral) truth, reason, and virtue. Their agenda has been to enlighten, educate, and perhaps even to instill moral values in their readers. The persuasive power of the modernist author resided in the assumption that there existed a single, literal reading of a textual object, the one intended by the author. As Rosenau (1992) put it:

> The modern author in society is a "legislator," defined as a specialist, a manager, a professional, an intellectual, or an educator . . . they "know" and "decide things" by weighing up the positive and negative and determining what is "true." [They] arbitrate in the sense of choosing between opposing points of view in controversy. What they select becomes "correct and binding." (Bauman, 1987, p. 27)

Part of the postmodern intellectual attitude is a repudiation of the modernist notion of textual authorship. An author may no longer claim to provide universal truth as a morally or politically neutral translation of reality. The act of authoring is now exposed as arising from within a peculiar perspective bound to issues of personal meaning, history, and power. Having listened to Barthes' (1977) proclamation of the "death" of the modernist author, the black South African, Zoe Wicomb (1991), has celebrated her rebirth as a *writer*; "As a writer [unlike an author] I do not have an agenda [in the sense of a list of things to accomplish]. But like everyone else I write from a political position" (p. 14).

The realization that the creation of story narrative is indeed political is implicit in the work of Nespor and Barylske (1991). Using a metaphor or reification, these authors described story narratives as *representational technologies*, tools or "devices tied to specific cultural uses" (p. 807). When, for example, teachers tell stories about themselves, they are not revealing or expressing, but crafting and constructing, those "selves." Nespor and Barylske (1991) elaborated by quoting Kondo (1990):

> Rather than bounded, essential entities, replete with a unitary substance and consciousness, identities become nodal points repositioned in different contexts. Selves, in this view, can be seen as rhetorical figures and performative assertions enacted in specific situations within fields of power, history, and culture. (cited in Nespor & Barylske, 1992, p. 811)

Similarly, the situated self, the persona constructed in the act of writing a story, can be viewed as a rhetorical figure employed in the interests of the writer. We may recognize this move toward regarding the devices of language as tools for constructing our views of "reality" as Wittgensteinian. Wittgenstein (1953/1968) reminded us that when we choose to employ alternative grammars and vocabularies, we are choosing to alter that reality. Rorty (1989) underscored the importance of using this redescriptive power of language to make new and different things possible and important. We must employ alternative descriptions of phenomena for the purpose of tempting others to accept and act upon those redescriptions of our own or other "selves" (Rorty, 1989, p. 41). Moreover, as Rorty noted, the devices of the storyteller, whether as ethnographer, journalist, autobiographer, dramatist, or novelist, are well suited for creating these powerful redescriptions.

One of these devices is the story form. The powerful allure of a format that invites the reader to join in solving a human problem, followed by an accumulation of meaning as the plot unfolds, and the relaxation of tension in a resolution of the central dilemma is well known not only to aestheticians, but also to consumers of novels, dramas, short stories, biographies, and autobiographies. Because its powerful formal properties distort reality, story narrative is *more* suspect than other forms of discourse. As Holquist (1990) put it,

> In a literary text, the normal activity of perception, of giving order to chaos, is performed to a heightened degree. . . . Every time we give order to the world: every time we write or read a literary text we give the greatest degree of (possible) order to the world. (p. 85)

Elegantly structured "high literature" prized by formalists often appeared too stunningly beautiful to be marred by acts of substantive criticism. Some poststructuralists, on the other hand, have championed stories that, even as they "sell" their redescriptions, invite discourse and critique rather than squelch it. These stories achieve this quality through rhetorical strategies that are distinct from (and at their best more delicate and indirect than) the tactics associated with other discursive forms. What are some of these strategies?

The human dilemma around which a story plot is erected is introduced within the context of what Iser (1974) called a *virtual world* (p. 42). The writer entices the reader into living vicariously within this hypothetical world, whether "fictional" or a version of actual events fashioned by the writer. Within the storysharing contract, the reader is asked to refrain from thinking of this storied world as a mirror image of reality, a literal construal of events. Instead, the reader is encouraged to travel outward into the hypothetical realm, although not to remain adrift in some unreal "aesthetic remove." The reader is offered a configuration of lived phenomena sufficiently distanced from present realities to stand against, and thus comment upon, the life world of the reader. In this manner "we [readers] may come to notice," as Rorty (1989) suggested, "what we ourselves have been doing" (p. 141), or (I would add) what is being done to us.

This realization can be dangerous, transgressive, and disruptive of our comfortable views of the world (Foucault, 1977). Storytellers can entice some readers into reconsidering comfortable attitudes and values and others into affirming latent perspectives not sanctioned by the dominant culture. The act of writing an artfully persuasive *educational* story is one with the potential for luring readers into reconstructing the selves of schoolpeople or into rethinking their own selves and situations as educators. For this invitation to be effective, the storyteller must maintain a delicate balance between two countervailing tendencies. If the writer is to comment persuasively upon the nearby world, she or he must be credible, offering observations that do not stray far afield from the lived experiences of the reader. The writer must strive for what Bruner (1987) called *verisimilitude* (p. 11), detailing familiar minutiae of daily life as lived within a particular moment of history and societal context. This quality implies a careful scrutinizing of the empirical world by the writer. On the other hand, the reader is coaxed into participating in the imaginative construction of literary reality through carefully positioned *blanks* (Iser, 1974, p. 113) in the writing. These blanks are pauses that the active reader must fill with personal meaning gathered from outside the text. They foster a kind of indeterminacy, an ambiguity of meaning that distinguishes literary activity from propaganda and other didacticisms.

The aim of storytellers therefore is not to prompt a single, closed, convergent reading but to persuade readers to contribute answers to the dilemmas they pose. For Bakhtin (1981), acts of writing that invite readers into this kind of dialogue possess the attribute of *novelness* (cited in

Holquist, 1990, p. 84). Novelness (often found in literature but not exclusively in novels) adheres to that body of utterances that are least reductive of variety for through it a multiplicity of voices – readers, writers, characters – offer varied interpretations of phenomena. The invention of the novel resulted in the demise of two myths: "the myth of language that presumes to be the only language, and the myth of a language that presumes to be completely unified" (Bakhtin, 1981, p. 68).

Of course, not all acts of storytelling possess novelness. Those that do not recognize change or that suppress diversity (for example, Socialist Realist literature) belong, according to Bakhtin (1981), to the genre of the *epic*: "The epic world is constructed in the zone of an absolute, distanced image, beyond the sphere of possible contact with the developing, incomplete and therefore re-thinking and re-evaluating present" (p. 17). Like most forms of non-literary discourse, epic writing yields *declarative texts* (Belsey, 1980, p. 91), texts meant to impart knowledge and thus to shut out other voices, to limit interpretive options. Epic writing, in Iser's (1974) lingo, is devoid of gaps to be filled in by the reader. An example of educational storytelling that is epic and declarative is the kind imagined by Berliner (1992). Berliner suggested that stories peopled with teachers and students be composed and used to explicate and illustrate findings previously derived and legitimized through research strategies based on the "hard sciences."

The declarative author-persuader, therefore, seeks direct control over the interpretations placed upon the text in the act of reading; the artful writer-persuader understands the necessity of relinquishing control, of allowing readers the freedom to interpret and evaluate the text from their unique vantage points. In other words, the writer grants to the reader a greater degree of *trust*. But such generosity is, alas, sometimes beyond the capacity of even (because of their fervid dedication to an agenda) the most emancipatory-minded writers. Indeed, a desire for control may partially account for the penchant of educational narrative researchers for covering exposed stories with blankets of didactic analysis. Consider, for example, this account (in Lancy, 1993) of the decision by McLaren, while writing *Life in Schools*, to augment his narrative with theory:

> McLaren (1989) . . . had doubts about how his journal was being interpreted: "I ran the risk of allowing readers to reinforce their stereotypes of what schooling was like in the 'blackboard jungle' " (p. ix). Hence, he turns his (auto)biography into a case study by incorporating it into an overview of Marxist/critical theory. . . . So . . . instead of the "interpretations being as numerous as readers," McLaren tells us how the journal *should* be interpreted. (Lancy, 1993, p. 182)

McLaren apparently assumed that the only way to lead his readers away from a state of restrained consciousness was to persuade them declaratively to view his characters from his own preferred perspective. Other emancipatory-minded writers, those more trusting of their readers, offer "novelness." They write, as Wicomb (1991) suggested, from an obvious political perspective but without an agenda, and still succeed in (artfully) persuading readers through narrative unadorned by declarative critique either to question stereotypical notions about the story's characters; or, paraphrasing hooks (1991), to put together the bits and pieces and see anew one's own self as a whole being. To elaborate on this point, I invite these characters of the storyteller into our discussion.

Story characters as reconstructed selves

About whose "selves" does the storyteller speak and the reader read? And why those particular "selves"? One set of answers can be found in the works of Richard Rorty (1989) and Clifford Geertz (1988). These writers emphasize the generation of empathic identification between society's strangers. Rorty expressed a need for powerful redescriptions of certain "selves" with whom it is difficult to feel a sense of human solidarity, "selves" looked upon as aliens who live outside the range of "us." For example, the technocratic superstructure of schooling institutions ensures that teachers, administrators, and their distanced and bewildering students are included in this list of existential foreigners. Following Rorty's view, sharing vivid depictions of their *modus vivendi* may serve to reduce this alienation among schoolpeople and with those outside the school. This humanistic goal of storytelling seems congruent with Geertz's (1988) hopes for the future of ethnography:

> The next necessary thing is to enlarge the possibility of intelligible discourse between people quite different from one another in interest, outlook, wealth, and power, and yet contained in a world where, tumbled as they are into endless connection, it is increasingly difficult to get out of each other's way. (Geertz, 1988, p. 147)

For some story readers and writers, however, solidarity and empathy are not enough. Keenly disturbed by a maldistribution of power, emancipatory-minded storytellers and readers focus on members of groups who have been disenfranchised and disempowered.[3] These storytellers aspire, as hooks (1991) suggested, to provide more than "chronicles of pain," for such "colorful spectacles" can easily be appropriated "to keep in place existing structures of domination" (p. 59). They aim to do more than merely "converse across societal lines" (Geertz, 1988, p. 147), especially when those lines serve to demarcate the boundaries between the powerful and the powerless. Instead, they hope subtly to persuade readers to ask questions about the interests served by these lines and about the necessity of their existence.

In Habermasian terms, understanding within the worldview of characters yields knowledge in the *practical* domain (Habermas, 1972). While such knowledge may facilitate social integration, these understandings are reached in the context of the limited state of social development at the time (Bredo & Feinberg, 1982). No consideration is given to the adequacy of these understandings in terms of broader interests of human development. This is not desirable within "openly ideological" (Lather, 1986) critical science nor within emancipatory-minded literature. Although these two approaches to socially conscientious inquiry honor different research protocols and rhetorical strategies, their primary interest is identical: namely, the general human interest of emancipation through the transformation of an unjust social system into one that is more democratic.

In order to accomplish this emancipatory goal, the writer cannot portray the self as operating within a moral and political vacuum. Instead, linkages must be established "between the structural dynamics of class, race [gender-based forms of hegemony], and the projects of human agents embedded in these historically constituted structures" (Sullivan, 1984, p. 124). Indeed, emancipatory-minded storytellers operate from the premise that these debilitating structures invade and, to some degree, condition the self. They must therefore be exposed if an alternate conception of the self is to be realized.

But what is the sociopolitical position of these selves vis-à-vis the writer? Rorty (1989) recommends a tradition of storytelling identified by Sartre (1948/1949). *Committed literature* (or *littérature engagée*) consists of stories told by privileged writers on behalf of members of oppressed classes, those who have been robbed of their voices and cannot (yet) speak for themselves. Dedicated to the fundamental project of power redistribution, socially committed writers choose as their primary focus issues of social justice, and, as their overriding goal, reader action toward enfranchising the disenfranchised. Rorty (as well as Sartre) identified examples of prominent writers outside the field of education – Charles Dickens, Victor Hugo, John Steinbeck, Upton Sinclair, Nadine Gordimer – who as members of privileged groups have published stories of oppressed and marginalized characters. In the educational sphere, one may consider works by Kozol (1991), Sparkes (1994), and Barone (1989).

Sparkes (1994) and others have offered justifications for acts of writing that cross over social boundaries of race, class, gender, and/or sexual orientation. These justifications include: (a) people who hold advantaged positions can more effectively challenge their privileged peers on behalf of the less privileged; (b) self-studies by members of marginalized groups may be coated with self-protective ideology (and therefore phenomenologically untrustworthy); (c) a vulnerable member of a marginalized community may not as yet possess the resources (time, interest, cultural capital) for telling her or his own story; and/or (d) the stories may reflect false consciousness (and therefore be politically untrustworthy). Why, advocates of committed literature ask, should we invest our trust in autobiographies of the downtrodden anymore than in tales about their lives told by empathic, but critical, privileged researchers? There is, moreover, Bakhtin's (1981) point that boundaries between selves are illusory, that there are no stable identities, and so we all inevitably speak in many possible voices, for ourselves and for each other. Fine (1992) has similarly cautioned against a romancing of oppressed selves as uncontaminated by dominant perspectives. No one, in other words, is sole proprietor of her or his own story.

In our postmodern age, these justifications require highlighting, for the weight of the *Zeitgeist* (Bakhtin and others notwithstanding) leans against writers who presume to tell the stories of other kinds of people. The thrust of the counterargument is seen in a quote from Owens (1989): "Perhaps it is in [the] project of learning how to represent *ourselves* – how to speak *to*, rather than for or about, others – that the possibility of a global culture resides" (p. 89). *Narratives of struggle* is the term hooks (1991) has used to describe an alternative tradition of emancipatory-minded stories, stories in which the writer speaks autobiographically as a member of an oppressed group. The selves that these narrators revisit are their own, or those of members within their own oppressed category of race, ethnicity, class, gender, or sexual orientation. The self-redescriptions, however, point in a specific political direction, for they arise out of a "coming to consciousness in the context of a concrete experimental struggle for self-actualization and collective . . . self-determination. . . . [These writers] enrich resistance struggles" (hooks, 1991, p. 54) as they, in a gesture that is simultaneously literary and liberatory, imagine their oppressed selves otherwise. Narratives of struggle include (among many) El Salvadoran writer Manlio Argueta's (1980/1983) *One Day of Life*, Toni Morrison's (1970) *The Bluest Eye*, and Richard Wright's (1945) *Black Boy*. Two examples from education are (auto)biographical accounts: Mike Rose's (1989) *Lives on the Boundary*, and Basil Johnston's (1988) *Indian School Days*.

My argument is for catholicity: I see a need for both socially committed literature and stories of struggle in the future of educational narrative research. Effective emancipatory-minded storytellers within each of these traditions seek to demystify and transform facets of the selves of the disenfranchised. Whether a compassionate, committed, observant stranger, or someone less privileged who comprehends and critiques the nature of the sociopolitical web that constrains her or him, or (as Bakhtin and others would prefer) a person who is an amalgam of privilege and oppression, an emancipatory-minded storyteller wrestles with a paradox: *She or he must trust her or his readers, grant them interpretive space, even as she or he artfully persuades them to reflect critically upon and reconstruct the selves of particular characters.* It is to the attitude assumed by the reader in the dialogue that we now turn.

Vigilant readings and emancipatory moments

The varied descriptions of writers of emancipatory-minded stories also apply to readers. Readers who identify with an oppressed group may achieve a unique outcome through reading about rhetorical figures who are metaphors for themselves. Self-re-cognition may result in an imaginative naming of one's condition. Such readings may also promote a previously absent sense of collectivity, an awareness of the presence of others whose life stories overlap with those of the reader (Richardson, 1990).

Readers within privileged groups may, on the other hand, be disturbed to find that their narrow interests are challenged. Persuaded to divert their eyes no longer, they may recognize their implication in an unjust system and feel compelled to "take stock of their responsibilities" (Sartre, 1948/1949, p. 80). Finally, following Bakhtin, who is ever wary of the totalization of any character, the reader may, at different moments, respond as both privileged and oppressed.

Whether privileged, oppressed, or both, skeptical poststructuralists are *revolutionary readers* (Belsey, cited in Wicomb, 1991). Revolutionary readers are reticent to relax their critical faculties, even in the presence of a potentially emancipatory story written by a storyteller with novelness as an aim. Literary persuasion may appear relatively benign when compared with the positioning of the declarative text that implicitly denies the presence of any values undergirding the writing process.

But is the artful persuader really that virtuous? Rorty (1989) quoted George Orwell's chilling observations concerning the rhetorical strategies employed within the literary text:

> "Imaginative" writing is as it were a flank attack upon positions that are impregnable from the front. A writer attempting anything that is not coldly "intellectual" can do very little with words in their primary meanings. He gets his effect, if at all, by using words in a tricky roundabout way. (p. 174)

Orwell admitted that in writing *Animal Farm* he was, in fact, doing the same kind of thing (attempting to persuade through rhetorical devices) as his opponents, the apologists for Stalin, were doing (Rorty, 1989, p. 174). Revolutionary readers recall the insistence of postmodern critics from Barthes to Derrida that even texts of well-intentioned authors possess a surplus of meaning as supplied by a dominant culture. Despite the style of persuasion-by-participation adopted by the literary text, the revolutionary reader honors the responsibility to uncover and inspect as much of that surplus as possible.

But sometimes, within certain rare conferences between reader, writer, and characters, there appears the splendid paradox of poststructuralist textual antagonists sharing a moment of trust. As Wicomb (1991) says:

> Had my education offered me the possibility of revolutionary reading, I would have done what I do with any commodity produced in the culture that I am told is good for me: sift out what I consider valuable from that which I find objectionable. (p. 13)

Wicomb suggests (through a reifying metaphor) that in our long overdue march toward deconstructivism, we must not forget that there are some stories worthy of being reassembled and valued.

Indeed, haven't we all listened to storytellers who invite us into astoundingly liberating acts of textual reconstruction, acts that remind us of the fundamental usefulness of storysharing? This is what happens during an occasion of narrative communion when I, the vigilant reader, find that my tired, habitual way of perceiving the selves of particular sorts of strangers (including, perhaps, the stranger that is me) is challenged. I accept the invitation of the storyteller to resituate those selves within the historical and cultural contingencies that shape them so that I may imaginatively identify with these heretofore strangers. I take the offer of perceiving in a strange new way the cruel social and institutional forces that have served to distort these selves and accept the invitation to imagine these rhetorical figures, and their analogues outside the text, remade within more empowering conditions. I, the reader, enter into a *conspiracy* with the storyteller (Barone, 1990), a politically based conversation about the relationship between world-at-hand and world-to-be-made, a sharing of ideals and ideas towards a "possible future" (hooks, 1991,

p. 55) in which the selves of the powerless are reconstituted into the selves of the empowered. Such a conspiracy cannot succeed without a suspension of distrust between the co-conspirators.

These conspiratorial moments are fragile, evanescent instants that occur within a unique constellation of historical and personal contingencies. They are rare, even if their effects can sometimes be long lasting. The sifting, to borrow Wicomb's term, takes patience; the valuable, trustworthy texts are like precious gems among objectionable silt. But emancipatory-minded readers may recall occasions in which his or her negotiations with writer and characters ultimately resulted in something akin to an *epiphany* (Denzin, 1989), a major transactional moment that disrupts the ordinary flow of life and makes problematic the usual definitions given to facets of one's world. An epiphany "leaves marks on people's lives . . . alters and shapes the meanings persons give to themselves and their life projects. . . . Having had this experience, the person is never quite the same again" (Denzin, 1989, p. 15).

Epiphanies (which also occur, of course, outside reading literature) are both rare and intensely personal, directly accessible only to the reader (or experiencer). Therefore, I can share only a few examples from my own life as an emancipatory-minded reader. I will briefly describe epiphanic moments I experienced in reading Richard Rodriguez' (1982) *Hunger of Memory*, Alex Kotlowitz' (1991) *There Are No Children Here*, and Pat Conroy's (1972) *The Water is Wide*.

Hunger of Memory is a narrative of struggle, or, in Rodriguez' words, an "intellectual autobiography." I have read and re-read this life story from my privileged perch as a white, male, middle-class university professor. Due to my ignorance of the existential issues that might confront a poor, academically adept Mexican American, my initial reconstruction of the self of the protagonist was an exercise filled with awe. Why, for example, had I never considered that a talented Hispanic's success in the Anglo world might be accompanied, as was Rodriguez', by several degrees of alienation – from his native language, from his family, and ultimately from his own feelings and emotions? Moreover, the author's lucid descriptions moved beyond the generation of empathic understanding as they sensitized me to certain issues surrounding bilingual education (and education generally). It is true that upon re-reading the text, I became disenchanted with it, more skeptical of the author's ultimate claims about the wisdom of a form of education that led to a denial of his primary form of being, to a separation from his parents and their culture, in favor of an intellectualism that gave him "ways of speaking and caring about that [separation]" (Rodriguez, 1982, p. 72). But conspiracies, like the effects of epiphanies, rarely last forever.

There Are No Children Here is not an autobiography, but literary journalism – a poignant, harrowing, convincing account of two African-American children growing up in an inner-city housing project. Its theme is innocence lost as the selves of these two brothers are pulled apart by powerful cultural forces. My moment with this story was generally one of horror. I felt I was participating in what Fine (1993) has called a "story of despair" (p. 36). This story is not a merely sensational, strictly emic "chronicle of pain" (hooks, 1991, p. 59). One hears not only the still-weak voices of the two young protagonists but also the voice of the author. Kotlowitz chooses not merely to recreate their horrific experiences for the reader but to contextualize them, to examine critically (in story language and format) some features of the political and cultural systems that engender such experiences. Radically subverting and challenging the dominant discourses, the writer ultimately persuaded me to revisit my stock of responsibilities, to become more engaged in educational activism aimed at attacking forces within "social institutions [such as the modern American school] which have made us cruel" (Rorty, 1989, p. 141).

I therefore reject any suggestion that, through my reading, a secure, white, middle-class male was merely indulging in a bourgeois act of cross-cultural voyeurism. Granted, reading these stories by Rodriguez and Kotlowitz was an observance from a distance. Still, my reading expedition represented not a kind of tourism of the soul, but a serious quest for comprehending, through particular cases, the forces of domination deplored by all citizens who yearn for democracy that is more than superficially political.

The last emancipatory-minded reading I will describe involved a conversation within an autobiographical novel written by a schoolteacher. I read Pat Conroy's (1972) novel *The Water Is Wide* two decades ago while still a high school teacher. Conroy's tale depicts one year in his life as a white schoolteacher of black children in an isolated school in South Carolina. Conroy confronts the constrained consciousness of administrators and others, victims themselves of a repressive, racist system, who confound his efforts at true education. Labeled a "troublemaker," Conroy was fired after 18 months. Although my situation was less extreme than Conroy's, I recall a profound identification with his plight. I realized that the distorted features of his social and institutional milieu were not locally contained; they roamed the expanses of American culture and schooling. I began to see them in my own workplace. I recall my initial entertainment of the now-obvious notion that teachers are themselves victims of oppression, and I began to wonder what could be done to alter that fact. Now calling on bell hooks (1991) to speak for me, I do not equate the challenges faced by an African-American woman with a white, male high school teacher. I do so because I cannot better express my sense of what this novel (along with other writings) gave to me:

> [N]ovels brought me close to myself, helped me to overcome the estrangement that domination breeds between psyche and self. Reading, I could vicariously experience, dare to know and feel, without threat of repression, retaliation, silencing. My mind became a place of refuge, a sanctuary, a room I could enter with no fear of invasion. My mind became a site of resistance. (p. 54)

Shortly afterward, as a result of experiences both vicarious and direct, I left high school teaching to explore the possibilities of resistance from a distance, within the habitué of a teacher educator. My explorations continue. But would they have commenced as early had I not confronted a vivid alternative to my fuzzy picture of the vaguely unacceptable conditions in my own professional life? A writer of a fictionalized version of his life story offered me a novel reading of my own. I was artfully persuaded to trust a writer who had trusted me, persuaded to conspire with him in a mutual struggle.

Closure

These three acts of educational storysharing, varied in elements such as genre, style, or relationship of writer to characters, are each an act of inquiry with integrity, a distinct moment in an ongoing educational dialogue. My point (in this non-storied form of discourse) is not to privilege the story over other discursive modes heard in that dialogue. Storytellers who aspire to novelness welcome, in due course, critique in all discursive forms, including historical, philosophical, or sociological theory, as well as counterstories that redescribe the conditions of the selves at hand. Indeed, the end of a story is best seen as an invitation to begin a new phase in the conversation. But, I have attempted to demonstrate that some stories deserve their own space, with inviolable boundaries surrounding the message that they attempt to convey in their chosen format and language. We do not always need, within the same textual breath, to deconstruct in another style and format the epiphanies they foster. Sometimes the conversation between writer, reader, and characters should be allowed to wane before additional voices interject themselves into the dialogue.

To value such emancipatory-minded stories, editors of educational books and journals will need to be willing to publish them, even though they are not enclosed within a textual envelope of traditional scholarly writing. It means that members of the educational research community (expanded to include teachers, school administrators, and students?) must learn to overcome a legacy of mistrust of all storysharing. (Is it surprising, that two of the three writers I referenced above – Kotlowitz and Conroy – write from outside that community?) Of course, judgments will still need to be made about the potential trustworthiness of each composition. Reader-references must ask whether other readers of the story are likely, in conference with writer and characters, to experience an emancipatory moment. This is hardly an easy task, given the complexities of writing and reading I have outlined here. But in my experience, the rewards of emancipatory educational storysharing – singular, liberating moments of heightened awareness in which new definition is given to the selves of others and to one's own being – are worth the effort.

Notes

1. Narrativists in the field of education sometimes conflate the terms narrative and story (e.g. Nespor & Barylske, 1991). In this essay, I do not. Narrative has been defined in various ways, but its root is in the Latin *narrare*, "to relate". Narrators, therefore, can be said to relate accounts of incidents and events. Many kinds of narrative accounts have been identified, including oral anecdotes and folklore, diaries, or historical treatises (Connolly & Clandinin, 1990). In this essay, narrative is defined in this broad sense, while story is one species huddled under that umbrella.

Of course, story can be a promiscuous term. Some radical rhetoricians of science even conflate the terms science and story, pointing to story-like dimensions of scientific texts (Lawson & Appignanesi, 1989; Nelson, 1987). While not denying the spectrum of rhetorical/literary possibilities, I choose the more traditional, Aristotelian definition of story. I use the term story to indicate a discourse with two particular attributes. The first is an eidetic structure, a particular sort of dynamic form. This form has been, over the years, segmented by literary critics into a varying number of phases. These phases, however, are generally viewed as integral parts that flow together within a single coherent and unified structure. An early phase involves the introduction and situation of characters within a human dilemma. The story then moves to a building phase in which complications arise and meaning continuously emerges until, in a final phase, a tentative, sometimes ambiguous, resolution to the dilemma is suggested. I am conscious of the middle-class, Eurocentric tendency here as I exclude narrative forms from other cultures that are not temporally organized (Nespor & Barylske, 1991; Rosaldo, 1989).

The second hallmark of a story, as I employ the term, is its participation in vernacular forms of speech. By this I mean that the storyteller tends to display everyday, informal language rather than speech that is narrowly technical or identified with a particular institution. Stories about teaching, therefore, are told, not in the argot of the social science professional, but in the language emanating out of the "dailiness" of classroom experience. This is not to posit a singular, totalized vernacular; various speech communities within a culture employ their own transinstitutional idioms. A female, Native American teacher in Window Rock, Arizona, may not employ the same style of language as a male, Jamaican teacher. Moreover, stories obviously represent only one of many sites of such everyday speech.

2. The session, entitled "Educational Discourse and Constructions of Profession," was organized by Margaret Marshall and Anthony G. Rud, Jr.

3. It may be argued that in an oppressive society this includes all of us, including those for whom we usually reserve the label "oppressor." Writers as diverse as Paulo Freire and James Baldwin have insisted that the oppressor is also the oppressed. The very act of oppression, this argument goes, demeans the oppressor, makes him less than fully human, prevents him from joining those who are able to gain mastery over their world without resorting to the narcotic of controlling others. Stories that investigate and reveal the webs of meaning in the lives of superficially powerful people without demonizing them are also emancipatory-minded stories.

References

Agger, B. (1990). *The decline of discourse: reading, writing, and resistance in postmodern capitalism.* New York: Falmer.

Argueta, M. (1983). *One day of life* (B. Brow, Trans.). New York: Vantage. (Original work published 1980)

Bakhtin, M.M. (1981). *The dialogic imagination: four essays.* Austin: University of Texas Press.

Barone, T. (1989). Ways of being at risk: the case of Billy Charles Barnett. *Phi Delta Kappan, 71,* 147–151.

Barone, T. (1990). Using the narrative text as an occasion for conspiracy. In E. Eisner & A. Peshkin (Eds.), *Qualitative inquiry in education: the continuing debate* (pp. 305–326). New York: Teachers College Press.

Barone, T. (1992). A narrative of enhanced professionalism: educational researchers and popular storybooks about schoolpeople. *Educational Researcher, 21,* 15–24.

Barthes, R. (1977). The death of the author. In R. Barthes (Ed.), *Images, music, text* (pp. 142–148). New York: Hill & Wang.

Bauman, Z. (1987). *Legislators and interpreters: modernity, post-modernity and intellectuals.* Ithaca, NY: Cornell University Press.

Belsey, C. (1980). *Critical practice.* London: Methuen.

Berliner, D. (1992). Telling the stories of educational psychology. *Educational Psychologist, 27,* 143–161.

Bredo, E. & Feinberg, W. (1982). *Knowledge and values in social and educational research.* Philadelphia: Temple University Press.

Britzman, D. (1991). *Practice makes practice: a critical study of learning to teach.* Albany: State University of New York Press.

Bruner, J. (1987). *Actual minds, possible worlds.* Cambridge, MA: Harvard University Press.

Connelly, F.M. & Clandinin, D.J. (1990). Stories of experience and narrative inquiry. *Educational Researcher, 19,* 2–14.

Conroy, P. (1972). *The water is wide.* Boston: Houghton Mifflin.

Denzin, N. (1989). *Interpretive interactionism.* Newbury Park, CA: Sage.

Fine, M. (1992). *Disruptive voices: the possibilities of feminist research.* Ann Arbor: University of Michigan Press.

Fine, M. (1993). A diary on privatization and on public possibilities. *Educational Theory, 43,* 33–39.

Foucault, M. (1977). *Discipline and punish: the birth of the prison.* New York: Vintage.

Geertz, C. (1988). *Works and lives: the anthropologist as author.* Stanford, CA: Stanford University Press.

Goodson, I. (1992). Studying teacher's lives: an emergent field of inquiry. In I. Goodson (Ed.), *Studying teacher's lives* (pp. 1–17). London: Routledge.

Grumet, M. (1988). *Bitter milk: women and teaching.* Amherst: University of Massachusetts Press.

Habermas, J. (1972). *Knowledge and human interest.* Boston: Beacon.

Holquist, M. (1990). *Dialogism: Bakhtin and his world.* London: Routledge.

hooks, b. (1991). Narratives of struggle. In P. Mariani (Ed.), *Critical fictions: the politics of imaginative writing* (pp. 53–61). Seattle: Bay.

Iser, W. (1974). *The implied reader.* Baltimore: Johns Hopkins University Press.

Johnston, B. (1988). *Indian school days.* Norman: University of Oklahoma Press.

Kondo, D. (1990). *Crafting selves: power, gender, and discourses.* Chicago: University of Chicago Press.

Kotlowitz, A. (1991). *There are no children here: the story of two boys growing up in the other America.* New York: Doubleday.

Kozol, J. (1991). *Savage inequalities: children in America's schools.* New York: Harper Collins.

Lancy, D.F. (1993). *Qualitative research in education: an introduction to the major traditions.* New York: Longman.

Lather, P. (1986). Issues of validity in openly ideological research: between a rock and a soft place. *Interchange: A Quarterly Review of Education, 17,* 62–84.

Lawson, H. & Appignanesi, L. (Eds.). (1989). *Dismantling truth: reality in the postmodern world.* London: Weidenfeld & Nicholson.

McLaren, P. (1989). *Life in schools: an introduction to critical pedagogy in the foundations of education.* White Plains, NY: Longman.

Morrison, T. (1970). *The bluest eye: a novel.* New York: Holt, Rinehart & Winston.

Nelson, J. (Ed.). (1987). *The rhetoric of the human sciences.* Madison: University of Wisconsin Press.

Nespor, J. & Barylske, J. (1991). Narrative discourse and teacher knowledge. *American Educational Research Journal, 28,* 805–823.

Owens, C. (1989). The global issue: a symposium. *Art in America, 77,* 86–89, 151–157.

Polkinghorne, D.E. (1988). *Narrative knowing and the human sciences.* Albany: State University of New York Press.

Richardson, L. (1990). *Writing strategies: reaching diverse audiences.* London: Sage.

Rodriguez, R. (1982). *Hunger of memory: the education of Richard Rodriguez.* Boston: David R. Godine.

Rorty, R. (1989). *Contingency, irony, and solidarity.* Cambridge: Cambridge University Press.

Rosaldo, R. (1989). *Culture and truth.* Boston: Beacon.

Rose, M. (1989). *Lives on the boundary.* New York: Penguin.

Rosenau, P. (1992). *Post-modernism and the social sciences: insights, inroads, and intrusions.* Princeton, NJ: Princeton University Press.

Ryle, G. (1949). *The concept of mind.* New York: Barnes & Noble.

Sartre, J.-P. (1949). *What is literature? and other essays* (B. Frechtman, Trans.). Cambridge, MA: Cambridge University Press. (Original work published 1948)

Sparkes, A. (1994). Life histories and the issue of voice: reflections on an emerging relationship. *International Journal of Qualitative Studies in Education, 7,* 165–183.

Sullivan, J.P. (1984). *A critical psychology.* New York: Plenum.

Tillman, L. (1991). Critical fiction/critical self. In P. Mariani (Ed.), *Critical fictions: the politics of imaginative writing* (pp. 97–103). Seattle: Bay.

Wicomb, Z. (1991). An author's agenda. In P. Mariani (Ed.), *Critical fictions: the politics of imaginative writing* (pp. 13–16). Seattle: Bay.

Wittgenstein, L. (1968). *Philosophical investigations* (3rd edn) (G.E.M. Anscombe, Trans.). New York: Macmillan. (Original work published in 1953)

Wright, R. (1945). *Black boy, a record of childhood and youth.* New York: Harper & Row.

Narrative strategies for case reports

NANCY ZELLER
East Carolina University

This paper explores what for many qualitative researchers is their most difficult task: writing a qualitative research report or case study. It explores the time and space conditions of two writing genres: narration and description. It argues that the new journalism, along with the nonfiction novel and ethnography, are useful narrative models for case reports. Several techniques managed well by new journalists and other narrative writers are discussed: (a) scene-by-scene construction; (b) characterization through ample use of dialogue; (c) point of view; (d) full rendering of details; (e) interior monologue; and (f) composite characterization. Two sample narratives illustrate the possible application of narrative techniques in a case report.

Researchers in the human sciences have shown an increasing interest in the rhetoric of research. Early expression of this interest occurred at a 1979 University of Chicago conference on "Narrative: The Illusion of Sequence." Subsequently, the University of Iowa established its Program on the Rhetoric of Inquiry (POROI) and has sponsored conferences and programs which focus on rhetoric in the human sciences (e.g., "The Rhetoric of the Human Sciences: Language and Argument in Scholarship and Public Affairs," March 1984; and "Conference on Narrative in the Human Sciences," July 1990). Researchers in a variety of academic and professional fields have contributed to the growing body of literature on the rhetoric of research and, more recently, on the use of narrative in research (e.g., Agar, 1990; Anderson, 1987; Atkinson, 1990; Bruner, 1986; Egan, 1986; Gee, 1985, 1989a, 1989b; Gudmundsdottir, in press; Hammersley & Atkinson, 1983; Krieger, 1984; Lightfoot, 1985; McEwan, in press; Mulkay, 1985; Van Maanen, 1988; Wolf, 1985; Zeller, 1990, 1993, in press). These researchers have identified and explored the use of narrative as a mode of communication more resonant with human experience than traditional social science research rhetoric and, thus, inherently more understandable.

My purpose is to explore the use of narrative writing strategies for qualitative case studies in education. I begin by examining the writing genre called *narration*. I then explore possible writing models that are narrative-based, focusing on "literary" (formerly "new") journalism as an especially appropriate model for case study research writing. Two fundamental assumptions underlie my paper: (a) the goal of qualitative research is to facilitate understanding, and (b) a case report should be a product of research, not merely a record.

Narration

Phyllis Bentley (1946) describes a writer as someone sitting on the top of a brick wall describing to someone below the action on the other side; this action is a "rolling pageant" (p. 8) going at various speeds – sometimes fast, sometimes almost stopped. The pageant consists of descriptions, scenes, and summaries, all of which form the narrative. Narration is the kind of discourse that answers the question, "What happened?" It tells a story which, according to McCorcle (1984), is what a case study should be: "Its narrative form may be the case study's most compelling

0951-8398/95 $10·00 © 1995 Taylor & Francis Ltd.

attribute. It is the case's story line that connects and enlivens all the various actors and processes" (p. 207).

Narration provides a sense of immediacy of an event unfolding before the reader's eyes. The writer provides many details that capture the reader's interest; but, more importantly, the events, the story, or the characters exist in a world whose clock is ticking. Description, a type of writing normally used to convey how something may be apprehended through the senses, engages the reader's interest by providing interesting details. Description also enables the writer to display the events, story, or characters against a particular setting – a place, a culture, a set of norms. Narration can be a total organizing strategy, subsuming or absorbing descriptions, scenes, and summaries. According to Brooks and Warren, (1970), while pure description presents the quality of an action, narration provides the movement. Description is a supporting strategy, rarely appearing in its pure form but often intertwined with scenes and summary to support narration.

Description has a place in qualitative research. Often there are sounds, smells, and, most importantly, sights that will help the reader understand the research setting and give the reader a sense of being there. Descriptive passages within the research report will enrich its texture and contribute generally to a better understanding of the case. Description is usually constructed differently from narration, which is organized within a time framework. In a descriptive passage, if what is being described is a sight, for example, the usual organizing strategy is spatial – from near to far, left to right, top to bottom.

In his discussion of types of novels, Edwin Muir (1929) provides an extended conceptualization of the time/space distinction between narration and description. According to Muir, there are two types of novels – dramatic and character – which differ in the following ways: the dramatic novel is personal and is associated with time; the character novel is social and is associated with space. The dramatic novel resembles music; the character, painting. In a dramatic novel, action is built up in time within the framework of a strict, logical plot; but in a character novel, action is reshuffled in space within the framework of a loosely woven plot. The most important distinction, however, is that in a dramatic novel, such as Dickens' *A Tale of Two Cities* (1859/1936), the characters move inexorably from a beginning to an end; while in a character novel, such as Forster's *A Room With a View* (1908/1947), the characters live in a society in relation to which they exist, act, and sometimes change. Muir comments that "the sense of time running out gives the real edge to the dramatic emotion. . . . In the novel of character, time is inexhaustible" (pp. 80–81). Referring to the intensity and ruthless forward motion of Dostoyevsky's dramatic novel, *The Idiot* (1868/1979), Muir observes: "Only a third of the story has been told, but the end is already throwing wild shadows over the action" (p. 75).

Narration, then, is the primary technique of the dramatic novelist. It is an important technique in nonfiction as well because, besides providing the excitement of events occurring in a given arena, its use can invest any subject with interest and meaning. For dramatic effect or emphasis, a writer may juxtapose events in time. One of the more familiar time manipulation techniques in narration is the flashback, whereby the author begins at some interesting point in a story, then relates events that occurred at an earlier time. Some narratives, such as that found in Marcel Proust's novel, *Swann's Way* (1913/1927), or Billy Wilder's (1950) film, *Sunset Boulevard*, consists entirely of a flashback. Some novelists, such as William Faulkner (e.g., *The Sound and the Fury*, 1929/1987) and Paul Scott (e.g., *The Raj Quartet*, 1966–1975 (4 vols)) manipulate time in more complicated ways.

For qualitative researchers, narration provides the perfect vehicle for solving reporting problems. The researcher may wish to tell a time-bound story, ensuring that the reader understands the exact sequence of events leading up to an incident. In addition, the researcher may want to invest the data with the logic, meaning, and interest provided by narration. In addition to using narration as an organizing strategy within a text, the qualitative research writer may elect to rely on narration (instead of a topical arrangement) as the total organizing strategy for the complete research report.

The following is an example of how one might use narration to report a class observation. This example presents one session in a junior college developmental math class.

THE MATH CLASS

It was 8:45 a.m. Developmental Math I, the lowest level math class offered by Landmark College, was scheduled to begin in fifteen minutes. It was a four-credit class, meeting one hour, four days a week. Crammed into the small, basement classroom were thirty-five tablet-arm chairs with graffiti on the writing surfaces. Blackboards stretched across the front and one side wall.

The classroom began filling slowly, with students plodding reluctantly to their seats. One boy laid his head on his desk and sighed. A foreign student from Yeman said he didn't like math, but that this class was "OK . . . the teacher is good."

At 8:57 the teacher, Karen Jackson, arrived. Most of the class was assembled: four boys, including two Arab students, and four girls, three of whom were Black, and one, White. A second White girl, a sleepy-looking blond, arrived five minutes late, and a Black male student came in twenty minutes late. The teacher questioned him extensively, but privately, about his lateness.

Ms. Jackson began class by making some announcements. Because of remodeling in the building the following week, the class would begin meeting in another room, the number of which Ms. Jackson wrote on the blackboard.

The next item was a review of the previous day's lesson: performing long division with two-digit numbers and understanding the meaning of the operation signs greater than ($>$), less than ($<$), and equals ($=$). In addition, the terms, dividend, divisor, and quotient, were redefined for students.

Ms. Jackson then asked students to solve (orally) simple, two-digit division problems which she wrote on the blackboard.

Although trained as an elementary teacher, she did not talk down to the students – quite the opposite – she acted as though it was perfectly natural that they wouldn't know the meaning of less than ($<$) or quotient or how to solve the problem (68 divided by 34).

Careful not to talk too much while facing and writing on the blackboard, Ms. Jackson gave a fifteen-minute lecture on long division, then assigned some related homework which the students were allowed to begin during class time so that she could help them.

As students began working their problems, she moved around the room and gave individual help. Starting in the front of the room and moving slowly to the back, she stopped to help every student. Sometimes she would stand silently for a moment or two, then ask a student if he knew what he was supposed to do. One student so confronted shook his head "yes," but, realizing that Ms. Jackson was still waiting to help him, blurted out after a minute, "but, I really don't understand this at all."

At 9:30 Ms. Jackson began handing out story problems, which she requires her students to work on every day. She also handed out two pages of math vocabulary terms she had copied from a textbook other than the class text, which she described as "boring."

As the students settled in to spend the last few minutes on their story problems, she announced, "I'm here to answer questions – don't struggle needlessly."

At 9:50 Ms. Jackson formally released the class; but a few students continued to work on their homework, and a couple more waited to talk to her after class.

In the preceding narrative, the events unfold much as they occurred in the class; the reader can experience the class session somewhat as the researcher did. The fact that the researcher makes no interpretive comments in the vignette gives the reader a chance to experience and respond directly to the statements and actions of the teacher and students and to draw his or her own conclusions about what has transpired. Of course, the *seeming* objectivity in such a narrative masks the researcher/writer's subjective involvement in the scene – the unconscious selection of events to observe and record and the conscious selection of events to report. Thus, a straightforward, ostensibly *objective* narrative can be somewhat deceptive in its impact, engendering in the reader the reaction that he/she had witnessed *reality* directly. Perhaps another kind of narrative is needed in qualitative research.

Narrative models

Stake (1978) suggests that for case studies a "writing style that is informal, perhaps narrative, possibly with verbatim quotation, illustration, and even allusion and metaphor" is more appropriate than a technical reporting style (pp. 6–7). Others (e.g., Agar, 1990; Anderson, 1987; Atkinson, 1990; Hammersley & Atkinson, 1983; Krieger, 1984; McEwan, 1991, in press; Mulkay, 1985; Van Maanen, 1988; Zeller, 1987, 1990, 1991, 1993, in press) suggest that case reporters consider such models as new ethnography, literary journalism, creative nonfiction, or even fiction in order to identify a narrative style reflective of the underlying assumptions of qualitative inquiry.

The writing techniques used in the nonfiction novel and ethnography result in powerful representations of individuals and their social milieu. The term *nonfiction novel* was used by Truman Capote (1965) to describe *In Cold Blood*, his penetrating study of the murder of a Kansas farm family. Much of Norman Mailer's later work, such as *Armies of the Night* (1968) or *The Executioner's Song* (1979), falls in the category of the nonfiction novel. Although Capote claimed that the nonfiction novel is a new art form that he created, earlier examples can be found, the most notable of which is James Agee's (1988) depression-era *Let Us Now Praise Famous Men*. Less famous, but more recent and relevant, examples of this genre include Kidder's (1989) *Among Schoolchildren* and Kotlowitz' (1991) *There Are No Children Here: The Story of Two Boys Growing Up in the Other America*.

Another model for case reporting is sensitively written ethnography. In this "new" ethnography, the social scientist's relationship to the people and events described reflects new attitudes and values; and, more important to the purpose here, the form and style of the ethnographic report are radically transformed through the use of fictional devices borrowed from short stories and novels. New ethnographers have learned that they need to scheme to conquer their material. Rosaldo (1984) likens the process to taking a photograph:

> It is as if one imagined that photographs told the unadorned real truth without ever noticing how they were constructed. Their images, after all, are framed, taken from particular angles, shot at certain distances, and rendered with different depths of field. (p. 3)

The writer, in other words, works in the background, unseen by the reader, manipulating materials to achieve certain effects. Jacques Barzun (1971) remarks that when an artist speaks of his *craft*, he means "quite literally that he is crafty" (p. 65).

Susan Krieger (1984) argues that sociologists can expand their options for "writing up social science field research by using methods of fiction" (p. 269). She finds that "social scientists often do what novelists do: they invent, they use illusion and inner vision, they focus on the unique and the particular" (p. 271). In writing her dissertation and resulting book *Hip Capitalism* (1979), a multiple-person, stream-of-consciousness narrative study of the co-optation of an underground radio station, Krieger (1984) admits that "the closest match in form for it that [she] could find was in the 'new journalism' " (p. 280).

Literary journalism

As Susan Krieger (1984) and others (e.g., Zeller, 1987, 1990, 1991, in press) have suggested, a powerful model for writing up case studies is found in *literary* (formerly *new*) journalism. Although no one knows who coined the term *new journalism*, most people agree with its chief advocate and exemplar, Tom Wolfe (1973), that new journalistic writing began appearing in the mid-1960s when people seemed overwhelmed by a cascade of information. The war in Vietnam, for example, became an enigma for Americans. In *Dispatches*, war correspondent Michael Herr (1977) described the central problem: "The press got all the facts (more or less), it got too many of them. But it never found a way to report meaningfully about death, which of course was really what it was all about" (p. 7). The new journalists, according to Hellman (1981), were able to respond to news that "continually threaten[ed] to overwhelm consciousness" with works which were "profoundly transforming literary experiments embodying confrontations between fact and mind" (p. x).

Hellman (1981) claims that "new journalism is a revolt by the individual against homogenized forms of experience, against monolithic versions of truth" (p. 8). Wolfe (1973) explains that he began to discover a new "artistic excitement in journalism" (p. 23) and the possibility of writing "journalism that would . . . read like a novel" (p. 9), more specifically, the novels of social realism" – those of Fielding, Smollet, Balzac, Dickens, and Gogol. Hellman (1981) argues that there is more to it – that:

> . . . finding a fragmented reality, [the new journalist] has chosen to use fiction as a way of knowing and communicating fact [because fiction] provides the most effective means of dramatizing the complexities and ambiguities of experience – the dynamic and fluid wholeness of an event as it is felt and ordered (made) by a human consciousness. (p. 18)

Dan Wakefield claims that the new journalism is

> . . . "imaginative" not because the author has distorted the facts, but because he has presented them in a full instead of a naked manner, brought out the sights, sounds, and feelings surrounding those facts . . . in an artistic manner that does not diminish but gives greater depth and dimension to the facts. (quoted in Hollowell, 1977, p. 45)

Hollowell (1977) argues that the new journalist "strives to reveal the story hidden beneath the surface of facts" (p. 23).

Because there appear to be similarities, in both belief and methods, between the new journalism and qualitative research, the writing strategies and techniques employed by the new journalists would seem appropriate models for case reporters. Wolfe (1973) has identified four writing devices central to the new journalism, devices which help the new journalists, when portraying real events and real people, achieve the immediacy or concrete reality found in fiction, especially novels of social realism. They are:

1. *scene-by-scene construction*, the telling of a story in scenic episodes;
2. character development through full recording of *dialogue*;
3. use of a *third-person subjective point of view*, experiencing an event through the perspective of one of its participants; and
4. full detailing of the *"status-life"* – or rank – of participants in a scene, their "everyday gestures, habits, manners, customs, styles of furniture, clothing, decoration, styles of traveling, eating, keeping house, modes of behaving towards children, servants, superiors, inferiors, peers, plus the various looks, glances, poses, styles of working and other symbolic details that might exist within a scene." (p. 32)

Each of these techniques deserves consideration.

Scene-by-scene construction

The new journalism differs from traditional journalism both in how data are gathered and in how stories are developed. Hollowell (1977) observes that in the usual news story, "the basic units are facts and quotations. . . . [But the new journalist] . . . attempts to reconstruct the experience as it might have unfolded" (p. 25). He constructs a scene, according to Dennis and Rivers (1974), "with the absolute detail and life of a playwright, then considers another, and another, and another" (p. 7). This technique is called scene-by-scene construction. A scene, then, is something like a miniature story, a unit of event that has a beginning, a middle, and an end. It contains, primarily, characters in action. The advantage of using scene-by-scene construction is described by Cassill (1975): scenes "bring the action and sometimes the dialogue of the characters before the reader with a fullness comparable to what a witness might observe or overhear if he had been present" (p. 26). The qualitative researcher can also benefit by constructing some of the units of event in a case study as if they were scenes in a story or play.

Characterization through dialogue

Most case reports, ultimately, are about people. Brooks and Warren (1970) argue that "to understand an action we must understand the people involved, their natures, their motives, their responses, and to present an action so that it is satisfying we must present the people" (p. 413). This process, characterization, can be achieved by using one or more of five types of material about a character: (a) appearance and mannerisms; (b) apparent motivation; (c) reactions of other persons; (d) action; and (e) speech. Even with careful attention to supporting material, the qualitative researcher will find it difficult to represent in writing a living person. A "character" is comprised of the writer's impressions, the selection and sequencing of those impressions, and the representation of that impression through language. The new journalists attempt to balance their often highly interpretive reports and achieve a sense of reality by rendering character chiefly through full recording of dialogue. Brooks and Warren argue, however, that it is not necessary to write a direct, verbatim transcription of what people say because conversation is "often stumbling, wandering, diffuse" (p. 609). The research writer cannot afford to "duplicate such a conversation; if he does so, the reader will not be readily able to follow the line of significance" (p. 609). What the case reporter needs to do is to provide "an impression of real life, a sense of pauses, the changes, the waverings of conversation" (p. 611). Brooks and Warren conclude that "this must be an impression and not a word-for-word recording" (p. 611). Qualitative researchers ponder a similar and related issue: to what extent should the researcher interpret the data (versus simply presenting the raw data – with readers providing their own interpretations)? Each case may call for a different approach, depending on the degree to which the data seem "transparent" or the degree to which a full reporting of the data will be compelling.

Point of view

The reader's attitude toward and understanding of a set of facts and events will usually be controlled by the writer through the technical management of point of view, which, according to Brooks and Warren (1970), addresses two questions: (a) Who is the narrator? and (b) What is his or her relation to the action? The narrator may have a "panoramic" or "omniscient" (p. 347) point of view or a limited "sharp focus" (p. 348) point of view whereby the writer "keeps his and the reader's attention focused on one character and on the character's relation to the action"

(p. 348). This character can be seen "as a kind of prism through which the action is refracted" (p. 348).

New journalists usually employ the "sharp focus" point of view and, despite critics who accuse them of keeping the writer in the foreground at all times, often prefer third-person to first-person narration. Wolfe (1973) points out that "in fact, most of the best work in the form has been done in third-person narration with the writer keeping himself absolutely invisible" (p. 42). Wolfe describes a new kind of subjective third-person point of view: "[Present] every scene to the reader through the eyes of a particular character, giving the reader the feeling of being inside the character's mind and experiencing the emotional reality of the scene as he experiences it" (p. 32). Wolfe, in addition, frequently employs a shifting subjective third-person point of view, selecting scene by scene or chapter by chapter the one character likely to invest the action with the greatest reality. In *The Right Stuff* (1983), his examination of the Mercury astronaut program, Wolfe begins his story from the point of view of a test pilot's wife, Jane Conrad, then shifts to that of her husband, Pete Conrad. A few chapters later, Wolfe shifts the point of view to that of test pilot Chuck Yeager who was passed over for the astronaut program because he did not have a college degree. The point of view later returns to Pete Conrad, then moves on to John Glenn and other Mercury astronauts. In the middle of his story, Wolfe even resorts to describing the first American space flight from the point of view of test subject Number 61 – a chimpanzee.

For the new journalists, point of view is supremely important – as it is for many qualitative researchers. Lincoln and Guba (1985) describe the relationship between researcher and respondent, "knower and known," as "interactive, inseparable" (p. 37), denying any possibility of objectivity. Of the new journalists, Hollowell (1977) makes the following similar claim: "The new journalist strives for a higher kind of 'objectivity.' He attempts to explode the myth that any report can be objective" (p. 22). Johnson (1971) argues that the mark of the new journalistic style is the writer's attempt to be "personalistic, involved, and creative in relation to the events he reports and comments upon. His journalism . . . has no pretense of being 'objective' and it bears the clear stamp of his commitment and personality" (p. 46). Hellman (1981) comments that the new journalist "typically approaches his subject matter from the vantage point of a relentless witness and detective . . . as an involved participant . . . or from the inside of the subjects themselves" (p. 7). Wolfe (1973) admits to using point of view in a Jamesian sense, "entering directly into the mind of a character, experiencing the world through his central nervous system throughout a given scene" (p. 19). When a reviewer called Wolfe a " 'chameleon' who instantly took on the coloration of whomever he was writing about," Wolfe countered: "He meant it negatively. I took it as a great compliment. A chameleon . . . but exactly!" (pp. 18–19).

The new journalists' use of the subjective third-person point of view, especially Wolfe's use of a shifting subjective third-person point of view, may be a valuable rhetorical device for case reporters because managing such a technique will force them to focus sharply on each scene or event or set of facts and will require them to decide who is likely to serve as the best "prism" to retrieve meaning from what often seems to be a hopeless muddle.

The following is an example of how a subjective third-person point of view could be used within a case report. The following account of a junior college developmental writing class session, as experienced by one of the students, results in a different kind of text (and reader experience) than that rendered by the more straightforward, "objective" account in the earlier vignette.

THE LEAST YOU SHOULD KNOW ABOUT ENGLISH
Sitting at one of the tables, Michele was waiting for the developmental writing class to begin. She couldn't get yesterday's pictures out of her mind . . . the deep, vivid blue sky . . . the intense flash of yellow and orange as it exploded . . . the billowy clouds of pure white smoke trailing the wildly careening pieces of the shuttle. She looked at her watch;

it was five till eleven. Just then she noticed that the writing teacher had arrived . . . he was still holding an armload of folders as he walked to the front of the room and looked thoughtfully at the 16 students who were seated in front of him – at tables that looked like halves of hexagons.

Michele didn't like the arrangement of the room, which was a long rectangle. The tables were lined up in two rows, one down each wall, and only one or two students were sitting at each table. Michele had chosen a seat in the back by herself. The tables closest to the front were empty.

She was still in a reverie about yesterday . . . she thought . . . if you hadn't known what it was, you would have thought it was so pretty . . . even when you did know, you had to admit it looked a lot like some special fireworks display.

The television was full of it last night . . . somehow it didn't seem right that they would show the relatives . . . she had felt uncomfortable watching their proud smiles turn to horror as they realized what was happening. "It's no wonder I didn't get this done," she thought. She rested her chin in the palms of her hands and tried to pay attention.

The teacher was taking attendance and handing back some graded assignments – an exercise on contractions and paragraphs from the previous class meeting. Michele was a little curious to see what he would have to say about her paragraph, which expressed her anger at having to take this remedial writing class.
[Michelle's essay]

> *Its my Option!*
>
> I was told in my Summer off after graduation; when I came up here, I would not pass Comp 101 (which was required for graduation) because of my poor marks in High School, SAT, etc. Which where I have to agree I goofed off until my Senior Year. They tried to put me in this 'beginning shit' which if I had taken, I would have been here for 4 years instead of 2 (associate degree??) since I would later be taking Comp, etc. They, I won't mention any names, Anyway he made me take a Test to get in Comp 101. He said I barely passed it: Anyway my point is – I'm paying to go to this place & I know I'm taking a risk of flunking the class – ITS MY OPTION. (You guys know you only want my damn money.) If a student wants a shot at Comp 101 or what ever he or she should be given the chance. I was denied the chance and now I feel screwed.

After handing back the students' papers and talking a little bit about some general problems with sentence structure, the instructor started a discussion of title pages. All the students were supposed to be working on an autobiography project. To prepare them for this assignment and to try to generate some enthusiasm for it, the teacher had described an autobiography written by a Chicago Bears' football player named Jim McMahon.

In her third semester of a medical assistant program at Landmark, Michele had a hard time getting excited about pro football. She looked at her paragraph again and was depressed by all the red marks, most of which she didn't understand: lc, FRAG, Sp, Diction, CS . . . what does all that mean? "Oh well," she thought, "I'll just go to the Study Skills Lab to get help correcting it."

This wasn't the first time she had expressed her anger about being put in a developmental class. The previous semester she met with her academic advisor to plan her next semester's schedule, but ended up, instead, talking about Developmental Reading II, a second level reading course which she had just completed.

"Why did I have to take Reading II, which I did not need?" she asked. "My first semester here I took psychology and got straight A's on all tests and homework and received an A out of the class. Reading II was a waste of my time and money just because I had a low SAT score in the reading division!"

. Michele slid back into the present. The instructor was asking students to comment about their progress on the autobiography project. Michele forced herself to listen to her classmates. When her turn came, she said, "Mine's not done yet . . . I'll bring it in Monday." She laid her head down on her arms as the instructor went on to another student.

After the discussion of the autobiography projects, the instructor introduced a dictionary assignment, explaining the various pieces of information provided by a standard dictionary citation. Just before allowing students some class time to work on their title pages, he collected the assignment that was due – the first draft of the autobiography.

While most of the students began to work at their seats, a couple came up to his desk and spoke to him quietly about special problems. Michele doodled on the back of her hand for a while, then asked the student in front of her how long his paper was.

"Guess I'd better start writing this thing," she said to herself and then opened her notebook to look at her outline.

At 11:50 the instructor reminded the students that their dictionary assignment and title pages would be due at the next class meeting; then, he released the class. Michele thrust her "Its My Option!" paragraph between the pages of her textbook, *The Least You Should Know About English*, slipped on her coat, and hurried back through the cold of a sunny January day to the warmth of the Pope Student Dining Center and lunch.

In their treatment of multiple, constructed realities, Lincoln and Guba (1985) state that "struggles with the concept of reality are as old as humankind" (p. 70). *Reality*, they continue, is "difficult to explain unless rooted in the meanings that are constructed and attached to everyday life by individuals" (p. 77). Many of us who are teachers and qualitative researchers embrace the notion of multiple realities; yet we marvel that two individuals – such as Michele and her teacher – can experience the same event (a class) in such markedly different ways. My aim in the preceding vignette was to suggest, by using a subjective, third-person narrative, the wide-ranging thoughts and feelings that distract many developmental students from learning.

Use of the third-person subjective point of view, of course, requires the researcher to ask respondents what they were thinking and feeling during events. To repeat Wolfe's (1973) words, the researcher needs to enter "directly into the mind" of respondents "experiencing the world through [their] central nervous system throughout a given scene," becoming "a chameleon . . . but exactly!" (pp. 18–19).

Details

Rendering details fully is an important technique in most kinds of writing. During the evolution of the new journalism, writers, according to Tom Wolfe (1973), found their reporting "more intense, more detailed" than anything else they were used to. It seemed important to them to be in the field, "to get the dialogue, the gestures, the facial expressions, the details of the environment . . . the full objective description, plus . . . the subjective or emotional life of the characters" (pp. 20–21). Wolfe believes that rank or status is of great importance to all people: "I think all humans function on the basis of status judgments every second of their lives" (quoted in Fishwick, 1975, p. 137); and he believes that status can be communicated most effectively through a full reporting of details.

In *The Right Stuff*, Wolfe (1983) uses many status life indicators, including the special language of the astronauts and some of his own created terms in a richly *repeating* pattern. Early in the book,

Wolfe uses the phrase *burned beyond recognition* as a dirge to drive home the brutal, physical reality that, each time he took a plane out, a young test pilot faced a one-in-four chance of not returning alive. A counterpoint to this phrase is his reference to the pilot's impressive, aristocratic *bridge coat*, worn at funerals, and an old Navy hymn, adapted for aviators, which ends, "O hear us when we lift our prayers for those in peril on the air" (p. 7). On five occasions in the first chapter, Wolfe writes "and they brought out the bridge coats and sang about those in peril in the air and put the bridge coats away" (pp. 7, 9, 10, 11), or something very similar.

In describing the ascension up the ladder of success for the pilot officer, with its progressive testing for *the right stuff*, Wolfe likens the climb to one up a *ziggurat* (the Babylonian terraced pyramid), and repeats this image throughout the book. The "fraternity" of flying is evoked with the use of such pilot slang as *fighter jock* (themselves), *pushing the outside of the envelope* (taking a plane slightly beyond its physical capabilities), *screwing the pooch* (making a mistake), *goodies* (perquisites), and *maintaining an even strain* (remaining calm). Edwards Air Force Base in California – the test pilots' heaven on earth – is referred to as the *dome of the world*, while Cape Canaveral qualifies for the ultimate Wolfe put-down, *low rent*. America's public failure with early rocket launchings prompts Wolfe to repeat, again dirge-like, that *our rocket always blows up*. Finally, according to Wolfe, most pilots of high-performance aircraft are committed drinkers and self-styled race car drivers; so Wolfe repeats the terms *Flying & Drinking* and *Drinking & Driving* throughout the book.

Qualitative researchers will find that collecting and presenting details pertaining to their respondents, particularly the "native language" and other "status life" indicators noted by Wolfe (1973, p. 32), will more fully inform the lives of these people than use of more traditional, but less well-defined, description. The end result will be characters who are believable.

Interior monologues and composite characterization

There are two additional narrative devices which may be of use to qualitative researchers: the interior monologue and composite characterization. Some of the new journalists prefer using an interior monologue over full recording of dialogue. Where traditional journalists ask respondents what they did and said, a new journalist is likely to ask them what they thought in every situation. Wolfe (1973) comments that when he and other new journalists were accused of entering people's minds, he responded "But exactly! I figured that was one more doorbell a reporter had to push" (p. 21). Nevertheless, the use of interior monologue involves risk for qualitative researchers. Besides the near impossibility of trying to represent accurately the running thoughts and feelings of another human being, there are certain ethical considerations. Is it proper to ask a respondent what he felt and thought when such-and-such occurred? Is it proper to include such revealed thoughts and feelings in such a public document as a research report or paper?

The writing technique of composite characterization, which Hollowell (1977) describes as "the telescoping of character traits and anecdotes drawn from a number of sources into a single representative sketch" (pp. 25–26), avoids the problem of confidentiality but is open to criticism for other reasons. In *Hustling*, her book on prostitution, writer Gail Sheehy (1970) created, in what became a highly controversial use of this technique, a composite prostitute whom she called "Redpants." Composite characterization has been attacked on the grounds that the unique, idiosyncratic voice of one human being is lost in the merging of speech, appearance and mannerisms, motivation, and actions of many related characters. An even bigger danger, and a difficult one to avoid in composite characterization, is that of stereotyping. One has only to conjure up a composite "woman" or "African-American" character to see the seriousness of the problem. With the stereotypical "prostitute" or "developmental writing student," the composite seems (but, of course, really isn't) less damaging. Hollowell (1977) argues, however, that the function of such a technique is "to present the life while protecting the privacy of perfectly decent people" (p. 31) and goes on to defend its use: "At its best, composite characterization allows the journalist to compress documented evidence from a variety of sources into a vivid and unified telling of the story" (p. 31).

Limitations of literary journalism

Literary journalism has, in Weber's (1974) words, "a special edge," and, to some degree, it distorts or magnifies life (pp. 16–17). The good side to this effect is that the writing endows life with a shape or clarity that couldn't otherwise be detected, and it involves the reader in the experience. Journalist Nat Hentoff (cited in Weber, 1974), in describing Norman Mailer's particular brand of new journalism in *The Armies of the Night*, comments that "it is not only that Mailer is so personally, so vulnerably involved in the events he is reporting, but also *his* involvement draws *you* in as no traditional news account possibly could" (p. 51).

The bad side to this magnification or distortion of life is that the writing deflects and refracts the material "in the filter of the self." Tom Wolfe's work, says Weber, "bears his individual, idiosyncratic mark." In Wolfe's case, "it's not really the facts, interior or exterior, that we read for but the fun house mirror . . . he holds up to them" (pp. 16–17). The trouble arises when the new journalist wants to tell the reader about *his* problems, not his subject's. Harold Hayes, editor of *Esquire* during the early days of new journalism, attacked the new journalists for their "assumption that the writer is at the center of events" (cited in Peer, 1975, p. 67). Wolfe (1973), as mentioned earlier in this paper, reacted to such criticism by pointing out that the best new journalism "has been done in third-person narration with the writer keeping himself absolutely invisible" (p. 42).

While it is true that many of the new journalists eschew the first-person point of view, as Wolfe (1973) claims, none manages to be "absolutely invisible" (p. 42). Gold (cited in Weber, 1974) argues that "the delight in self, the lack of delight in subject matter, implies a serious ultimate judgment which ought to be faced by the . . . journalist: What matters? . . . Does anything matter but me?" (p. 285). Arlen (cited in Weber, 1974) also finds something "troubling and askew in the arrogance . . . that so often seems to compel the New Journalist to present us our reality embedded in his own ego" (p. 22).

There are other limitations to literary journalism. Wolfe (1973) himself admits to practical drawbacks and describes the various costs involved:

> Legwork, "digging," reporting is . . . beneath [the dignity of the genteel essayist]. It puts the writer in such an awkward position. He not only has to enter the bailiwick of the people he is writing about, he also becomes a slave to their schedules. Reporting can be tedious, messy, physically dirty, boring, dangerous even. But worst of all . . . is the continual posture of humiliation. The reporter starts out by presuming upon someone's privacy . . . adapting his personality to the situation . . . being ingratiating, obliging, charming . . . enduring taunts, abuse . . . behavior that comes close to being servile or even beggarly. They are willing to cross the genteel line and head through the doors marked Keep Out. (pp. 43–44)

Besides describing well the principal limitations of literary journalism, Wolfe touches on the ethical problem confronting both the new journalists and qualitative inquirers regarding treatment of respondents. The dilemma the new journalists and case reporters both face in trying to maintain integrity in their research, while at the same time safeguarding the well-being of respondents, is not easily solved; it must be viewed as a serious limitation in *both* disciplines.

Another limitation to literary journalism may be its oversimplification of complicated events or issues and its failure to focus clearly on a subject. Film critic Pauline Kael claims that the new journalism is "non-critical," that it merely gets people "excited" about an event – they "are left not knowing how to feel about it except to be excited about it" (cited in Wolfe, 1973, pp. 37–38). Kallan (1977) argues that Wolfe "constructs an appealing rhetorical reality wherein there are simple, absolute, almost 'hilariously' obvious explanations for everything" (p. 5). This style, argues Kallan, "denies the wisdom of multiple causation since it dictates that single answers and explanations be given" (p. 10).

A subtle, but important, problem in literary journalism concerns the distinction between fiction and fictive techniques. The new journalists apply fictive techniques to real people and events to heighten interest and authenticity. In using fictive techniques, they sometimes stray into fiction proper. The reason Gail Sheehy was attacked by journalists over her creation of the composite character "Redpants" was that this character was not an actual person. Sheehy had created an artificial character who had no single human referent. This is what fiction writers do. When Gay Talese created an interior monologue for one of his subjects, he too was attacked by journalists, who accused him of *piping* or making up (i.e., fictionalizing) his story. They argued, with some justification, how could Talese *really* know what his respondent was thinking during this event (Robinson, 1970)?

The most serious charge against literary journalism, however, may be that because it is a hybrid form, it is vulnerable both as literature and journalism (or inquiry). Weber (1974) explores this limitation:

> However the New Journalists view themselves, what they are up to is neither exactly literature nor exactly journalism but a rough mixture of the two – and that's the heart of the critical problem. The New Journalism is vulnerable on both sides. . . . To the degree that journalism pushes toward literature it opens itself to attack both as second-rate literature and second-rate journalism . . . a bastard form . . . exploiting the factual authority of journalism and the atmospheric license of fiction. . . . Its aim isn't to convey information . . . but create entertainment. . . . The result, despite repeated claims to accuracy, is widespread disregard of the New Journalism as serious journalism, let alone serious literature, and the inclination to view it as yet another branch of the entertainment industry. (pp. 23–24)

Needless to say, if talented, professional writers such as Tom Wolfe, Norman Mailer, and Hunter Thompson can be attacked for spawning both second-rate journalism and second-rate (or worse) literature, these same criticisms could be leveled against qualitative case reporters who adopt the writing strategies of literary journalism.

Conclusion

The rhetoric I am proposing for qualitative research raises many questions: Is it reasonable and practically possible, for example, for an investigator to guarantee anonymity for programs, institutions, or respondents? Can trustworthy data collection, data analysis, and peer review take place in a situation where anonymity has been assured? Is the temptation to stray into the realm of imaginative writing too great for case reporters who use such fictive techniques as the interior monologue, composite characterization, and the subjective third-person point of view? Finally, is it really possible to ensure the *integrity* of "mutually shaped" qualitative case reports?

The benefits to be derived from borrowing from literary journalism seem obvious; but the limitations are many and not to be taken lightly. There are safeguards, however, for qualitative researchers who wish to try the strategies of the literary journalists in their own case report writing.

To guard against the danger of straying into fiction when using fictive techniques, case reporters should avoid creating composite characters and, even more, writing interior monologues. The third-person subjective point-of-view technique also has some potential for leading writers into the land of imaginative literature and should, therefore, be used with caution.

The serious problems relating to both the ethical treatment of informants and the writer's self-absorption may be solved in part by the qualitative researcher's normal process of mutual shaping – of providing for extensive review by respondents and other interested commentators. Case reporters should continue to seek many reactions to their reports so that they may both safeguard the privacy of respondents and ameliorate or dilute the egocentrism embedded in the techniques of literary journalism – they need help to overcome the limitation that Weber (1974) describes as the writer's need "to drag everything back to *his* cave, to stamp everything, character, events, language, with the imprint of his person" (p. 23).

Following the dictates of sound research within the qualitative paradigm (particularly satisfying the trustworthiness criteria identified by Lincoln & Guba, 1985) will protect the case reporter against the danger of creating second-rate inquiry, while following the dictates of good writing (creating an effective structure and providing for unity, coherence, development, and clarity) and avoiding techniques which tend to fictionalize events or people will provide some protection against creating second-rate writing. The problems of oversimplification and failing to provide an adequate focus can be avoided if the case reporter stays alert to these dangers.

References

Agar, M. (1990). Test and fieldwork: exploring the excluded middle. *Journal of Contemporary Ethnography, 19*, pp. 73–88.

Agee, J. (1988). *Let us now praise famous men*. Boston: Houghton Mifflin.

Agee, J. & Evans, W. (1941). *Three tenant families: let us now praise famous men*. Boston: Houghton Mifflin. Original 1941; reprinted in 1960 & 1968 by Houghton-Miff.

Anderson, C. (1987). *Style as argument: contemporary American nonfiction*. Carbondale: Southern Illinois University Press.

Atkinson, P. (1990). *The ethnographic imagination: textual construction of reality*. London: Routledge.

Barzun, J. (1971). *On writing, editing and publishing*. Chicago: University of Chicago Press.

Bentley, P. (1946). *Some observations on the art of narrative*. London: Home & Van Thal.

Brooks, C. & Warren, R. (1970). *Modern rhetoric* (3rd ed.). New York: Harcourt, Brace & World.

Bruner, J. (1986). *Actual minds, possible worlds*. Cambridge, MA: Harvard University Press.

Capote, T. (1965). *In cold blood*. New York: Random House.

Cassill, R.V. (1975). *Writing fiction* (2nd ed.). Englewood Cliffs: Prentice-Hall.

Dennis, E. & Rivers, W. (1974). *Other voices: the new journalism in America*. San Francisco: Canfield.

Dickens, C. (1936). *A tale of two cities*. New York: New American Library of World Literature.

Dostoyevsky, F. (1979). *The idiot* (D. Magarshack, Trans.). Harmondsworth: Penguin. (Original work published 1868).

Egan, K. (1986). *Teaching as story telling: an alternative approach to teaching and curriculum in the elementary school*. Chicago: University of Chicago Press.

Faulkner, W. (1987). *The sound and the fury*. New York: Norton.

Fishwick, M. (Ed.). (1975). *New journalism*. Bowling Green: Bowling Green University Popular Press.

Forster, E.M. (1947). *A room with a view*. London: E. Arnold.

Gee, J. (1985). The narrativization of experience in the oral style. *Journal of Education, 167*, 9–35.

Gee, J. (1989a). The narrativization of experience in oral style (reprinted, revised). *Journal of Education, 171*, 75–96.

Gee, J. (1989b). Two styles of narrative construction and their linguistic and educational implications. *Journal of Education, 171*, 97–115.

Gudmundsdottir, S. (in press). The narrative nature of pedagogical content knowledge. In H. McEwan & K. Egan (Eds.), *Perspectives on narrative and teaching*. New York: Teacher's College Press.

Hammersley, M. & Atkinson, P. (1983). *Ethnography: principles in practice*. London: Tavistock.

Herr, M. (1977). *Dispatches*. New York: Alfred A. Knopf.

Hellman, J. (1981). *Fables of fact: the new journalism as a new fiction*. Urbana: University of Illinois Press.

Hollowell, J. (1977). *Fact and fiction: the new journalism and the nonfiction novel*. Chapel Hill: University of North Carolina Press.

Johnson, M. (1971). *The new journalism, the underground press, the artists of non-fiction, and changes in the establishment*. Lawrence: University of Kansas Press.

Kallan, R. (1977, December). *Tom Wolfe and the use of argument*. Paper presented at the 63rd Annual Meeting of the Speech Communication Association, Washington, DC.

Kidder, T. (1989). *Among schoolchildren*. Boston: Houghton Mifflin.

Kotlowitz, A. (1991). *There are no children here: the story of two boys growing up in the other America.* New York: Doubleday.

Krieger, S. (1979). *Hip capitalism.* Beverly Hills: Sage.

Krieger, S. (1984). Fiction and social science. *Studies in Symbolic Interaction, 5,* 269–287.

Lightfoot, S. (1985). *The good high school: portraits of character and culture.* New York: Basic.

Lincoln, Y. & Guba, E. (1985). *Naturalistic inquiry.* Beverly Hills, Sage.

Mailer, N. (1968). *Armies of the night: history as the novel, the novel as history.* New York: New American Library.

Mailer, N. (1979). *The executioner's song.* Boston: Little, Brown.

McCorcle, M. (1984). Stories in context: characteristics of useful case studies for planning and evaluation. *Evaluation and Program Planning: An International Journal, 7,* 2.

McEwan, H. (1991, April). *Narrative understanding in the study of teaching.* Paper presented at the annual meeting of the American Educational Research Association, Chicago.

McEwan, H. (in press). Narrative understanding in the study of teaching. In H. McEwan & K. Egan (Eds.), *Perspectives on narrative and teaching.* New York: Teachers College Press.

Muir, E. (1929). *The structure of the novel: Hogarth lectures on literature.* New York: Harcourt, Brace.

Mulkay, M. (1985). *The word and the world: explorations in the form of sociological analysis.* London: George Allen & Unwin.

Peer, E. (1975). New journalism now. *Newsweek, 85(13),* 67.

Proust, M. (1928). *Swann's way.* (C.K. Scott, Trans.). New York: Modern Library (original work published 1913–27, 7 Vols).

Robinson, L. (1970). The new journalism: a panel discussion with Harold Hayes, Gay Talese, Tom Wolfe, and Professor L.W. Robinson. *Writer's Digest,* January, Reprinted in Weber (1974), pp. 66–75.

Rosaldo, R. (1984, March). *Where objectivity lies: the rhetoric of anthropology.* Paper presented at the Conference on the Rhetoric of the Human Sciences: Language and Argument in Scholarship and Public Affairs, University of Iowa, Iowa City.

Scott, P. (1971). *The Raj quartet:* collective title for a set of four novels: *The jewel in the crown* (1966), *The day of the scorpion* (1968), *A division of the spoils* (1975), & *The towers of silence* (1971). New York: Avon.

Sheehy, G. (1970). *Hustling: prostitution in our wide open society.* New York: Delacorte.

Stake, R. (1978). The case study method in social inquiry. *Educational Researcher, 7,* 6–8.

Van Maanen, J. (1988). *Tales of the field: on writing ethnography.* Chicago: University of Chicago Press.

Weber, R. (1974). *The reporter as artist: a look at the new journalism controversy.* New York: Hastings.

Wilder, B. (Director) (1950). *Sunset Boulevard* [Film].

Wolf, D. (1985. Ways of telling: text repertoires in elementary school children. *Journal of Education, 167,* pp. 71–87.

Wolfe, T. (1973). *The new journalism.* New York: Harper and Row.

Wolfe, T. (1983). *The right stuff.* New York: Bantam.

Zeller, N. (1987). *A rhetoric for naturalistic inquiry.* Unpublished doctoral dissertation, Indiana University, Bloomington.

Zeller, N. (1990, July). *A rhetoric for naturalistic inquiry: writing the case report.* Paper presented at the Conference on Narrative in the Human Sciences, Project on the Rhetoric of Inquiry, University of Iowa, Iowa City.

Zeller, N. (1991). *A new use for new journalism: writing the case report.* Paper presented at the annual meeting of the American Educational Research Association, Chicago.

Zeller, N. (1993). *The transformation power of narrative.* Paper presented at the Sixth Annual Qualitative Research in Education Conference, University of Georgia, Athens.

Zeller, N. (in press). Narrative strategies in educational research. In H. McEwan & K. Egan (Eds), *Perspectives on narrative and teaching.* New York: Teacher's College Press.

The story so far: personal knowledge and the political

IVOR F. GOODSON
University of Western Ontario

This paper looks critically at a number of forms of inquiry that are now developing in the field of teacher education. Narrative methods and storying are two associated genres that have emerged forcefully in the past decade as ways of seeking to represent the lived experience of schooling. It is because of the very potential of these methodologies to bring us closer to the experience of schooling that our scrutiny should focus sharply upon both the strengths and weaknesses of these methods. To help the process of identifying the cultural place of stories and narrative, the paper seeks to link the emergence of such genres inside teacher education with broader cultural patterns within contemporary societies. In particular, the use of personal stories in the global media is examined; and as a result, a series of questions is asked and issues are raised. Finally, some conclusions regarding the role of stories and narrative in educational research are provided. Here, some antidotes to the absence of historical and theoretical context are developed.

In this paper, I explore forms of inquiry becoming influential within teacher education. In particular, I will focus on forms of inquiry variously called "stories," "narratives," "personal knowledge," "practical knowledge," or in one particular genre, "personal practical knowledge." I find myself highly sympathetic to the urge to generate new ways of producing, collaborating, representing, and knowing. These approaches offer a serious opportunity to question many of the implicit racial, class, or gender biases which existing modes of inquiry mystify whilst reproducing (see Giroux, 1991). Storying and narratology are genres that move researchers beyond (or to the side) of the main paradigms of inquiry – with their numbers, variables, psychometrics, psychologisms, and decontextualized theories. The new genres have the potential for advancing educational research in representing the lived experience of schooling.

Because of their potential, the new genres of research require close scrutiny. Whilst they have obvious strengths, they also have weaknesses which may prove incapacitating. If this is so, we may be advocating genres of inquiry in the name of empowerment, whilst at the same time effectively disempowering the very people and causes we seek to serve.

Personal knowledge and the cultural logic of postmodernity

Before embracing personal knowledge in the form of narratives and story, it is important to locate this genre within the emergent cultural patterns of contemporary societies and economies. Whilst the pace of change at the moment is rapid, a good deal of evidence points to an increasingly aggrandizing centre or state-sponsored "voices" at the level of interest groups, localities, and peripheries. From the perspective of these groups, these efforts may look like steps to the empowerment of oppressed aboriginals, physically and mentally challenged persons, gays and lesbians, and other deserving groups. This is all long overdue, but we need to be aware of the overall social matrix of these activities. Empowerment can go hand in hand with overall social control.

0951-8398/95 $10·00 © 1995 Taylor & Francis Ltd.

Alongside these emerging new voices, a systematic attack on median or secondary associations is underway on schools, universities, libraries, welfare agencies, and the like – an attack on many of the existing agencies of cultural mediation and production. Economic restructuring is being closely allied to cultural redefinition. There is emerging a clear reduction of contextual and theoretical discourse, coupled with an overall sponsorship of personal and practical forms of discourse and cultural production. The overall effect will be substantially to redraw existing modes of political and cultural analysis. We may end up with what Harvey (1989) calls the *tyranny of the local* alongside what we might call the specificity of the personal. General patterns, social contexts, and critical theories will be replaced by local stories and personal anecdotes.

Denzin (1992) has commented on this in his critique of the rehabilitated "life story movement."

> The cultural logics of late capitalism valorize the life story, autobiographical document because they keep the myth of the autonomous, free individual alive. This logic finds its modern roots on Rousseau's *Confessions*, a text perfectly fitted to the cultural logics of the new capitalist societies where a division between public and private had to be maintained, and where the belief in a pure, natural self was cherished. The logic of the confession reifies the concept of the self and turns it into a cultural commodity. The rise to power of the social sciences in the twentieth century corresponded to the rise of the modern surveillance state. That state required information on its citizens. Social scientists, of both qualitative and quantitative commitments, gathered information for this society. The recent return of the life story celebrates the importance of the individual under the conservative politics of late postmodernism. (pp. 8–9)

Hence, in the cultural logic of late capitalism, the life story represents a form of cultural apparatus that accompanies an aggrandising state and market system. In the situation of "working for" the subject/state, consumer/market confrontation will be immediate. The range of secondary associations and bureaucracies that currently "buffer" or mediate this pattern of social relations will be progressively reduced. The cultural buffer of theory, critique, and political commentary will likewise wither. It will not be the state that withers (as in Marxist theory) but the critical theories and cultural critiques that stand against the state. In the "end of history" we shall indeed see the closure of cultural contestation as evidenced in theoretical and critical discourse. In its place will stand a learned discourse comprising stories and practices – specific to local situations but divorced from understandings of social context and social process. In the next section I review how this cultural redefinition is emerging in the media.

The media context of personal knowledge

This section examines the promotion of more personal stories by the media. The promotional strategies in this context pose questions about in whose interests the move to more personal knowledge is being undertaken. There is, after all, an "opportunity cost" to the time being spent on personal stories – in a finite world of time. Less time is thereby spent on other aspects, most notably on more wide-ranging political and social analysis.

The move towards story-telling is becoming pronounced in the media. This can be seen clearly in the media of countries that have retained, until recently, a strong tradition of political and cultural analysis. Michael Ignatieff (1992), a Canadian working in Britain and one of the most elegant cultural analysts, recently wrote in *The Observer*, "Whatever we hacks may piously profess, the media is not in the information business. It is in the story-telling business" (p. 21). He then details a range of new developments in the British media that evidences this trend. Story-telling and personal anecdotes are the powerful new fashion about which he writes:

> As if to make this plain, ITN's *News at Ten* is reintroducing its "And finally" endpiece, "traditionally devoted to animals, children and royalty." After footage from Sarajevo, we'll be treated, for example, to the sight of some lovable ducks on a surfboard. The ducks are then not just to cheer us up but to reach those subliminal zones of ourselves which long to believe that the horror of Sarajevo is just so much nasty make-believe.
>
> The audience's longing for stories about ducks on surfboards is only one of the trends which is taking the media away from even notional attention to the real world. The other is the media's growing fascination with itself. The last few weeks have seen this obsession inflate to baroque extremes of narcissism. When Trevor McDonald gets the *News at Ten* job and Julia Somerville does not; when Sir David English vacates one editor's chair and Simon Jenkins vacates another; when Andrew Neil snarls at the "saintly" Andreas Whittam-Smith and the saint snarls back, I ask myself: does anybody care but us hacks? (p. 21)

He notes that, "there's a price to pay when the media systematically concentrates on itself and ignores the world outside." (Ignatieff, 1992, p. 21) The opportunity cost of story-telling is that personal minutiae and anecdotes replace cultural analysis. Above all, the "story" is the other side of a closure on broad analysis, a failure for imagination. He writes:

> In this failure and in the media's amazing self-absorption, I see a shrinking in journalism's social imagination. When I know about the 1980's I owe to a journalism which believed that the challenge was to report Britain as if it was an unknown country: Bea Campbell's *Road to Wigan Pier*, for example, or Ian Jack's *Before the Oil Ran Out*. In place of genuine social curiosity, we have the killer interview, the media profile, the latest stale gossip. It's so fashionable we can't even see what a capitulation it represents. (p. 21)

The reasons for the promotion of the anecdote and personal story are broadly cultural and political but also specifically economic. They relate to emerging patterns of globalization and corporatization. Broadly speaking, the British media is following American patterns in pursuit of American sponsorship. American capital is thereby reproducing the American pattern of decontextualized story-telling.

We find in the British *News at Ten* an example of the new initiatives in broadcasting style:

> [It] is part of a new-look bulletin, which will, in the words of one ITN executive, become "more formulaic with a more distinctive human interest approach." Viewers, it seems, like certainty both in the format of a bulletin and the person who presents it. Lessons have been learnt from American TV news by senior ITN managers such as chief executive Bob Phillis, editor-in-chief Stewart Purvis and *News at Ten* producer Nigel Dacre (brother of Paul, the new editor of the *Daily Mail*). (Brooks, 1992, p. 69)

The reasons for the convergence with American styles of story-telling are addressed later.

> By 1994, ITV companies must become minority shareholders in ITN. American TV companies, CNN, CBS and NBC, have already cast their eyes over ITN, though only one of them is likely to take a stake. It is no coincidence that *News at Ten* will have more of an American look – the single anchor, like Dan Rather or Peter Jennings, for example.
>
> In short, ITN and *News at Ten* are being dressed up to be more attractive not just to viewers, but also to prospective buyers. (Brooks, 1992, p. 69)

In America, it is obvious that the "story" is being employed specifically to close off sustained political and cultural analysis. John Simpson (1992) wrote about "the closing of the American media." In this closure, the "story" took pride of place in cutting America off from international news and political analysis. Simpson analyzed the CBS news:

> After reports on drought in the western United States and the day's domestic political news, the rest of CBS's news broadcast was devoted to a regular feature, "Eye on America." This evening's item was about a man who was cycling across America with his son, a sufferer from cerebral palsy. It was designed to leave you with a warm feeling, and lasted for three minutes, 58 seconds; longer than the time devoted that night to the whole of the rest of the world.
>
> It is no surprise that soon there will almost certainly be no American television network correspondent based anywhere in the southern hemisphere. Good-bye Africa; good-bye most of Asia; good-bye Latin America. (p. 9)

As one might expect from a Briton, Simpson concludes that the only repository of serious cultural analysis is on British television which, as we have seen, is being restructured according to American imperatives. The circle is being closed:

> The sound of an Englishman being superior about America is rarely uplifting; but in this case the complaints come most fiercely from the people who work for American television themselves. They know how steep the decline has been, and why it has happened. All three networks have been bought up by giant corporations which appear to regard news and current affairs as branches of the entertainment industry, and insist they have to pay their way with advertisers just as chat-shows and sit coms do. Advertisers are not good people for a news organization to rely on: during the Gulf War NBC lost $25 million in revenue because companies which had bought space in the news bulletins canceled their advertisements – they were afraid their products would appear alongside reports of American casualties.
>
> The decline of the networks is depressing. CBS is one of the grandest names in journalism, the high-minded organisation which broadcast Ed Murrow's wartime despatches from London and Walter Cronkite's influential verdicts on the Vietnam war and Watergate. NBC's record is a proud one too. Recently it announced it was back in the news business and would stop broadcasting stories that were simply features. But NBC News seems very close to the rocks nowadays, and it does not have the money to send its teams abroad in the way it did until a couple of years ago. The foreign coverage will mostly be based on pictures from the British television news agency Visnews, and from the BBC. (Simpson, 1992, p. 9)

We have entered the period of "authoritarian capital," and Simpson argues that the "story" is the indicator of this denouement. If this is so, the promoters of storying have strange bedfellows:

> Earl and Irma, meanwhile, are still there in front of their television sets, serenely unaware of what is happening around them. Decisions which affect their lives are being taken every day in Frankfurt, Tokyo and London, but no one tells them about it. Most of the companies which advertise on television just want them to feel good so, therefore, do the people in charge of providing them with news. The freest society in the world has achieved the kind of news blackout which totalitarian régimes can only dream about. (Simpson, 1992, p. 9)

In one sense, the enshrinement of the personal story as a central motif for knowledge transmission links up with another theme in current restructuring, namely, the reconstruction of the middle ground in the social and economic system. By sponsoring voices at the periphery, the centre may well be strengthening its hand. Hence, empowerment of personal and peripheral voices can go hand in hand with aggrandizement and a further concentration of power at the centre. As Alan Wolfe has pointed out in his book *Whose Keeper?*:

> . . . a debate that casts government and the marketplace as the main mechanisms of social organization leaves out all those intermediate institutions that are, in fact, the most important in people's lives: family, church, neighbourhood associations, workplace ties, unions and a variety of informed organizations. (quoted in Dionne, 1992, p. 18)

The current appeal to personal and "family values" in the United States undoubtedly is driven by a realization of this kind of dissolution of mediating social structures:

> The appeal of this vague phrase is that fundamentally it reminds people that good society depends not only, or even primarily, on their economic well-being, but also on this web of personal-social relationships that transcend the marketplace and transcend government. (Rosenthal, 1992, Sec. 4, p. 1)

A focus on storytelling emerged early in the movies. By 1914, William and Cecil DeMille had developed a technique of storytelling that would "follow the old dramatic principles, but adapt itself to a new medium," and "find its own compensations for its lack of words . . . to make a train of thought visible enough to be photographed" (Berg, 1989, p. 48). By 1916, this had evolved to the point where a ghostwriter for Samuel Goldwyn could write, "by the time I started the Goldwyn Company it was the player, not the play which was the thing" (Berg, 1989, p. 68). Likewise in the world of fantasy promoted by the movies, stories are the central motif for colonizing and redirecting lived experience. This has been so since very early on, as the Goldwyn quotes indicate:

> A painless way to make sense of this new world was suggested by one of the modernizing forces itself: the movies. The movies offered many forms of guidance to confused Americans, particularly to immigrant urban dwellers; they became a virtual manual for acculturation. But one of the most important and most subtle services the movies offered was to serve as a popular model of narrative coherence. If reality was overwhelming, one could always carve it into a story, as the movies did. One could bend life to the familiar and comforting formulas one saw in the theatre. ("Now Playing," 1991, p. 32)

From these beginnings, movies explored new terrains for formularizing and domesticating reality.

In American life, beginning in the 1920s, a number of media began to exploit the storying theme, first initiated in the movies. The tabloid press and then magazines and television began to provide a range of real-life plots from kidnappings and murder to political scandals, to crimes in executive suites, to election campaigns, to the Second World War, to the cold war, to Watergate, to the recent Soviet coup attempt, to Operation Restore Hope:

> Today, virtually all the news assumes a narrative configuration with cause and effect, villian and hero, beginning, middle and provisional end, and frequently a moral. Events that don't readily conform, the savings and loan scandal, for example, seem to drift in foggy limbo like a European art film rather than a sleek commercial American hit. ("Now Playing," 1991, p. 32)

It might well be that the savings and loan scandal could have been made to conform to a very exciting story line, but it was in fact pushed off into foggy limbo. This probably raises the key question of the power of storying to make vivid and realistic certain story lines whilst suppressing others. It is clear that murders, fires, and kidnappings are exciting material for story lines but many of the things that go on in American society somehow or other do not form a reasonable story line. It is interesting, therefore, that an influential newspaper like *The New York Times* should see the savings and loan scandal as not worthy of a story line. It appeared to accept the assumptions which underpin the genre.

I return again to *The New York Times* for an extended statement on the importance of storying in the news:

> That is why reading the news is just like watching a series of movies: a hostage crisis is a thriller, the Milwaukee serial murders a morbidly fascinating real-life *Silence of the Lambs*, the Kennedy Palm Beach case a soap opera, a fire or hurricane a disaster picture.
>
> One even suspects that Americans were riveted by the Clarence Thomas–Anita Hill hearings last week not because of any sense of civic duty but because it was a spellbinding show – part *Rashomon*, part *Thelma and Louise*, part *Witness for the Prosecution*.
>
> But as with movies, if "formularizing" reality is a way of domesticating it, it is also a means of escaping it. Michael Wood in his book *America in the Movies*, described our films as a "rearrangement of our problems into shapes which tame them, which disperse them to the margins of our attention" where we can forget about them. By extending this function to life itself, we convert everything from the kidnapping of the Lindbergh baby to the marital misadventures of Elizabeth Taylor into distractions, cheap entertainments that transport us from our problems.
>
> But before disapproving too quickly, one is almost compelled to admit that turning life into escapist entertainment has both a perverse logic and a peculiar genius. Why worry about the seemingly intractable problems of society when you can simply declare, "It's morning in America" and have yourself a long-running Frank Capra movie right down to an aw-shucks President? Why fret over America's declining economic might when you can have an honest-to-goodness war movie that proves your superiority? Movies have always been a form of wish fulfillment. Why not life?
>
> When life is a movie, it poses serious questions for those things that were not traditionally entertainment and now must accommodate themselves. Politics, for instance. Much has already been made of the fact that Ronald Reagan came to the White House after a lifetime as a professional actor. Lou Cannon, in his biography of Mr. Reagan, *President Reagan: The Role of a Lifetime*, details just how central this was to Mr. Reagan's concept of the Presidency and what it suggests about the political landscape. ("Now Playing," 1991, p. 2)

The important point about this quote is that the storying genre is far from socially and politically neutral. As already noted, the savings and loan scandal was somehow not a valid story line. Likewise, the great exploiters of story lines, the John Waynes, the Ronald Reagans, tend to be of a particular political persuasion and of a particular sensitivity to the dominant interest groups within American society. Storying, therefore, becomes a form of social and political prioritizing, a particular way of telling stories that in its way privileges some story lines and silences others. Once the focus shifts, not to real events but to "what makes a good story," it is a short distance to making an argument that certain political realities "would not make a good story," whilst others would. By displacing its focus from real-life events into storying potential, it is possible to displace some unwanted social and political realities. Even when unwanted realities intrude in deafening ways, such as the LA riots, it is possible to story them in ways that create a distance of sorts. In Umberto Eco's words, it is possible to move from a situation where realities are scrutinized and analysed to the world of American life where "hyper realities" are constructed (Eco, 1986).

Storytelling and educational study

Because the media often employs stories to close off political and cultural analysis, this does not weaken the value of storying and narrative in educational study. I would, however, suggest that it is cause for pause in two ways. First, if stories are so easily used in this manner in the media, it is plainly possible that they might act in this same way as educational study. Secondly, as is made clear in some of the foregoing quotes, the way we "story" our lives (and therefore the way we present ourselves for educational study, among other things) is deeply connected to story lines derived from elsewhere. In American life especially, but increasingly elsewhere, forms of narrative and storying, the classic "story lines" are often derived from television and newspapers. In this sense, Ronald Reagan is not alone; he made such a representative president because of his capacity to catch and dispatch the central story lines of American life. His "It's morning in America" campaign slogan sounded right and true. It was a powerful story line, and it was not seriously contested by political or cultural analysis. But with the power of hindsight, was it not also a gigantic lie which inaugurated an economic depression?

Stories need to be closely interrogated and analysed in their social context. Stories, in short, are most often carriers of dominant messages, themselves agencies of domination. Oppositional stories can be captured, but they are very much in the minority and are often themselves overlaid or reactive to dominant story lines. As Gordon Wells (1986) has warned us, an expression of reality is largely:

> . . . a distillation of the stories that we have shared: not only the narratives that we have heard and told, read, or seen enacted in drama or news on television, but also the anecdotes, explanations, and conjectures that are drawn upon in everyday conversation. (p. 196)

Or as Passerini (1987) noted, "when someone is asked for his life-story, his memory draws on pre-existing story-lines and ways of telling stories, even if these are in part modified by the circumstances" (p. 28). Put another way, this means that we often narrate our lives according to a "prior script," a script written elsewhere, by others, for other purposes.

Seen in this way, the use of stories in educational study needs to become part of a broader project of reappropriation. It is not sufficient to say we wanted "to listen to people," "to capture their voices," "to let them tell their stories." A far more active collaboration is required. Luisa Passerini's work on Turin's working class and on women's personal narratives is exemplary in this regard (Passerini, 1987; 1989). As Weiler (1991) has summarized,

> Passerini's emphasis on recurrent narrative forms begins to uncover the way people reconcile contradictions, the ways they create meaning from their lives, and create a coherent sense of themselves through available forms of discourse. At the same time, she is concerned with the "bad fit" or "gap" between "pre-existing story lines" and individual constructions of the self through memory. As individuals construct their past, they leave unresolved contradictions at precisely those points at which authoritative discourse conflicts with collective cultural meanings. (pp. 6–7)

At the centre of any move to aid people, teachers in particular, to reappropriate their individual lived experiences as stories is the need for active collaboration. In the case of teachers, this will sometimes be in association with educators located in the academy, especially in Faculties of Education.

The relationship of studies of teachers' stories to the academy sits at the centre of major ethical and methodological issues involved in any effort toward the collaborative use of stories. Of course, views of the academy cover a wide spectrum from the classic stance based on "disinterested pursuit of knowledge" through to the 1968 Situationist International slogan that "the intelligentsia is powers' hall of mirrors." I take a position that stresses the *interestedness* rather than disinterestedness of the academy.

Howard Becker (1970) has judged that:

> In any system of ranked groups, participants take it as given that members of the highest group have the right to define the way things really are. In any organization, no matter what the rest of the organization chart shows, the arrows indicate the flow of information point up, thus demonstrating (at least formally) that those at the top have access to a more complete picture of what is going on than anyone else. Members of lower groups will have incomplete information and their view of reality will be partial and distorted in consequence. Therefore, from the point of view of a well-socialized participant in the system, any tale told by those at the top intrinsically deserves to be regarded as the most credible account obtainable of the organizations' workings. (p. 126)

Becker (1970) provides a rationale that explains why accounts "from below" may be unwelcome, and this has particular force when we think about schooling and its associated bureaucracies:

> Officials usually have to lie. That is a gross way of putting it, but not inaccurate. Officials must lie because things are seldom as they ought to be. For a great variety of reasons, well-known to sociologists, institutions are refractory. They do not perform as society would like them to. Hospitals do not cure people; prisons do not rehabilitate prisoners; schools do not educate students. Since they are supposed to, officials develop ways of both denying the failure of the institution to perform as it should and explaining those failures which cannot be hidden. An account of an institution's operation from the point of view of subordinates therefore casts doubt on the official line and may possibly expose it as a lie. (p. 128)

For these reasons, the academy normally accepts the

> . . . hierarchy of credibility. . . . We join officials and the man in the street in an unthinking acceptance of the hierarchy of credibility. We do not realize that there are sides to be taken and that we are taking one of them. (p. 129)

Becker also reminds us that the terrain of research involves not only differentiated voices but stratified voices. It is important to remember that the politicians and bureaucrats who control schools are part of a stratified system where "those at the top have a more complete picture of what is going on than anyone else" (p. 126). It would be unfortunate if, in studying teachers' stories, we ignored these contextual parameters which so substantially impinge upon and constantly restrict the teacher's life. It is, therefore, a crucial part of our ethical position as researchers that we do not "valorize the subjectivity of the powerless" in the name of telling "their story" (Denzin, 1992, p. 2). To do so would be merely to record constrained consciousness, a profoundly conservative posture and one, as Denzin (1992) has noted, that explains the popularity of such work during the recent conservative political renaissance. In my view, teachers' stories should, where possible, provide not only a *narrative of action* but also a history of *genealogy of context*. I say this in full knowledge that this approach is open to the substantial danger of changing the relationship between "story giver" and "research taker" and of tilting the balance of the relationship further towards the academy.

These dangers must be faced if a genuine collaboration between the life story giver and the research taker is to be achieved. In a real sense, *it cannot be all give and no take.* How is the research taker in a position to give and provide the basis for a reasonably equitable collaboration? I have argued elsewhere (Goodson & Fliesser, 1994) that what we are searching for in developing genuine collaboration in studying teachers' stories is a viable *trading point* between life story giver and research taker. The most important element in developing this trading point is the differential structural location occupied by the researcher. The externally located academic researcher has the time and resources to collaborate with teachers in developing genealogies of context. A good deal of work now emerging on teachers' lives and careers develops insights about structure that help locate the teacher's life within the deep social structure and embedded milieu of schooling. This work and these contexts provide a prime trading point for the external researcher. One of the most valuable aspects of a collaboration between teachers as researchers and externally located researchers is that the collaboration takes place between parties that are differentially located in social structure. In this sense, each of the two collaborators sees the world through a different prism of thought and practice. This difference, far from providing a barrier to collaboration, can be valuable when trading points are sought.

In many ways, the work of Sue Middleton (1992) summarizes these aspirations rather well: "Teachers, as well as their students, should analyse the relationship between their individual biographies, historical events, and the constraints imposed on their personal choices by broader power relations, such as those of class, race and gender" (p. 19). In awakening to history in our studies of teachers' stories, I have felt for some time that life history work is a most valuable avenue for collaborative, intercontextual work (Goodson, 1992). The distinction between life stories and life histories is an important one to restate. The life story is a personal reconstruction of experience, in this case by the teacher. Life story givers provide data for the researcher often in loosely structured interviews. The researcher seeks to elicit the teacher's perceptions and stories but is generally passive rather than actively interrogative.

The life history also begins with the life story that the teacher tells but seeks to build on the information provided. Hence, other people's accounts might be elicited, documentary evidence and a range of historical data amassed. The concern is to develop a broad intertextual and intercontextual mode of analysis. This provision of a wider range of data allows a contextual background to be constructed.

Crucial to the move to life history is a change in the nature of collaboration. The teacher becomes more than a teller of stories and becomes a more general investigator; the external researcher is more than a listener and elicitor of stories and is actively involved in textual and contextual construction. In terms of give and take, I would argue a more viable trading point can be established. This trading point, by focusing on stories *in context*, provides a new focus to develop our joint understandings of schooling. By providing this dialogue of a *story of action within a theory of context*, a new context is provided for collaboration. The teacher researcher can collaborate in investigating not only the stories of lives but the contexts of lives. Such collaboration should provide new understandings for all of us concerned with the world of schooling.

Personal knowledge and educational research

As we have seen, story telling has been a sign in the media of a move away from cultural and political analysis. Why then might we assume that it would be any different in educational and social research? After all, educational research has tended to lag behind mainstream cultural and political analysis in its cogency and vitality. Let us go back a step. Storytelling began to be used because the modes of cultural and political analysis were biased, white, male, and middle class. Other ways of knowing and representing grew at the periphery of research to challenge the biased centre. However, those oppositional discourses, having achieved some success in representing "silenced voices," have remained ensconced in the particular and the specific. They have, in short, not developed their own linkages to cultural, political analysis.

The assumption of much postmodernist thinking is that by empowering new voices and discourses, by telling stories, we will rewrite and reinscribe the old white male bourgeois rhetoric, and so it may be. But, so what? New stories do not by themselves analyse or address the structures of power. As the commonsensical level, is it not worthy of pause to set the new stories and new voices against a sense of the centre's continuing power? The Western version of high modernity is everywhere ascendant. We have an unparalleled *end of history triumphalism* with most of the historical challenges vanquished. Is the new ascendent authoritarian capital a likely vehicle for the empowerment of the silenced and the oppressed? I think not, particularly since capital has historically been the vehicle for the very construction and silencing of the same oppressed groups. Is it not more likely then that new discourses and voices that empower the periphery at one and the same time fortify, enhance, and solidify the old centres of power? In short, are we not witnessing the old game of divide and rule?

The collection of stories, then, especially the mainstream stories that live out a "prior script," will merely fortify patterns of domination. We need to move from life stories to life histories, from narratives to genealogies of context, towards a modality that embraces *stories of action within theories of context*. In so doing, stories can be "located," seen as the social constructions they are, fully impregnated by their location within power structures and social milieux. Stories provide a starting point for active collaboration, "a process of deconstructing the discursive practices through which one's subjectivity has been constituted" (Middleton, 1992, p. 20. Only if we deal with stories as the *starting point* for collaboration, as the *beginning* of a process of coming to know, will we come to understand their meaning: to see them as social constructions which allow us to locate and interrogate the social world in which they are embedded.

Acknowledgment

An earlier version of this paper was presented at the American Educational Research Association Annual Meeting, Atlanta, GA, April 1993.

References

Becker, H.S. (1970). *Sociological work: method and substance*. Chicago: Aldine.
Berg, A.S. (1989). *Goldwyn: a biography*. New York: Knopf.
Brooks, R. (1992, July 19). And finally . . . *News at Ten* goes tabloid. *The Observer*, p. 69.
Denzin, N.K. (1992, April). *Deconstructing the biographical method*. Paper presented at the 1992 American Educational Research Association Annual Meeting, San Francisco.
Dionne, E.J., Jr. (1992, July 19). The disillusion with politics could be dangerous. *Guardian Weekly*, p. 18.
Eco, U. (1986). *Travels in hyper reality*. San Diego, Harcourt Brace Jovanovich.
Giroux, H. (1991). *Border crossings*. London: Routledge & Kegan Paul.
Goodson, I.F. (Ed.). (1992). *Studying teachers' lives*. London: Routledge.
Goodson, I.F. & Fliesser, C. (1994). Exchanging gifts: collaborative research and theories of context. *Analytic Teaching*, *15*, p. 47–52.
Harvey, D. (1989). *The condition of postmodernity*. Oxford: Basil Blackwell.
Ignatieff, M. (1992, July 19). The media admires itself in the mirror. *The Observer*, p. 21.
Middleton, S. (1992). Developing a radical pedagogy. In I.F. Goodson (Ed.), *Studying teachers' lives* (pp. 18–50). London: Routledge.
Now playing across America: real life, the movie. (1991, October 20). *The New York Times*, p. 32.
Passerini, L. (1987). *Fascism in popular memory: the cultural experience of the Turin working class*. Cambridge: Cambridge University Press.
Passerini, L. (1989). Women's personal narratives: myths, experiences, and emotions. In Personal Narratives Group (Eds), *Interpreting women's lives* (pp. 189–197). Bloomington: Indiana University Press.
Rosenthal, A. (1992, July 26). What's meant and what's mean in the "family values" battle. *The New York Times*, sec. 4, p. 1.
Simpson, John (1992, July 18). The closing of the American media. *The Spectator*, p. 9.
Weiler, K. (1991). *Remembering and representing life choices: a critical perspective on teachers' oral history narratives*. Medford: Mimeo, Tufts University.
Wells, G. (1986). *The meaning makers*. London: Hodder & Stoughton.

Conflicts of selves: nonunitary subjectivity in women administrators' life history narratives

LESLIE REBECCA BLOOM
PETRA MUNRO
Iowa State University
Louisiana State University

The study of life history narratives has established itself as a rich source for examining the construction of a gendered self-identity. Rejecting humanist notions of a unitary self, the authors take up a feminist, postmodern position in which subjectivity is thought to be nonunitary – always active and in the process of production. Three recurrent themes in the life history narratives of four female administrators are examined: contradictory gender discourses, resistance to patriarchy, and stories of the body. In acknowledging the sites of conflict and fragmentation in women's lives, the authors explore diverse modes of self-representation and the role of nonunitary subjectivity in subverting fixed-meaning claims.

Introduction

To engage in feminist life history work is to enter conflicted terrain. We simultaneously seek to create and disrupt the notion of the subject. Our concern is to theorize the subject as a "site of identity production" (Gilmore, 1994, p. 14) which recognizes the subject as constructed at the nexus of multiple subject positions. Embracing "nonunitary" readings of subjectivity encourages the rejection of humanist concepts of a unitary self. Nonunitary readings also acknowledge women's conflicted subject positions in a world where they are typically represented as objects rather than subjects of knowledge.[1] By focusing on life history narratives, we hope to better understand nonunitary subjectivity and the process of negotiating gendered roles when the self is nonunitary.

For women educators who choose to become administrators, the task of constructing themselves as subjects is particularly conflicted. These women must work within a professional context that is male-dominated and male-defined (Antler & Biklen, 1990; Lieberman, 1988) and that is shaped by a bifurcated discourse of educational leadership in which women and leaders are treated as two mutually exclusive categories (Blount, 1993). Despite these obstacles, women are slowly regaining a presence in school administration; but the persistent absence of and marginalization of their voices within school administration discourse still restricts our understanding of how women shape administrative leadership.

In this paper, we seek to understand how women administrators negotiate the tensions that are produced when their professional roles conflict with their gendered senses of self; we also seek to interpret how these same women both resist and produce cultural identities defining what it means to be an administrator.[2] To this end, we examine a selection of stories from the life history narratives of four women administrators, two of whom were the life historians[3] in Petra's research of women educators' life histories (Munro, 1991, 1993) and two of whom were the life historians for Leslie's study of feminist methodology and interpretation (Bloom, 1993).[4] Specifically, we focus on their stories of becoming and being administrators.[5] Through close readings of passages, we attempt to make sense of self-representation in the narratives as a means through which nonunitary subjectivity is created, recreated, explored, and expressed.

Life history narratives

The word "narrative" is used to mean different things in different contexts; adding the phrase "life history" does not lessen the ambiguity. We use the phrase "life history narratives" as a synonym for oral histories, informal narratives, personal narratives, and life stories. While there are minor differences among these terms (Denzin, 1989), each connotes that the narratives to be studied are about the lives of persons; that they focus on the experiences of the narrators; and as Dégh (1985) notes, that they are structured and patterned by "laws, customs, and cultural knowledge of society" (p. 106). While life history narratives may have nontraditional elements, for the most part they adhere to socially shaped narrative conventions.[6]

The importance of using life history narratives as data in feminist research has been discussed extensively in a number of disciplines. Perhaps the most comprehensive discussion is found in *Interpreting women's lives*, edited by The Personal Narratives Group (1989). The editors maintain that life history narratives "are particularly rich sources because, attentively interpreted, they illuminate both the logic of individual courses of action and the effects of system-level constraints within which those courses evolve" (p. 6). Other advantages of studying life history narratives focused on women include the following: they illustrate the relationship between the individual and society; they demonstrate how women negotiate their "exceptional" gender status in their daily lives; and they make possible the examination of the links between the evolution of subjectivity and the development of female identity.

Nonunitary subjectivity

The examination of nonunitary subjectivity[7] is one of the main interests of much recent feminist scholarship. As Weedon (1987) and others (e.g., Braidotti, 1991/1991; Cixous, 1975/1976; Henriques, Hollway, Urwin, Venn, & Walkerdine, 1984; Irigaray, 1974/1985) explain, redefining subjectivity as nonunitary refutes the humanist assumption that humans have "an essence at the heart of the individual which is unique, fixed and coherent and which makes her what she *is*" (Weedon, 1987, p. 32). Toril Moi (1985) maintains that the very concept of the "seamlessly unified self" posited in the western humanist tradition is part of the phallic logic which likes to see itself as "gloriously autonomous, . . . banish[ing] from itself all conflict, contradiction and ambiguity" (p. 8). Such claims for the existence of the individual essence in humanist ideology deny the possibilities of changes in subjectivity over time. They mask the critical roles that language, social interactions, and pivotal experiences play in the production of subjectivity and ignore gender as a social position that influences the formation of subjectivity. Because of these limits in humanist concepts of subjectivity, many feminists embrace the idea that an understanding of nonunitary subjectivity is critical to feminist research.

In feminist postmodern theory, subjectivity is thought always to be active and in the process of production, or nonunitary. Smith (1993) explains that the focus on nonunitary subjectivity means that, for some, the self "has become more verb than noun, more process than entity, emergent at any moment in language, discourse, ideology" (p. 393). Weedon (1987) sees subjectivity as an active process that is "constantly being reconstituted in discourse each time we think or speak" (p. 33). De Lauretis (1984) further emphasizes that subjectivity is always in a state of process; it is "an ongoing construction, not a fixed point of departure or arrival from which one then interacts with the world" (p. 159). For bell hooks (1990), subjectivity contributes to the individual's ability to take a radical stance toward the world, one that seeks to change systems of domination through speech and action. These understandings of nonsubjectivity as a process and way of being in the world remind us that the self must be considered precarious – always open to new ways to understand the world and the self, to act in and upon the world, and to think about experiences.

The attempt to theorize nonunitary subjectivity in women's narratives indicates a desire for interpretive research to contribute to a transformational politics. As Davies (1992) suggests, empirical work to help women comprehend their nonunitary subjectivity will in turn allow them to gain greater understanding of the ways in which patriarchal discourse "inscribes in the body and emotions" of women (pp. 55–56). Walkerdine (1990) asserts that empirical research is important for understanding how the process of subjectivity "actually works in the regulative practices of daily life" (p. 193). Davies's and Walkerdine's beliefs that researching nonunitary subjectivity may help transform women's lives gives us hope that our research will contribute to this transformation, especially as it concerns women's work as school administrators.

Keeping nonunitary subjectivity at the forefront of our analyses of the narra-tives of Cleo, Bonnie, Sandy, and Robin, we examine three recurrent themes in their stories about being administrators: (a) how moving from a female-dominated teaching environment to a male-dominated administrative environment results in the taking up of multiple and contradic-tory discourses about their gender identities; (b) how they resist patriarchy by redefining power and authority in their lived experiences as administrators; and (c) how the body is a site in which conflicts about gender identity and professional identity are often controlled and negotiated.

The life historians

Space does not permit us to provide a more complete contextualization of the life historians which we consider essential to life history methodology. However, we provide the following abbreviated descriptions of their career histories. All of the life historians with whom we worked were at one time classroom teachers who became administrators. Petra worked with Bonnie and Cleo; Leslie worked with Sandy and Robin.

Cleo began her career as an administrator in the 1960s after working as a high school social studies teacher. Her success in bringing about curricular change as a department chair resulted in her promotion to District Curriculum Coordinator, a position she held until the early 1980s. She is now retired. Bonnie began her teaching career as a secondary social studies teacher in the early 1970s. She narrates her "teacher's story" within the context of her work in VISTA, the civil rights movement, and union activism. Three years ago, after a lengthy struggle, she became department chair. For her, enacting change is central to her life. Sandy, after over 20 years of teaching high school English and Spanish, began her career in administration slowly; she split her time between classroom teaching and running faculty development workshops part-time. In 1989, when she became the first full-time Director of Faculty and Staff Development in the school system, she also became the only woman in the higher administrative ranks. Robin is chair of the special education department at a large high school. With a group of teachers from multiple disciplines, she has implemented a program of collaborative teaching so that learning and physically disabled students can participate in regular classrooms.

From teaching to administration: taking up multiple discourses

Bonnie, Cleo, Sandy, and Robin each told stories about becoming school administrators. They found the transition difficult not only because of the barriers that keep women out, but also because of their own conflicted feelings about becoming administrators. In their stories of becoming administrators, they shared how they struggled with the complex and contradictory expectations of them as women, as teachers, and as professionals moving into positions of authority. As Cleo explained, the gender barrier was obvious and taken for granted:

> In secondary, there weren't many women administrators because they assumed they would never be given the job because the men always got the jobs. Now there were women elementary principals, but there were far more male principals than female. . . . If there was [one] man teacher in the elementary school, it was assumed that at some time, he would be a principal. You could have 30 women teachers, and there was no assumption that they would be looking into administration. But you know this.

Commenting on these same barriers, Robin explains that male dominance in the field makes being a woman administrator particularly frustrating:

> Certainly frustrations are greater in the administrative realm, being a woman, and not as great in the teaching role. Maybe that's because kids are more accepting of people than adults are. It doesn't matter to the kids I teach who or what I am as long as I care about them. Whereas with the administrative world, which is a real male-dominated hierarchy, that's a lot more frustrating.

Sandy shares Robin's sense of frustration:

> I think that as a career woman who really takes herself seriously . . . it is really so aggravating . . . but all I have to work with at my level is men. You know, maybe if I had another 15 years, I could find an incompetent female at the top too – but right now what I see are incompetents and they're all men. It's tough to be a school leader, a visionary. And what they've asked me to do is cover their asses . . . which I think is very sexist.

As these three examples demonstrate, becoming an administrator was a career change laden with tension. That each of the women expressed conflicted feelings about becoming an administrator alerted us that this site of transition was a particularly appropriate place in which to explore nonunitary subjectivity. In the following section, Petra focuses on Cleo's story of becoming an administrator.

Cleo

Born in the South in the 1920s, Cleo characterizes her childhood as one in which "it was clear you just did certain things like wearing white gloves and a hat, even if it was just to the corner store." Her life history narratives describe how she struggled to escape from the social and gender norms of her family and the South. Dominant in her narratives is her desire to live her own life:

> I wanted to get out. So that I could be myself. I don't know that I was rebellious; I just didn't want everything I did clouded by the way my mother thought it should be. But I wasn't really rebelling against her as a person. I was rebelling against a controlled life.

Taking flight from the marriage plot (Aisenberg & Harrington, 1988), Cleo describes her travels and adventures and her eventual pursuit of degrees in history and economics in the 1940s. Central to her success in these intellectual subjects was her understanding of herself as "one of the boys." I was intrigued with the agency and rebellion Cleo expressed in these narratives of shedding the white gloves, becoming educated in predominantly male disciplines, and resisting societal expectations. These narratives satisfied in me a desire to interpret Cleo's life as an example of how women can resist traditional gender roles and can construct themselves as subjects. However, when I asked her how she decided to become a teacher, she explained that it happened "probably the way people stumble into most anything." This response lacked the agency of her earlier stories, and because of this, helped me to realize that both my unitary interpretations of her stories as resistance and Cleo's unitary self-representation of herself as rebellious combined to mask the conflicts unavoidable for women like Cleo who struggle to rebel against gender norms. While such masking may make the narrator feel empowered and help the feminist interpreter locate agency, the irony is that both these positions threaten to erase female subjectivity by reproducing masculinist discourses and humanist assumptions about the self. It was with an emerging understanding of these lived contradictions that I turned to Cleo's stories of becoming an administrator.

I initially interpreted Cleo's promotion as an example of how women disrupt the stereotype of women teachers as lacking motivation and career aspirations, what Dan Lortie (1975) has termed "flat career lines" (p. 99). I saw her move into administration as an attempt to place herself in a position from which she could enact change and live an intellectual life. Her story intrigued me because it spoke to my understanding of women teachers as active agents of change and resistors of gender stereotypes.

However, what I interpreted as resistance to gender norms, Cleo named something else. My initial understanding of her move "up the career ladder" as resistance conflicted with her assertion that she did not seek a promotion to administration as a District Coordinator of Curriculum:

> It was something I did; it wasn't that I wanted to move to some other plateau. . . . I wasn't trying to reach the top in either teaching or administration; I had no desire to be the top Joe. . . . I didn't apply for [the position], I was asked.

In my desire to locate resistance in teachers, a desire encouraged by Cleo's construction of herself as rebellious against gender norms, I initially did not hear the fragmenting of her subjectivity reflected in the above excerpt about becoming an administrator. I struggled to understand why, despite her prior representation of herself as "wanting to live her own life," she resisted conceptualizing herself as an active agent in regard to becoming an administrator. Perhaps what was troubling to me was that her story of deference positioned her as a willing "daughter" to patriarchy's desired subservience. In essence, such deference engages women in a discourse which silences their agency and which therefore thwarted my desire to find resistance. Statements about her career such as: "It wasn't conscious"; "I didn't plan ahead"; "I was a drifter" prompted me to reread her narratives. I needed to put aside my understanding of resistance as public and oppositional and, instead, look more closely at her lived experience and come to terms with the idea that Cleo could have agency and act in rebellion while she could simultaneously be deferential. Only in this way would I be able to acknowledge the ways that nonunitary subjectivity not only emerges out of conflicting gender norms but also helps us to negotiate them as well.

I think that I could alternatively read Cleo's statement that she did not actively seek a promotion as a strategy for easing her conflicted feelings about taking up a position usually reserved for men. Denying that she actively sought to become an administrator allows her to maintain her identity as a teacher, a subject position less contested for women. The importance of maintaining her identity as a teacher is evident in a statement in which she adamantly names herself a teacher: "I'm still with teacher groups. I am not with administrators. I'm with the same group of women as when we started and most of us were teaching. Now we're all retired. But they're all teachers. Classroom teachers." Thus, Cleo's ambivalence about "moving up" the career ladder into administration could also be seen as a way to disrupt traditional male norms that devalue teaching (female) and prize administration (male). In effect, her ambivalence challenges the traditional patriarchal tales of natural and desired ascendancy to positions of power.

Biklen (1983) describes something similar in her ethnographic work with women teachers. She explains that for many women teachers moving "up" into administration is seen as *diminishing* the quality of their work as educators, rather than advancing it, because they become distanced from the classroom. The decision to stay in the classroom reflects a commitment to a set of values that resonates more closely with the values of female selfhood than does the decision to accept an administrative position. It also functions to avoid the potential erasure of female subjectivity when one takes up the male-defined position of administrator. Consequently, Cleo's early rebellions, her deferral of her success to others, and her investment in the discourse of teaching rather than administration not only highlight sites of conflicted subjectivity but also suggest how nonunitary subjectivity is of vital importance in women's lives for resisting gendered norms. Equally critical, Cleo's story demonstrates that subjectivity does become conflicted when one has experiences that challenge received views of what it means to be gendered in this culture and in a particular profession.

Narratives of administration: redefining power and authority

For many women, becoming an administrator means continually negotiating gender roles. To be a woman administrator is to function in a culture in which power and authority are defined by patriarchal and masculinist norms. More importantly, our very understandings of terms like power and authority are located in and dependent on gendered understandings in which male behavior is constituted in opposition to female behavior (Butler, 1990). To be female is to not have authority. Thus, to be a female administrator is necessarily a contradiction in terms.

For Cleo, Bonnie, Sandy, and Robin to be recognized as competent administrators, they must resist presenting themselves in stereotypically female ways. As women socialized to cultural femininity, becoming authoritative in the ways that patriarchy socializes men is rife with conflicts; it may mean that they participate in their own exclusion and silence their own gendered voices (Pagano, 1990). The narratives in this section suggest how nonunitary subjectivity evolves in women's struggle to be "competent" as professionals while not "disappearing." Central to this struggle and the evolution of subjectivity is the redefinition of authority and power to resonate more with female selfhood. Interpreting these contested sites of female selfhood and professional authority provides not only a clearer understanding of nonunitary subjectivity but also suggests alternative understandings of power and authority. In this section, we share stories from the lives of Bonnie and Robin; Petra will examine Bonnie's narrative and Leslie will examine Robin's.

Bonnie

In the fall of 1990, Bonnie became the department chair of an all-male social studies department. As both she and her principal remarked on separate occasions, "blood was spilled on the ground" over that decision. Bonnie explains the controversy: "There might have been some fear in an all-male department. I think they were not looking forward to me moving out of the teaching position I had been in for 15 years." Inasmuch as her social studies colleagues may have attempted to block her promotion, Bonnie credits other males, particularly her principal, for helping her get the promotion:

> Some men are willing to give assertive women the help they need and encouragement to move into leadership positions. . . . Some of these men have put me out in front, and they've always been there to say, "We'll give you whatever support you need."

As a department chair and part of the administrative team, Bonnie continually confronts stereotypical masculinist expectations of how to express power and authority: assumptions of hierarchy as natural, power as consolidation, and authority as the willingness of others, or even coercion of others, to give up their power. In contrast, Bonnie's understanding of power is embedded in her dislike of authority for authority's sake: "I guess I believe in strong authority, provided that it is authority that is used judiciously and that I can understand it and work with it. I can't understand authority for authority's sake, and I will challenge it." From Bonnie's perspective, power and authority are interdependent. Power is derived from one's authority, yet authority is not derived solely from one's position of power. Authority should be achieved through judicious use of power and, therefore, misuse of authority should be confronted.

But confrontation, as Bonnie defines it, is often misunderstood. For her, it is a means to talk through differing standpoints on issues with colleagues. That the talk may get confrontational does not trouble Bonnie who assumes that, when colleagues differ, they do so based on commitments to principles and deeply held beliefs. Therefore, Bonnie believes it is critical to talk through differences in order to understand another's standpoint: "It takes a long time to develop the kind of trust that you can have different points of view, but that doesn't necessarily mean you're working with the enemy."

As Carol Gilligan and her colleagues (Gilligan, Lyons, & Hanmer, 1990) suggest, for some women, disagreement or confrontation can be a sign of relationship because it indicates a desire to understand the position of the other. However, Gilligan's perspective conflicts with dominant ideology in which women are expected to subsume their own thoughts in order to nurture those of others rather than to confront them for greater understanding. This became a concern in Bonnie's interview for department chair:

> Even in the interview, one of the things they asked was "What will happen if your department wants to go one way on an issue and the administration is opposed to it or has a different view? What would you do?" I said, "You mean 'no' isn't negotiable?"

When women do not repress disagreement or when they openly challenge "misuse of authority," they are considered aggressive and unnatural. Consequently, Bonnie's often confrontational style and her challenges to authority were interpreted in her school district as resistance to building consensus rather than as efforts to forge relationships and gain deeper insights into differing standpoints.

Thus, as Bonnie negotiates her role as an administrator with what she believes is an appropriate manner to manifest authority in productive ways, she is cast into the devalued and disdained role of "the aggressive female." However, what Bonnie may be approaching in her desire for open, albeit confrontational, dialogue is the basis for a notion in which power is not used to consolidate authority but to disperse authority in order to enlarge a group's collective investment in change.

Robin

Robin also hopes to enact change and to participate in school reform by redefining power and authority. While Bonnie redefines power and authority by creating understanding through confrontation and challenges to existing authority, Robin redefines power and authority by taking on the role of facilitator. Like Bonnie, Robin understands the conflicted terrain one enters as a woman in administration:

> Women have not been very successful in this country in breaking into those admin-
> istrative positions. Deans and assistant principals, yes, that's fine. But not in real, real
> roles of a school leader or a school principal or a system superintendent. So the
> whole idea that you change how schools are governed, I think, will have a major
> impact depending on what gender is involved because I think that women typically
> are much more geared to participatory management than are men, purely because
> of, I think, the way that – I mean, I think that it is a leadership style that is very natural
> for us.

Robin is chair of a special education department and facilitator of a group of teachers whose goal is to implement a regular education initiative. At first, Robin thought of her role as department chair as being a "manager who managed, who did the nuts and bolts things." However, Robin later became more comfortable with herself as someone who is responsible for "being current" and for "helping her department have access to information" by giving them an article or two each month from journals they do not have time to read. Her underlying motivation in doing so, she explained, was to get them excited and knowledge-able about innovations that they could all take part in without imposing changes on them. She says:

> I see that my role in this building is to facilitate what it is they want to see happen
> in the classroom or in their programs. And we meet in small groups to talk about it.
> So the department is, as a whole, a pretty cohesive group of people. And that is not
> a credit to me at all; it's a credit to the people.

By using the term "facilitator" to describe her administrative role, Robin's narrative func-tions in contradictory ways and again demonstrates how subjectivity is a process that evolves through experience.[8] Robin's goal of creating a context in which teachers take responsibil-ity for designing and implementing changes in curriculum reflects some of the literature regarding educational change, such as site-based management, action research, and teacher collaboration, in which authority is decentralized in order to empower teachers. However, when women administrators take on the role of being a facilitator, a term that is associated stereotypically with women, there is a complex gender dynamic. As a facilitator, she risks erasing herself as an expert. This, in turn, reproduces cultural norms that women are not creators of knowledge and should not have authoritative voices. There is a potential, then, for internal conflict in women who express authority through facilitation because they know that they are expected to express authority and are evaluated on their ability to embody male norms of authority and professionalism.

Being a facilitator, however, resonates with Robin's understanding of how to relate to people in respectful and collegial ways. She neither silences her own voice in taking on the role of facilitator nor abnegates the authority that fits a department chair; rather, she uses facilitation and authority to promote investments in the programs being implemented collaboratively. Consequently, she redefines both the terms "facilitator" and "authority" in ways that allow her to express herself as a professional and that change the landscape in which she and her colleagues function.

Bonnie's and Robin's ways of redefining power and authority differ, yet what they desire is similar: a professional environment in which they can participate and enact systemic change within a context of community and without giving up what it means for them each to enjoy being women. That they respond differently to their administrative roles reminds us that subjectivity is always grounded in the individual, is recreated continually in relation to others, and is fragmented and evolves according to daily experiences and investments in self-representation (Hollway, 1989). That Bonnie and Robin share a desire for understanding and community in their professional relations, however, suggests that the conflicts women face being in a patriarchal administration profoundly mediate their evolving process of subjectivity – not only fragmenting it but also creating it in ways that give them personal satisfaction.

Unbearable contradictions of being: regulation of the professional female body

Another commonality that we noticed when we shared our work with each other was how the life historians experienced the regulation of their bodies as a site of gender identity at work. We were reminded of the first women who were allowed to attend Oxford provided that they listened to the lectures from behind screens outside the door so that they would not disrupt the men. Women's bodies are still treated as outlaws in academe and women themselves are still subjected to regulation by the male gaze. As the following story will demonstrate, being both professional in an administrative setting and being a woman creates what feels like an impossible incongruity. No wonder, as Valerie Walkerdine (1990) suggests, "some of us split apart in various ways, or have different conscious and unconscious methods for dealing with the unbearable contradictions" (p. 144). In this section, Leslie will focus on Sandy's reaction to her male colleagues about a conflict at work.

Sandy

During the spring of 1991, Sandy was having an especially difficult time in her job. She had been asked to attend a number of meetings with school administrators and teachers' union leaders so that she could design a workshop to instruct teachers on how to file a grievance against the school administration. She felt that the meetings were unproductive. When

Sandy confronted them about their inability to make any useful decisions, there was a great deal of anger and tension. As she explained: "After a total of about six hours of discussion . . . the meeting ended with [other administrators] being just totally, rabidly angry with me. It became real obvious to me that there was a lot of old boy networking going on." From the experience of confronting the union leaders and school administrators, Sandy discovered that, in challenging their power, she had to face her own disempowerment and vulnerability. Further, this experience affirmed for her that when dealing with conflicts between women and men at work, being a woman meant having limited discourses available to resolve the friction:

> It's hard for a woman [to be assertive], for fear of being typed as "bitchy" . . . and so what you've got is sort of an automatic means of intimidating women who are in high positions that is very effective, even though unspoken. And just a few words or even the raise of an eyebrow on the part of a man can give that message to a woman . . . that she may be – you have to always ask yourself, "Am I being unreasonable? . . . Is the position that I'm taking reasonable so that it isn't one of these intuitive, emotional kinds of responses?"

Sandy's questions about how, as a woman, she should speak, act, and react in the presence of male bosses and colleagues are profound. They illustrate how patriarchal power disempowers strong, intelligent, capable women like herself. Her questions about her own reasonableness and her fear of responding with intuition and emotion remind us how, under patriarchy, misogynist concepts of women as "bitchy" and "irrational" work as a "truth-effect" which is part of the regulation of women (Walkerdine, 1990, p. 135). Such fictions about what it means to be a female inscribe themselves even on quite "reasonable," "thoughtful," and "controlled" women like Sandy, filling them with self-doubt and self/woman-hate. These reactions, in turn, compromise their self-esteem, further destabilize their subjectivity, and foster the creation of work environments that feel hostile to them. Under patriarchy, as Sandy puts it, women's assertiveness may be equated with bitchiness, and bitchiness means unreasonableness; therefore, women are denied access to a discourse in which assertiveness signifies healthy career ambition, competence, and seriousness.

How are men able to intimidate women by "the raise of an eyebrow" or a "few words"? How is the intimidation so effective that it takes place automatically and may, therefore, be "unspoken"? If we understand the "raised eyebrow" as symbolic of a form of discipline for women who speak or behave as women, then Foucault's (1977/1984) genealogy of discipline and punishment is helpful for locating how the male "raised eyebrow" acts as a form of discipline.

Foucault (1977/1984) suggests that, with all forms of discipline, it is the body that must be subjugated. First, we need to recall, as Foucault does not, that the body is the site of gender difference. With this in mind, Foucault's claim that the body is the subject and object for discipline can be extended to make the claim that the female body is the subject and object for discipline by male bodies. Therefore, as members of the workforce in a patriarchal society, women are expected to be productive within the construct of normative male productivity and professional behaviors; however, to achieve this norm, they must be disciplined. Discipline, in this case, takes the form of subjugating femaleness or the female body – even if that femaleness is fictionalized, as Walkerdine (1990) asserts. The raised male eyebrow is one such subtle strategy for exercising power and disciplining women. The discipline serves to remind women that they may not speak as women. They may not give "intuitive" or "emotional" responses because these are the fictionalized "truth-effects" of women.

Because women under patriarchy have internalized the negative image of speaking as women, it even becomes unnecessary for the eyebrows to be raised or for words to be spoken; the disciplining occurs inside each woman, painfully inscribing her with self-censorship and profoundly shaking her subjectivity. In this way, male norms and their underlying misogyny function as regulative ideals for women although they conflict with women's own senses of self.

Thus, for Sandy, being able to talk openly at these meetings means being able to resist judging her own woman's voice as different, unnatural, and inferior. Sandy knows that stepping over the gender divide at work is dangerous business, but she also knows that suppressing herself means living an unbearable contradiction of being. She told me that she thought she had a choice between two options: She could assert her power which will result in being seen as a "bitch," or she could play it "flirty" and "feminine" so that the male power is not threatened and she might get more accomplished. In the end, she decided to "play it straight and not be afraid to be assertive . . . even at the chance that people would interpret it as I'm bitchy." The result of this strategy, she later told me, was that she "gained a new place of growth" because being assertive and not apologizing for it helped her to realize that it was not she who was "fucked up" but the system that repressed women's ability to do their jobs well.

The control of women's bodies is a constant reminder to women that they are women's bodies first, people second. The current emphasis on professionalization in education is an exemplar of this continued objectification that we believe particularly affects women in administration. As Barbara Beatty (1990) points out, the concept of "professionalism" is in part an imposition of masculine models of work and career advancement. The push for the "professionalization" of education, with the emphasis on "dress for success" for example, becomes one more form of control in which women must take on characteristics of men in order to be seen as professional. The notion of "professionalization," therefore, functions as another form of control and self-regulation. Again, the conflict is clear: To be valued, women have to be professionals; but to be professionals means complying with a male discourse. And when women comply with male discourses, ideologies, and norms, we know the conflicts within ourselves.

Conclusions

Having situated our work as postmodern, we now find ourselves in the rather ironic position of needing to write a conclusion to this chapter. Perhaps the best way to approach this is to share with you what we have learned both from conducting life history research and from the process of writing this chapter together.

In this chapter, we have drawn from current feminist and postmodern theories to interpret segments of four women's life history narratives. What we learned from this is that nonunitary subjectivity is indeed a powerful and affirmative way to understand the female self because it moves us away from unitary humanist/masculinist readings of the self. Nonunitary subjectivity was a particularly helpful theoretical framework for analyzing life history narratives because it enabled us to examine how the life historians variously negotiated their gendered roles, professional identities, and daily experiences from the perspective that conflicts and negotiations are part of a positive female praxis of growth and change and not a disabling confusion. Because women have all too often been regarded as having mental illnesses for not complying with normative acts, thoughts, and speech (Smith, 1990), we have come to believe that understanding nonunitary subjectivity as a positive complexity in women's lives is critical in feminist life history research. Our work has further confirmed for us the importance of continuing to conduct feminist life history research in education because this methodology is particularly suited for showing how uneven gendered relations permeate educational settings and discourse. An increased understanding of the lives of women educators and administrators may teach us ways that women and men can make significant progress toward eliminating sexism, racism, homophobia, and other forms of oppression in order to create profoundly different school climates from those that currently exist.

The focus on interpreting nonunitary subjectivity in life history narratives also deepened our understanding of how interpretation, like subjectivity, is constantly in flux and constructed through a continuous process of interactions. As we talked through interpretations, often agreeing but sometimes arguing and attempting to persuade each other of alternative interpretations, we were profoundly aware of the importance of recognizing how our own conflicted subjectivities, our interactions with each other, and our daily experiences influenced our interpretations (see Bloom, Munro, & Pagano, 1993). Therefore, while some might argue that in qualitative inquiry the subjectivity of the researcher has either been sufficiently discussed or can be formulaically accounted for, we are more convinced than ever of the importance of recognizing that the situatedness of subjectivity should never be veiled, discounted, or reduced.

Finally, we hope that this chapter illuminates, first, how women administrators such as Sandy, Robin, Cleo, and Bonnie negotiate cultural norms and sexist stereotypes and, second, a method by which subjectivity might be interpreted. What we also hope this chapter demonstrates is that interpreting life history narratives must be understood as a process that increases, rather than lessens, the understanding of the lives examined. Life history research, we believe, needs to allow the complexity, ambiguity, and contradictions of lived experience to disrupt the traditional coherence of the text. Similarly, it is a process that should generate, rather than answer, questions about what it means to do interpretive work. We are not dismayed by the idea that our readings of these women administrators' narratives have made more enigmatic what it means for us to do interpretive work. We come away from this project asking questions such as: What does it mean to engage in interpretive work in which there are no fixed meaning claims? How do we construct our final texts in ways that resist authoritative final interpretation? What would a text look like that acknowledges and invites readers to participate in the interpretive process? How can we as authors represent the intersubjective process of our collaborative work?

Of course, we do not pretend to have the answers to these questions. Instead, we continue to open ourselves to the possibilities of engaging in feminist life history research through which we seek not only to understand women's non-unitary subjectivities and to examine uneven power structures but also to create a context in which life history research is open to conflicts of selves.

Acknowledgment

We would like to thank Cleo, Bonnie, Robin, and Sandy for their generosity of time and spirit without which our work would not be possible. We would also like to thank those individuals who attended our American Educational Research Association 1993 presentation on this research for their helpful comments and critical suggestions.

Notes

1. Using gender as the main analytic category in feminist research is problematic. It has the danger of seeming to use the terms "female" and "women" as if all women's experiences are the same (regardless of ethnicity, race, sexual orientation, religion, or ableness) and, therefore, leaves us open to charges of essentialism. In this paper, we use gender as the main analytic category; however, we do so not to imply that there is an essential, unchanging female character but to make the strategic case that because women as a group still live in uneven, oppressed, or victimized relations under patriarchy, to do away with the category of women is politically unwise. As Fuss explains, "retaining the idea of women as a class, if anything, might help remind us that the sexual categories we work with are no more and no less than social constructions, subject-positions subject to change and to historical evolution" (1989, p. 23).

2. We join other current researchers such as Casey (1993), Etter-Lewis (1993), Grumet (1988), Lewis (1993), Miller (1988), Pagano (1990), and Witherell and Noddings (1991) who write about the importance of the subjective meanings that educators give to their lives.

3. We use the term "life historian" rather than respondent or informant to acknowledge the depth and extent of their participation in our research projects.

4. This paper is the result of over two years of ongoing discussion between the authors concerning the narratives of the life historians and the theoretical questions raised by doing interpretive work. Just as we interrogate the narratives for nonunitary subjectivity, our ongoing discussions reflect our goal to resist fixed-meaning claims and to acknowledge the intersubjectivity of interpretation. We regret that one of the constraints of publishing life history narratives is that the text reflects neither the collaborative process of interpretation nor the collaborative process of writing.

5. Interpreting women's administrative roles was not the primary focus of either of our original research projects. However, the conflicts experienced in trying to negotiate "identity" as female administrators were frequently described by the women with whom we worked. They expressed how difficult it was to forge an identity as a female administrator when they understood power, change, and leadership in different ways than they were taught. In our collaborative writing, we chose to focus on the conflicts over identity as administrators because the issue was so critical in their lives and seemed an ideal site in which to explore the life historians' nonunitary subjectivity.

6. While producing narratives may give women a forum for self-expression, the use of traditional narrative conventions to express women's experiences has raised some concerns by feminist theorists. Teresa de Lauretis (1987) warns women that because narrative conventions work as unconscious ideologies on individual subjects, patriarchal and other harmful ideologies are often represented, produced, and reworked in the texts and stories women write and tell, thus causing them to participate in their own oppression. Rachel DuPlessis (1985) argues that narrative conventions limit women from fully expressing lived experiences and emotions. Sidonie Smith (1987) explains that because autobiographical narratives are constructed according to ideologies of male selfhood, women's subjectivity cannot be narrativized in traditional narrative forms. Linda Brodkey and Michelle Fine (1991) express concern that the use of narrative conventions encourages women to represent themselves as empowered subjects, which may mask patriarchal oppression. These critiques of narrative conventions are critical in feminist narratology; therefore, throughout this article, we address how dominant ideologies are reproduced, resisted, and subverted in the narratives of the administrators.

7. The term subjectivity is succinctly defined by Chris Weedon (1987) as "the conscious and unconscious thoughts and emotions of the individual, her sense of herself and her ways of understanding her relation to the world" (p. 32).

8. The term "facilitator" is used by all of the respondents which may indicate either the assimilation of current professional discourse or a mode of authoritative interaction that resonates with their own sense of self.

References

Aisenberg, N., & Harrington, M. (1988). *Women of academe: outsiders in the sacred grove.* Amherst, MA: University of Massachusetts Press.

Antler, J., & Biklen, S. K. (Eds.). (1990). *Changing education: women as radicals and conservators.* Albany: State University of New York Press.

Beatty, B. (1990). "A vocation from on high": kindergartening as an occupation for American women. In J. Antler & S. K. Biklen (Eds.), *Changing education: women as radicals and conservators* (pp. 35–50). Albany: State University of New York Press.

Biklen, S. (1983). Women in American elementary school teaching. In P. Schmuck (Ed.), *Women educators* (pp. 223–242). Albany: State University of New York Press.

Bloom, L. R. (1993). *"Shot through with streams of songs": explorations of interpretive research methodology.* Unpublished doctoral dissertation. Indiana University, Bloomington.

Bloom, L., Munro, P., & Pagano, J. (1993, October). *The gift of gossip: talking through women's lives.* Paper presented at the Conference on Curriculum Theory and Classroom Practice, Dayton, OH.

Blount, J. (1993). One postmodern perspective on educational leadership: and ain't I a leader? In S. Maxcy (Ed.), *Postmodern school leadership* (pp. 47–59). Westport, CT: Praeger.

Braidotti, R. (1991). *Patterns of dissonance: a study of women in contemporary philosophy* (Elizabeth Guild, Trans.). New York: Routledge. (Original work published in 1991)

Brodkey, L., & Fine, M. (1991). Presence of mind in the absence of body. In H. Giroux (Ed.), *Postmodernism, feminism, and cultural politics* (pp. 100–118). Albany: State University of New York Press.

Butler, J. (1990). *Gender trouble: feminism and the subversion of identity.* London: Routledge.

Casey, K. (1993). *I answer with my life.* New York: Routledge.

Cixous, H. (1976). The laugh of the Medusa (K. Cohen & P. Cohen, Trans.). *Signs: Journal of Women in Culture and Society, 1,* 875–899. (Original work published 1975)

Davies, B. (1992). Women's subjectivity and feminist stories. In C. Ellis & M. G. Flaherty (Eds.), *Investigating subjectivity: research on lived experience* (pp. 53–76). Newbury Park, CA: Sage.

Dégh, L. (1985). "When I was six we moved west . . .": The theory of personal experience narrative. *New York Folklore. 11*(1–4), 99–108.

de Lauretis, T. (1984). *Alice doesn't: feminism, semiotics, cinema.* Bloomington: Indiana University Press.

de Lauretis, T. (1987). *Technologies of gender: essays on theory, film, and fiction.* Bloomington: Indiana University Press.

Denzin, N. K. (1989). *Interpretive biography.* Beverly Hills, CA: Sage.

DuPlessis, R. B. (1985). *Writing beyond the ending: narrative strategies of twentieth-century women writers.* Bloomington: Indiana University Press.

Etter-Lewis, G. (1993). *My soul is my own: oral narratives of African-American women in the professions.* New York: Routledge.

Foucault, M. (1984). Excerpts from *Discipline and Punish* (Alan Sheridan, Trans.). In P. Rabinow (Ed.), *The Foucault reader* (pp. 170–225). New York: Pantheon Books. (Original work published in 1977)

Fuss, D. (1989) *Essentially Speaking: Feminism, Nature and Difference* New York and London: Routledge.

Gilligan, C., Lyons, N., & Hanmer, T. (1990). *Making connections: the relational worlds of adolescent girls at Emma Willard School.* Cambridge, MA: Harvard University Press.

Gilmore, L. (1994). The mark of autobiography: postmodernism, autobiography, and genre. In K. Aschley, L. Gilmore, & G. Peters (Eds.), *Autobiography and postmodernism* (pp. 3–21). Amherst: University of Massachusetts Press.

Grumet, M. R. (1988). *Bitter milk: women and teaching.* Amherst: University of Massachusetts Press.

Henriques, J., Hollway, W., Urwin, C., Venn, C., & Walkerdine, V., (Eds.). (1984). *Changing the subject: psychology, social regulations and subjectivity.* London and New York: Methuen.

Hollway, W. (1989). *Subjectivity and method in psychology: gender, meaning and science.* Newbury Park, CA: Sage.

Hooks, B. (1990). *Yearning: race, gender, and cultural politics.* Boston: South End Press.

Irigaray, L. (1985). *Speculum of the other woman* (G. C. Gill, Trans.). Ithaca, NY: Cornell University Press. (Original work published in 1974)

Lewis, M. (1993). *Without a word: teaching beyond women's silence.* New York: Routledge.

Lieberman, A. (1988). *Building a professional culture in schools.* New York: Teachers College Press.

Lortie, D. (1975). *Schoolteacher.* Chicago: University of Chicago Press.

Miller, J. (1988). The resistance of women academics: an autobiographical account. In W. F. Pinar (Ed.), *Contemporary curriculum discourses* (pp. 486–494). Scottsdale, AZ: Gorsuch Scarisbrick.

Moi, T. (1985). *Textual/sexual politics: feminist literary theory.* London: Routledge.

Munro, P. (1991). *A life of work: stories women teachers tell.* Unpublished doctoral dissertation, University of Oregon, Eugene.

Munro, P. (1993). Continuing dilemmas of life history research: a reflexive account of feminist qualitative inquiry. In D. Flinders & G. Mills (Eds.), *Theory and concepts in qualitative research: perspectives from the field* (pp. 163–177). New York: Teachers College Press.

Pagano, J. (1990). *Exiles and communities: teaching in the patriarchal wilderness.* Albany: State University of New York Press.

Personal Narratives Group (Eds.). (1989). *Interpreting women's lives: feminist theory and personal narratives.* Bloomington: Indiana University Press.

Smith, D. E. (1990). *The conceptual practices of power: a feminist sociology of knowledge.* Boston: Northeastern University Press.

Smith, S. (1987). *A poetics of women's autobiography: marginality and the fictions of self-representation.* Bloomington: Indiana University Press.

Smith, S. (1993). Who's talking/Who's talking back? The subject of personal narrative. *Signs, 18,* 392–407.

Walkerdine, V. (1990). *Schoolgirl fictions.* London: Verso.

Weedon, C. (1987). *Feminist practice and poststructuralist theory.* Oxford: Basil Blackwell.

Witherell, C., & Noddings, N. (Eds.). (1991). *Stories lives tell: narrative and dialogue in education.* New York: Teachers College Press.

Life history and narrative: questions, issues, and exemplary works

J. AMOS HATCH
RICHARD WISNIEWSKI
University of Tennessee

This chapter reports findings from an analysis of answers to questions sent to a group of narrative and life history scholars. Respondents were asked to reflect on distinctions between "life history" and "narrative," the relationship of narrative and life history to other qualitative approaches, issues connected with work in these fields, and the relationship of life history and narrative to poststructuralism. They were also invited to nominate significant works about life history or narrative approaches as well as outstanding scholarship utilizing these approaches. Findings are discussed in relation to literature in the life history and narrative field, including the chapters in this volume.

Introduction

Life history and narrative approaches have emerged as important research areas over the past decade. While not new, interest in these methods has never been greater. Life history and narrative offer exciting alternatives for connecting the lives and stories of individuals to the understanding of larger human and social phenomena. For many scholars familiar with other qualitative methodologies and for others exploring the possibilities for inquiry in a postmodern age, consideration of these approaches raises many questions. In preparing this chapter, we identified some important questions and asked individuals experienced in doing and writing about narrative and life history to respond. We also asked them to identify excellent examples of life histories or narratives as well as work discussing methods, ethics, and theory related to these approaches. In this chapter, we present the questions sent to our expert group, report a summary analysis of their responses, and provide a discussion of these responses in relation to the chapters in this book and other literature in this area. We include two appendices in which full references to the works identified as exemplary by our respondents are listed.

Guiding questions

As we planned this project, we recognized the limitations and incongruity[1] of using a questionnaire, no matter how open ended, to gather information about an important genre of qualitative inquiry. Nonetheless, we saw this strategy as the best available way to gather expert opinion and generate discussion about a field of emerging interest. We sent six questions to everyone in the database of the *International Journal of Qualitative Studies in Education* listed under "life history" or "narrative" and to everyone not listed we could identify by being familiar with their work or references to it. The questions follow:

1. What, if any, distinctions can be made between "life history" and "narrative"?
2. What distinguishes life history or narrative work from other types of qualitative research?
3. What are the major issues connected with life history or narrative work?
4. What is the relationship of life history or narrative to poststructuralism?
5. What are three important works about life history or narrative?
6. What are three important examples of life history or narrative work?

The questions were sent to a total of 79 individuals and 22 responded.[2] While we were hoping for more responses, those received were of exceptional quality. They provide valuable insights into the "state-of-the-art" of narrative and life history scholarship. We use the above questions to frame this chapter and include, in appendices, full references to the works identified as exemplary in response to the last two questions.

What, if any, distinctions can be made between "life history" and "narrative"?

Everyone responding, except Bill Ayers, opted to describe distinctions at various levels between life history and narrative. Ayers wrote:

> This is not a useful distinction to me. Both approaches to inquiry are unabashedly genre blurring. They tend to tear down walls – anthropology, sociology, history, linguistics – and why should we resurrect them? Each relies on story, on subjective accounts, on meaning as it is constructed by people in situations. Each focuses on life as it is lived – an experience not easily fitted into disciplines, categories, or compartments. Each assumes a dynamic, living past, a past open to interpretation and reinterpretation, to meaning-making in and for the present.

Despite this important statement and the acknowledgment by most others of the similarities in the approaches, several useful differences were evident in the responses.

Life histories as a type of narrative

Several individuals (who, like us, are structuralists at heart) offered a distinction based on taxonomic relations. All who were explicit about the superordinate–subordinate relationship between the two had life history as a type of narrative. Examples of responses taking this approach include: "Life history is often presented as though it were a special case of the more general class of 'narratives'" (Rob Walker); "It seems to me that a . . . simple distinction between narrative and life history is that one is much broader in scope than (and subsumes) the other: while all life histories are narratives, not all narratives are life histories" (Nancy Zeller). Michelle Foster suggests that confusion could be avoided by using the term "*autobiographical narrative* to indicate that one means life history narratives and to distinguish them from other kinds of narratives." Anticipating question two concerning the relationship between qualitative research and life history and narrative, Mary Jean Herzog organized the following straightforward classification:

    I. Qualitative Research
       A. Narrative
          1. Life history.

Stories as ways of knowing

Narrative was characterized by many respondents as "a way of knowing." As they made distinctions between life history and narrative, the place of story was important. Andrew Sparkes wrote:

> The ways that stories are used differ. Life histories often take them more at face value and work off them in terms of content to generate interpretations. Narratives focus more on how stories are formed and structured by the wider culture in terms of their telling, and during the face-to-face interaction that generates their telling.

In narrative work, there is a particular emphasis on "*how* we tell our stories rather than *what* is told. *How* we tell our stories, the narrative form, becomes a window to ways of knowing" (Petra Munro). Yvonna Lincoln summarized this perspective:

> As Polkinghorne uses the term narrative, it may also mean a way of knowing, as for instance in the sense that we make sense of our lives not in terms of "factoids," but rather in terms of stories we tell about ourselves and our significant others, and the meanings that are implicit in those stories, particularly the meanings which we ourselves have made of the events of our lives. . . . Thus, life history is always the history of a life, a single life, told from a particular vantage point, while narrative may be a style of telling, a particular way of constructing the story of several individuals or a group; a particular way of writing which has strong focus on the rhetorical structure, discursive structure, and "feeling tone" (as Studs Terkel calls it).

Life histories as individual, contextually situated stories

Several others agreed with Lincoln that life history is always the history of a single life. In terms of scope, some noted that narrative is well suited for making sense of "particular experiences," while life history is designed to "explain, describe, or reflect upon a life – making meaning of a person's life" (Linda Tillman Rogers). Bill Tierney supported this view: "Life history revolves around questions pertaining to one's life. Narrative may simply pertain to a moment in a text, a story about an episode in one's life (or a group, or an organization, etc)."

Pauline Chinn defined life history as follows: "A life history is composed of self-referential stories through which the author-narrator constructs the identity and point(s) of view of a unique individual historically situated in culture, time, and place." Chinn's emphasis on situatedness was a theme taken up by others using this approach to making life history distinct from narrative:

> While there are a variety of forms of life history, they all include an essential combination of life story accounts (i.e., autobiographical accounts – oral and/or written), and the accounts of others, including the researcher, for the purposes of "triangulation" into a history rather than being a personal life story. (Richard Butt)

> In so much as life histories are stories of people's lives, they are narratives; but it is the connection of one's life events to social events that distinguishes life history from other forms of narrative. The life is seen as being lived in a time, place, and under particular social circumstances rather than a simple collection of events. (Paul Schempp)

The most important distinction between life history as method and narrative as method is the role of context. I think of life history research as taking narrative one step further; that is, life history places narrative accounts and interpretations in a broader context – personal, historical, social, institutional, and/or political. Thus, life history studies go beyond "the personal." Related to this, I also see a difference with respect to the broad purposes of life history and narrative research. Narrative focuses on making meaning of individuals' experiences; life history draws on individuals' experiences to make broader contextual meaning. (Ardra Cole)

What distinguishes life history or narrative work from other types of qualitative research?

Focus on the individual

Our respondents identified a focus on the individual as the predominant characteristic that sets life history and narrative work apart from other qualitative approaches. Yvonna Lincoln articulated this distinguishing characteristic as follows:

Life history and narrative are always rooted in the sense-making systems of individuals. . . . You would not, or could not, probably expect studies of communities or societies (as you would expect from more common sociological foci) or tribes or ethnic groups (as you would expect from traditional anthropology) from either of these two kinds of studies.

Understanding individual lives or individual stories is central to the research processes and products of life history and narrative. Data for this type of work "have to be collected by interacting with the narrators. Therefore, the material of the life history comes from the participants themselves" (Michelle Foster). Individual lives are the units of analysis of life history work and individual stories are the stuff of narrative analysis. In Norman Denzin's words:

The focus with the life history–narrative approach is on the stories people tell one another. The focus on stories and their narrative analysis distinguishes this type of work from other qualitative methods like interviewing, direct observation, and partici-pant observation.

The products of life history or narrative projects provide different perspectives on individu-als than are possible in other qualitative genres:

The ability of life history to focus upon central moments, critical incidents, or fateful moments that revolve around indecision, confusions, contradictions, and ironies, gives a greater sense of process to a life and gives a more ambiguous, complex, and chaotic view of reality. It also presents more "rounded" and believable characters than the "flat," seemingly irrational, and linear characters from other forms of qualitative inquiry. (Andrew Sparkes)

The tension between this focus on the individual and the contextually situated nature of individual experience was addressed as part of our respondents' acknowledgment of the centrality of the individual in this work. Bill Tierney discussed how this tension gets played out in the different qualitative approaches he employs:

> Life history is singular. When I undertake a life history, I try to understand how larger concepts (culture, society, time) get defined and worked out by one individual. When I do case studies, ethnography, or interviews, I might use the larger concepts to understand a particular idea/dilemma.

Petra Munro warned of the potential dangers of decontextualizing individual lives:

> This focus on the individual is to gain a deeper understanding of the complex relations between ideology and culture, self and society. Life history requires a historical, cultural, political, and social situatedness in order to avoid the romanticization of the individual, and thus reproduction of a hero narrative which reifies humanist notions of the individual as autonomous and unitary.

Personal nature of the research process

Related to its emphasis on the individual, our respondents saw the processes of doing narrative and life history work as distinctly more personal than other types of qualitative investigation. In order for the work to be well done, researcher and participant work closely together to come to a shared understanding of the participant's story. As Pauline Chinn explained, "The element that distinguishes narrative and life history work from other kinds of qualitative research is its dialogical, discursive nature. Narrator and researcher achieve mutual understanding, or intersubjectivity." Chinn acknowledged that while perfect intersubjectivity is impossible, the relationship between researcher and narrator is nonetheless much closer than in other modes of qualitative research. Ardra Cole agreed, noting several elements that make relationships closer: "the personal and intrusive nature of the research, the role of personal histories as a data source, and the primary emphasis on verbal and/or written personal accounts as an information gathering tool." Cole also mentioned that because of the personal nature of the work, "research participants tend to be more involved in the design, conduct, and analysis of the inquiry." More involvement in the research process was another dimension of difference between life history and narrative approaches and other qualitative research modes mentioned by individuals responding to our questionnaire:

> Life history has greater potential to develop collaborative modes of engagement in which greater control and status is given to the subject. In relation to this, it has greater potential to develop knowledge that has relevance and meaning to the subjects or story tellers. (Andrew Sparkes)

Sparkes' statement about relevance and meaning leads to a discussion of the practical orientation that many of our respondents saw as distinguishing life history and narrative.

Practical orientation

Because of their central focus on individual lives as lived, these approaches were seen by our respondents as producing "findings" that have more practical value for wider populations of readers than other forms of qualitative research. Mary Jean Herzog noted "the orientation to practice and change and also the real world" as a distinguishing characteristic of this approach. Two British scholars independently identified as characteristic the ability of life history to place theoretical understanding in a practical light, making it possible to bridge gaps between understandings from micro and macro perspectives:

Of supreme importance is the way in which life history can get at lived experience and in so doing can make the familiar strange. It can reveal what theory means in practice. To use obvious examples, what it means to belong to a particular social class, gender or "race," to have certain sexual orientations, or to be in such and such a job can be illustrated in a way that is especially meaningful and accessible to other people. In other words, it links the micro and the macro. (Pat Sikes)

Given that the life history has to constantly move between the changing biographical history of the individual and the social history of his/her lifespan, it can provide powerful insights into the process of change. Likewise, it is better able to bestride the micro–macro interface than most other forms of qualitative research. (Andrew Sparkes)

Emphasis on subjectivity

A final area in which distinctions were drawn between life history and narrative and other qualitative methods is in the former's emphasis on subjectivity. Many respondents noted the power of life history and narrative to go beyond "scientific" or "empiricist" standards that they believe continue to dominate other qualitative methodologies. Yvonna Lincoln described life history and narrative as "always and without exception phenomenological, naturalistic, only loosely coupled (if at all) to 'scientific' notions of causality and/or generalizability." Rob Walker went even further:

My interpretation is that much qualitative research remains essentially empiricist. It uses words rather than numbers as its substrate, but in most other respects it continues to maintain itself within the same kind of paradigm space as survey research or testing (for instance). "Narrative" offers a point from which to leap out of the dominant empiricist paradigm to something else (I am not at all sure what yet), for the questions about generalization and objectivity that define empiricism look quite different when they are asked in terms of narrative inquiry.

Bill Ayers summarized the sentiments of many as he connected the subjectivity that is definitional of life history and narrative to its value as a means for understanding the human condition:

Life history and narrative approaches are person centered, unapologetically subjective. Far from a weakness, the voice of the person, the subject's own account represents a singular strength. Life history and narrative are ancient approaches to understanding human affairs – they are found in history, folklore, psychiatry, medicine, music, sociology, economics, and of course, anthropology. Their relative newness to us is a reminder of how often we tail behind.

What are the major issues connected with life history or narrative work?

Researcher–participant relationships and issues of voice

Most of those responding to this question mentioned the importance of ethical considerations in establishing relationships with informants in life history and narrative work. Paul Schempp put it succinctly: "Will the person feel fairly treated by my work?" Respondents worried about the vulnerability of subjects of life histories or narrative inquiries. Exposing one's self to another in the research process involves issues of (in our respondents' words) trust, truth telling, fairness, respect, commitment, and justice. Yvonna Lincoln, citing Shulamit Reinharz, suggested that "such research proceeds on a 'lover model,' where mutual respect, ongoing relationships, and trust are some of the basic commitments of this kind of research posture."

Relatedly, respondents identified issues in the areas of authorship, ownership, and voice. In this kind of work: Who speaks for whom and with what authority? Whose story is it? Who owns the products of the work? Who is the author? What are the purposes of life-history taking? What does the researcher gain from the research? The subject? These questions reflect our respondents' concern for establishing mutually beneficial relationships between researchers and subjects. Lisa Smulyan wrote:

> Clarifying, negotiating, and renegotiating the relationship between the researcher and the subject of the life history and narrative [is an important issue]. How do we carry out a collaborative, mutually beneficial project while working through issues of knowledge, power, control, and privacy; how, as a researcher, can I contribute as much as the subject of my work is giving?

Petra Munro extended this concern to include the possibility that when telling the stories of less powerful others researchers may be operating on assumptions that work to keep unequal power relations in place:

> Life history and narrative have been central to challenging official histories by providing a more inclusive view of social relations. Yet, a central tension in life history work is the desire to "give voice" without producing the very unequal power relations we are critiquing. How does the notion of "giving voice" actually underscore our perceptions of those with whom we conduct research as disempowered?

The irony of hurting those we seek to help is evident in another concern tied to researcher–participant relations. Linda Tillman Rogers charged researchers with responsibility for the possibly negative emotional and psychological consequences for participants who are sharing their life stories:

> Reflection is a powerful tool; the researcher, simply by being there causes a form of "knowing" an event differently. Many people survive or, indeed, endure by deliberately not being aware of all the complexities and dangers – the slings and arrows of discontent. . . . The reflective act does make clear the nature of the problem, but existential reality – what we *really* do and *really* know – is often not comforting. . . . Therefore, what is the researcher's obligation?

This and other issues of researcher–participant relationship are connected to the discussions that follow.

Balancing individual stories and social-historical contexts

A second issue domain was again summarized by a question from Paul Schempp: "How was this person's life influenced by his/her society and vice versa?" We noted above that a focus on the individual is a distinguishing characteristic of this work, and "how to fit life histories, self-stories, and personal experiences stories into the larger cultural processes that shape and inform these tales of self, always fitting stories to their historical moment" (Norman Denzin) was seen as an important issue. Lisa Smulyan framed the issue as follows:

> [At issue is] balancing the story of the individual in all of its uniqueness with the larger social, political, economic contexts which frame it and are, in turn, reinforced or challenged by the individual's actions and responses. How do we place the individual within her social context and demonstrate the powers and forces that shape her experience and also provide a rich description of her story, her shaping of her world?

Criteria for judging quality

A number of respondents noted as an issue that criteria for making judgments about the quality of scholarship used with other research approaches do not fit narrative and life history. Andrew Sparkes identified as an issue,

> The problematic nature of the criteria for judging "good" work in both [life history and narrative]. Both reject orthodox foundational views of validity and reliability; but, at the end of the day, we still have to pass judgment. For example, what makes a "good" narrative or life history? Is just a good story enough? What must be added to story to make it scholarship? What makes for authentic life history?

Others agreed that "orthodox" views do not work:

> But at the very least, the silliest issues in such research would be traditional ideas of internal and external validity, replicability, and objectivity. It's not that those issues don't get done well in this form of research; they are simply not in the same universe. (Yvonna Lincoln)

Finding criteria to determine whether life history and narrative qualify as scholarship and then to judge its quality was identified as another important issue in the field. Mary Jean Herzog noted that for many scholars an elemental issue is the "debate about whether stories can be construed as research." Others were concerned about "issues of the truthfulness of the story, the authority of the researcher to interpret a life, and the difficulty of keeping the complexity of a life – not reducing it to a simplified, coherent text" (Leslie Rebecca Bloom). Issues of credibility and trustworthiness were identified as areas in which criteria for judging the quality of life history and narrative work need to be explored.

Crisis of representation

A final set of issues foreshadowed the fourth question in our survey about the relationship of life history and narrative to poststructural thought. Richard Butt offered:

> The major issue for me is the challenge that poststructural and postmodern critiques have leveled at the whole notion of "the self" and whether indeed, it, per se, or its current conceptualizations are justified as tenable assumptions upon which most life history, life story, life course research is predicated.

Butt cautioned that "narrative inquiry has not been clearly grounded in its scholarly history – especially its relationship to the postmodern critique." Others described similar concerns around poststructuralist reservations related to representing lives in text:

> At the moment, the major issue pertains to the representation of the data in the text. Although this is an issue in all qualitative work, the crisis of representation is writ large when we work solely with life history data. By definition, we are working with one person's life. How we present that life, who is the "author" and how subject–researcher get defined are issues that go to the heart of doing qualitative work in a postmodern world, and they are best dealt with in life history work. (Bill Tierney)

Others saw opportunities in the postmodern moment to go beyond traditional qualitative textual representations. Norman Denzin noted that now may be a time for "moving beyond purely structural approaches to narrative to a deeper hermeneutic informed by the logics of postmodernism." Andrew Sparkes expressed a parallel opinion:

> Given the postmodern turn, I feel that we need to explore different ways of representing the other and ourselves as researcher-author in life histories. At the moment, we rely mostly on realist tales that are author evacuated texts. But what about creating impressionist tales, dramas, fictions, and poetic representations of lives?

More on the relationship of poststructuralism to narrative and life history is directly addressed in our next question.

What is the relationship of life history or narrative to poststructuralism?

No one responded that the two are mutually exclusive; therefore, life history and narrative approaches and poststructural thought are related. No one claimed that the two are synonymous. Not all life histories or narratives are "poststructural," and not all poststructural work is in life history or narrative forms. This question drew the fewest responses of any of our questions. Seven respondents chose not to answer without explanation, and two answered with "I don't know" and "I can't answer this question. The answer is . . . so complex that it would take a whole book to sort it out." We have organized the responses we received into three related categories: lives as text; the nonlinear life, the incoherent self; and theory and analysis.

Lives as text

In the "Crisis of representation" discussion above, several respondents signaled the important connections between postmodern conceptions of text and its ability to represent, or not, lived experience. This connection was raised again as we asked about the relationship of poststructuralism and life history and narrative approaches.

For some, the poststructural critique means that life historians and narrative inquirers need to take special care in establishing relationships with their subjects, in constructing their texts, and in framing the presentations of their texts for readers. Two respondents described the connections as follows:

> Poststructuralism tends to reject the possibility that those conducting . . . autobiographical narrative research can accurately represent reality since poststructuralism questions whether we researchers can gain access to an independent reality. (Michelle Foster)

> Poststructuralist critiques have heightened our awareness for ways in which social science researchers reduce respondents' lived experiences to texts for the sole benefit

of the researcher. This raises questions about authorial responsibility and power and
the importance of the ethical responsibility (beyond "do not harm") toward those
who have invested their time with us. (Leslie Rebecca Bloom)

Other respondents saw life history work as a positive response to the crisis of representation. For example, Richard Butt responded:

> The postmodern focus is on the text per se, not on life beyond text. . . . The relation-
> ship of the researcher to the autobiographer is through the text. With life history or
> life story work, the relationship with the person as a cointerpreter is important. It is
> less disembodied, less impersonal.

Pat Sikes made the case that life history work predates poststructuralist thought and notes
that issues raised by poststructuralists have been concerns of life his-torians for 70 years:

> Life history explicitly acknowledges the existence of multiple, and possibly conflict-
> ing, personal realities and perspectives. In doing this, it also acknowledges the part
> (often) played by the researcher in selecting the field of study and in interpreting the
> data. Nowadays, these characteristics may well be described in terms of the post-
> modernist paradigm, but it is, I think, important to remember that life history dates
> back to the 1920s. Maybe the role of the researcher was not recognized in the same
> way then, but the seeds were there.

There seemed to be a consensus around the notion that poststructuralist tenets related to
the tenuous relationships between texts and lives-as-lived ought to inform narrative and life
history methods and influence the construction and presentation of research products.

The nonlinear life, the noncoherent self

Another set of concepts that was seen by our respondents as related to life history and
narrative work has to do with poststructuralist perspectives on identity. Individual constructions of "self" or of "a life" were seen as complex, situational, fragmented, nonunitary,
nonlinear, noncoherent, and constantly in flux. Since individuals' expressions of self and
their stories of their lives are the data of narrative and life history inquiries, the poststructural
critique must be reconciled by scholars doing this kind of research in the postmodern
moment. Peter McLaren's statement reflected others' concern with the complexity poststructuralism brings to the task of the researcher:

> Poststructuralism situates "subjectivity" and "identity" within multiple competing and
> conflicting narratives and theories of narration. We inherit narratives already codified
> by others and populated with others' meanings. As selves, we narrate our world to
> give it form and meaning; but at the same time, we are being narrated because the
> forms we use to narrate are not our own – they belong to other times, other places,
> other contexts. Narrative speaks to the performative aspect of history. We act out
> history, but history also "acts" us by providing us with narrative codes and syntax with
> which we live and make sense of our lives.

Leslie Rebecca Bloom identified feminist poststructural work as having impacted on life
history and narrative scholarship by moving researchers away from

> . . . the humanist concepts of the self as a neat, coherent package to a more complex
> idea of the self as fragmented and nonunitary. This complicates life history

research. . . . If we have nonunitary subjectivity, we can no longer chart the life in a simple, linear fashion in which one logical step leads to the next. . . . When the representations are complex, we, as interpreters, find that the lives are more open to multiple interpretations, and therefore, our interpretations become less authoritative.

Seeing the same constraints, Andrew Sparkes concluded that life history is well suited for dealing with poststructural issues of identity:

The poststructural position seems to be that the individual has no permanent, essential, or fixed identity, but assumes different identities at different times so that identifications are continually in a state of flux, a fleeting multiplicity of opportunities. Should we feel we do have a unified identity, then this is only because we construct a comforting "narrative of self" about ourselves. If this is the case, then I feel that life history work has much to offer the poststructural project. For example, given its focus upon the construction and reconstruction of identities and the self over time, it could provide important insights into how the "narrative of the self" is developed and how it is transformed continuously in relation to the ways that we are represented in the cultural systems that surround us.

As with the crisis of representation, scholars seem to be divided about whether poststructural notions of self and identity make narrative and life history work extremely problematic or make this kind of inquiry a valuable tool for sorting out the complexity. As we will discuss later, it is likely that both are correct.

Theory and analysis

A final domain of relationship identified by our respondents involved the connections between poststructural theory and analytic stances associated with life history and narrative. As can be seen in the responses above, several individuals noted that "life history and narrative research are imbedded in the general tenets of poststructuralism" (Ardra Cole). Some were more specific about the utility of applying "poststructuralism as a technique for interpreting narratives" as well as "an orientation toward life history research in general" (Leslie Rebecca Bloom). In the spirit of poststructural thought, such an application gives researchers (and readers of life histories and narratives) tools for deconstructing the stories that make up the lives under examination. Petra Munro described the deconstructive potential of poststructurally based analyses:

Poststructuralism is a theoretical perspective which assumes knowledge as partial, power as dispersed, and identity as always in flux. For those who reject unitary subjectivity, poststructuralism becomes a useful theoretical perspective to analyze constructs like power, knowledge, subjectivity as they are constructed in discourses and within personal narratives.

Finally, Andrew Sparkes saw a different kind of connection between poststructural theory and life history work. He argued that poststructuralist theory could itself be informed by the findings of life history research:

Life history data would put some valuable meat on the theoretical bones of the poststructural skeleton, which for some, has spent too long in armchair theorizing and little time interacting with the people who are supposedly reacting to and living in a poststructural or postmodern period in which "all is text."

What are important works about and examples of life history or narrative?

Rob Walker began his response with, "They probably have yet to be written." That is true at some level, but Walker and almost all of our other experts were able to identify at least three sources (many named more) of information about narrative and life history and three or more examples that they believe provide models of high-quality work. We have prepared appendices that include full bibliographic references to the books, articles, and chapters identified: Appendix A has the references to works *about* life history and narrative; Appendix B is a list of works identified as important *examples of* life history or narrative.

It was interesting to us to see the wide variety of responses to both questions. Since the majority of our respondents have some connection to education, we expected materials on teachers' lives to be well represented, and these were widely cited, especially by Canadian and British scholars. We were pleased, however, to see references to texts with roots in many academic disciplines, including: anthropology, sociology, psychology, feminist studies, philosophy, history, rhetoric, and literary criticism. In addition, excellent exemplars were identified from the literary genres of biography, autobiography, and fiction. It seems evident that (a) our respondents are well read and eclectic in their reading; and (b) the literatures related to life history and narrative are diverse and broad based. These appendices offer novice scholars a starting place for their explorations and give more experienced researchers a wider lens through which to view the landscape of narrative and life history work.

Discussion

What's in a name?

It is difficult to make absolute distinctions between "life history" and "narrative" examining responses to our questionnaire and the literature reviewed in preparing this chapter. To add to the confusion, the two terms fit into a larger category of related or synonymous terms such as autobiography, biography, interpretive biography, autobiographical narrative, life history narrative, oral narrative, life narrative, personal narrative, stories, life stories, self stories, personal experience stories, auto-ethnography, ethnographic fiction, personal history, oral history, case history, and case study.[3] Part of the reason for this array of terms may be that these types of scholarship have a history of use in disciplines as diverse as anthropology, sociology, medicine, psychology, history, political science, literature, and others (Langness & Frank, 1981). Many of the scholars utilizing life history or narrative approaches have been on the margins of mainstream academic thought in their individual disciplines, and few have made attempts to join forces with others from outside their academic homes. Hence, theories and methods, while sharing basic aims and assumptions, developed different emphases and vocabularies.

Life history proponents trace their roots back to at least the 1920s. During that decade, anthropologists first used life history approaches to describe Native American cultures (e.g., Michelson, 1925; Radin, 1926). In 1927, Thomas and Znaniecki published their seminal sociological life history work, *The Polish Peasant in Europe and America*. The 1930s saw the emergence of a new field, a marriage between anthropology and psychology, that emphasized life history analysis (see, Sapir, 1932). Out of this movement came Dollard's (1949) *Criteria for the Life History*, an attempt to blend the principles of cultural study and psychoanalysis. In anthropology, a subgroup interested in life history has turned to phenomenology and hermeneutics to improve interpretive understandings of the human condition (e.g., Crapanzano, 1980; Watson, 1976).[4]

Polkinghorne (this volume) mentions Freud's case studies and the work of the Chicago School symbolic interactionists as examples of classic narrative analyses. Those who chose to use the term narrative to identify their work are likely to refer to scholars who have challenged the taken-for-granted connections between text and life-as-lived, for example, Agger (1990), Bakhtin (1981), Derrida (1967/73), Fisher (1989), Lyotard (1984), and Ricoeur (1991). Life history and narrative traditions are, of course, not mutually exclusive; for example, life historians are interested in the deconstructivist, postmodern perspective, and narrative inquirers utilize criteria developed in the anthropological life history tradition to guide their studies.

We have identified several definitions in the literature that highlight points of emphasis in life history and narrative studies. Again, these points are not distinctly within one tradition and not the other, but they suggest important identifying characteristics:

> *Life history* – "any retrospective account by the individual of his/[her] life in whole or in part, in written or oral form, *that has been elicited or prompted by another person*" (Watson & Watson-Franke, 1985, p. 2, emphasis in original).
>
> *Life story* – "the story we tell about our life" (Goodson, 1992, p. 6).
>
> *Life history* – "the life story located within its historical context" (Goodson, 1992, p. 6).
>
> *Life history* – "sociologically read biography" (Bertaux, quoted in Measor & Sikes, 1992, p. 210).
>
> *Storied narrative* – "the linguistic form that preserves the complexity of human action with its interrelationship of temporal sequence, human motivation, chance happenings, and changing interpersonal and environmental contexts" (Polkinghorne, this volume).
>
> *Narrative* – "both phenomenon and method. Narrative names the structured quality of experience to be studied, and it names the patterns of inquiry for its study" (Clandinin & Connelly, 1994, p. 416).
>
> *Oral narrative* – "both a process and product that mediates the boundaries between history, language, and literature. . . . [It] offers an intimate perspective of a narrator's interpretation and understanding of her/his own life" (Etter-Lewis, 1993, p. xii).

Life history work emphasizes the importance of the researcher in the process of gathering, interpreting, and reporting biographical information. Goodson (1992, this volume) and many of the respondents to our questionnaire point out that an analysis of the social, historical, political, and economic contexts of a life story by the researcher is what turns a life story into a life history. In this volume, Barone takes the position that not all "emancipatory-minded" stories need to be "theorized" to be useful, a position that does not represent all narrative inquirers but which challenges Goodson and the more common life history perspective.

Based on J. Bruner (1986), Polkinghorne and other narrative proponents make a distinction between two types of cognition (paradigmatic and narrative) associated with two types of narrative inquiry: analysis of narratives and narrative analysis. The former uses narratives (stories) as data and produces taxonomies and categories much like those found in other qualitative studies. Narrative analysis gathers descriptions of events and happenings and generates a narrative as a research product (see Polkinghorne, 1988, this volume). Following this logic, it seems to us that narratives generated via narrative analysis procedures would look more like "life stories" than the "life histories" of those adhering to Goodson's position.

That narrative includes both process and product, phenomenon and method, is emphasized throughout the narrative literature and in our questionnaire responses. J. Bruner's (1986) notion of narrative knowing is central here. Narrative cognition, even though it has been ignored or devalued by proponents of more "scientific" approaches, is the way each of us comes to understand and communicate human action. Narrative knowledge is organized as stories, and this knowledge is best expressed in storied narrative forms. The processes of doing narrative inquiry involve sharing narrative knowledge through the telling of stories; the products are the stories of self we choose to tell. Narrative as a way of knowing is important to life history research; it defines narrative inquiry.

Life history, narrative, and qualitative research

Some have suggested that while the qualitative paradigms have increased their respectability, narrative and life history approaches remain suspect even within the qualitative field because their "data are subject to incompleteness, personal bias and selective recall" (Butt, Raymond, McCue, & Yamagishi, 1992, p. 91). When personal stories are the prime sources of data, and often the products of inquiry, those (qualitative researchers among them) bound to thinking of "science" as paradigmatic knowledge will be reluctant to accept life history and narrative inquiry as legitimate. Given these constraints, our respondents and the literature reviewed place life history and narrative comfortably within the qualitative camp.

The literature reviewed supports the characteristics identified in our analysis of questionnaire responses as distinguishing life history and narrative from other qualitative methods: a focus on the individual, the personal nature of the research process, a practical orientation, and an emphasis on subjectivity. In an interesting turn, the focus on the individual is being critiqued by some as potentially dangerous. Denzin (1992) argues that life stories can be construed as cultural capital within the logic of late capitalism. He sees social scientists as agents of the modern surveillance state, collecting self stories as information that keeps the myth of the autonomous individual alive. Goodson (this volume) builds on Denzin's assertions, using the news media to make his case that "stories that live out a 'prior script' will merely fortify patterns of domination". He argues that life histories (life stories located in a social, historical, and political context) avoid the trap of disempowering those we seek to empower.

The personal nature of life history and narrative is emphasized by Clandinin and Connelly as they selected the term "personal experience methods" to describe this genre of research in the *Handbook of Qualitative Research* (Denzin & Lincoln, 1994). They summarize: "Personal experience methods inevitably are relationship methods. As researchers we cannot work with participants without sensing the fundamental human connection among us" (Clandinin & Connelly, 1994, p. 425). As our questionnaire respondents noted, with these human connections comes responsibility. When researchers ask for personal experience stories, they are asking participants to engage in an activity that may bring unexpected insights that may change participants' view of past experiences (Watson & Watson-Franke, 1985). The closer the relationship, the more likely that deep insights will be elicited. Grumet (1991) warns that the personal nature of such work can put the participant at risk: "Even telling a story to a friend is a risky business; the better the friend, the riskier the business"

(p. 69). In a similar vein, Butt and his colleagues remind us that researchers need to be aware of the potential for invading the privacy of our participants and "practicing therapy without a license" (Butt et al., 1992, p. 93). In this volume, Blumenfeld-Jones addresses this topic, offering "fidelity" as a criterion for establishing and honoring research relationships.

The literature supports our respondents' view that narrative and life history are characterized by a practical dimension. Methods and products are seen as revealing the experiences of real people, in real situations, struggling with real problems (Hauser, 1995; Witherell & Noddings, 1991). In his essay on biographical method, Smith (1994) places such work in the domain of reflective practice, arguing that:

> Engaging in life-writing inquiry is, in part, a craft, an instance of practice. In my interpretation of these views, I believe an essentially pragmatic perspective arises. I believe that the stories and ideas that one creates should be useful for solving further problems in one's professional life. (p. 302)

Scholars taking a critical perspective see the practical dimensions of narrative and life history work in the creation of emancipatory possibilities for the disenfranchised and disempowered (e.g., Barone, this volume).

The emphasis on subjectivity in the research process sets life history and narrative inquiry apart from other qualitative methods. This was clear in our respondents' statements and is evident in the chapters of this book (see especially, Emihovich; Bloom & Munro). The centrality of subjectivity is one of the issues taken up in the next section.

Issues

Our respondents' answers to our request for issues in this arena yielded four categories of responses: relationships and issues of voice; individual stories and social-historical contexts; criteria for establishing quality; and the crisis of representation. We address the first three categories in this section, leaving the crisis of representation for the final section on poststructuralist thought.

Issues derived from relationship and voice have three dimensions: epistemological, political, and moral. Whose story is it? What is the relationship of the researcher's story to the story told in the final text? These questions are at the core of methodologies that depend on close personal relations between story givers and story takers. Clandinin and Connelly (1994) explain: "Researcher relationships to ongoing participant stories shape the nature of field texts and establish the epistemological status of them" (p. 419). They continue, "These intensive relationships require serious consideration of who we are as researchers in the stories of participants, for when we become characters in their stories, we change their stories" (p. 422). Stories of a life told by one person to another are joint productions; they are in a real sense "co-authored" (E. M. Bruner, 1986; J. Bruner, 1990). The researcher's position in relation to the stories of participants ought to be acknowledged, examined, and explicated (see Measor & Sikes, 1992).

We agree with authors in this volume that writing narratives and life histories is a political act (see especially Emihovich; Nespor & Barber; Bloom & Munro). Who benefits? Whose voice is privileged? Who chooses the story to tell? These are questions related to the politics of this type of research. While some would contend that narrative and life history approaches provide opportunities for "the production and circulation of first accounts with a direct popular authorship" (Popular Memory Group, 1982, p. 251), we agree with Nespor and Barber (this volume) that the complexities of political relationships within the research process make this assertion less powerful than one would hope.

There is no doubt that participants are vulnerable when they agree to enter into relationships with life history or narrative researchers. The moral dimension of these inherently close relationships requires researchers to fulfill certain obligations to their informants. On the most basic level, "Researchers have an obligation to protect people from being managed and manipulated in the interest of research" (Measor & Sikes, 1992, p. 211). Grumet (1991) establishes that "telling is an alienation, that telling diminishes the teller," then argues:

> So if telling a story requires giving oneself away, then we are obligated to devise a method of receiving stories that mediates the space between the self that tells, the self that told, and the self that listens: a method that returns a story to the teller that is both hers and not hers: that contains her self in good company. (p. 70)

In this volume, both Emihovich and Goodson argue for collaboration as a means for dealing with the researcher's moral obligations.

Butt and colleagues ask a question that is at the center of the issue of individual stories versus stories imbedded in social-political analysis: "How can we simultaneously represent commonality and uniqueness?" (Butt et al., 1992, p. 94). If individual stories are the stuff of narrative and life history research, ought these to be connected to the larger contexts of society, and if so, how? There is some contention about the place of individual, "untheorized" stories as legitimate research (see Barone, this volume). Earlier, we noted Goodson's (1992) distinction between life stories and life histories. Goodson's distinction is an important one. Applying theoretical frameworks from a variety of perspectives provides ways to represent commonality and uniqueness; operating without them leaves open the possibility of solipsism and the elevation of the idiosyncratic. The Personal Narratives Group (1989) addresses this issue in relation to women's individual experiences of system-wide gender inequities: "We maintain that personal narratives are particularly rich sources because, *attentively interpreted*, they illuminate both the logic of individual courses of action and the effects of system-wide constraints within which these courses evolved" (p. 6, emphasis added). We see the power of life history and narrative accounts in the dialectic between the unique experiences of individuals and the constraints of broad social, political, and economic structures. It may be possible artfully to weave these constraints into life stories so that they are barely visible, but their presence is essential.

"Will any old story suffice?" This is the central question in Phillips' (1994, p. 13) critique of narrative research. Phillips sees this as a parallel question to traditional science's, "Will any old explanation suffice?" His answer to the first question is that the narrative research community apparently believes that any story will do because it has not developed a "shared understanding of the criteria of adequacy or of epistemological warrant" (p. 15). Phillips finds lacking narrative proponents' explanations that this research genre is based on different assumptions and that it should be judged by different criteria than traditional notions of validity and reliability. He concludes with a warning: "There are many contexts in which the issue of truth of narratives needs to be dealt with more thoroughly before widespread use can be condoned" (p. 21).

While we agree that concern is warranted and that criteria of quality are important, we see a flaw in Phillips' argument that he is apparently unwilling to step outside his paradigmatic boundaries and accept that there are other ways of thinking about issues of "truth," "epistemological warrant," and "criteria for adequacy" that go beyond the standardized notions of reliability, validity, and generalizability. This is not the place to attempt to construct a comprehensive set of criteria of quality or to try to detail the various attempts we have found in the literature.[5] Instead, we present a list of criteria for quality narrative and life history work, noting the sources for those interested in studying them further. The list includes the following:

Adequacy (Connelly & Clandinin, 1990)
Aesthetic finality (Connelly & Clandinin, 1990)
Accessibility (Barone, 1992)
Authenticity (Blumenfeld-Jones, this volume; Lincoln & Guba, 1986)
Believability (Blumenfeld-Jones, this volume; J. Bruner, 1986)
Closure (Connelly & Clandinin, 1990)
Credibility (Barone, this volume)
Compellingness (Barone, 1992)
Continuity (Connelly & Clandinin, 1990)
Explanatory power (Connelly & Clandinin, 1990; Polkinghorne, this volume)
Fidelity (Blumenfeld-Jones, this volume; Grumet, 1988)
Moral persuasiveness (Barone, 1992)
Persuasiveness (Barone, this volume)
Plausibility (Connelly & Clandinin, 1990; Polkinghorne, this volume)
Resonance (Blumenfeld-Jones, this volume)
Sense of conviction (Connelly & Clandinin, 1990)
Trustworthiness (Lincoln & Guba, 1986; Zeller, this volume)
Verisimilitude (Barone, this volume; J. Bruner, 1986; Polkinghorne, 1988)

Poststructuralism and the crisis of representation

The poststructuralist position on the relationship of text to lives as lived was identified by our respondents as an important issue. The remainder of this discussion focuses on this and other poststructuralist concerns.

E. M. Bruner (1984) distinguishes between a life as lived, a life as experienced, and a life as told:

> A life lived is what actually happens. A life as experienced consists of the images, feelings, sentiments, desires, thoughts, and meanings known to the person whose life it is. . . . A life as told, a life history, is a narrative, influenced by the cultural conventions of telling, by the audience, and by the social context. (p. 7)

Life historians and narrative inquirers usually only have access to lives as told. From a poststructuralist perspective, these tellings are problematic for many reasons. First, the act of telling one's story is an act of creating one's self. In *Nausea*, Sartre (1964) asserts that "Nothing really happens when you live. The scenery changes, people come in and go out, that's all. There are no beginnings. Days are tacked on to days without rhyme or reason, in interminable monotonous addition" (p. 39). A life (the story of a life) is created in the consciousness to give order and meaning to events that have no "intrinsic or immanent relations" (Freeman, 1993, p. 95). The telling of the story is in a real sense the construction of a life.

Second, Ricoeur and others assert that since one of the central products of narrative is narrative identity, "that makes identity somewhat unstable, insofar as many stories can be woven from the same material" (Wood, 1991, p. 4). The life as told may be different at different times, with a different audience, or when told with a different purpose. In addition, as Polkinghorne (1988) has noted: "We are in the middle of our stories and cannot be sure how they will end; we are constantly having to revise the plot as new events are added to our lives" (p. 150). Narrative identities are dynamic, partial, fragmented, and context dependent. The problems for the narrative researcher are obvious.

Third, participants and researchers are bound by discourse structures to a limited range of expression and understanding. These discourse conventions shape and in many ways limit how we construct our own versions of a life (life as experienced), how we organize and express our selves through story (life as told), and how such a life can be understood and represented in text (see Emihovich, this volume; McLaren, 1993). In some cultures, the notion of "self" is not even a part of the conventional discourse. Understanding such a phenomenon gives salience to the taken-for-granted influence of discourse structures on what can be understood and communicated.

A fourth problem is the researcher's subjective involvement in the construction of the life history or narrative. Just as tellers have their own purposes for framing their stories in certain ways, so do story receivers have their own agendas and priorities, hidden or not, consciously held or not. Appearing to be the "objective" researcher "masks the researcher/ writer's subjective involvement in the scene – the unconscious selection of events to observe and record and the conscious selection of events to report" (Zeller, this volume). Researchers need to acknowledge and monitor their participation in the construction of the storied lives of their informants.

Finally, there is the problem of the limitations of text to represent a life as lived. Denzin (1989) provides this summary of an influential deconstructivist's ideas:

> Derrida (1972) has contributed to the understanding that there is no clear window into the inner life of a person, for any window is always filtered through the glaze of language, signs, and the process of signification. And language, in both its written and spoken forms, is always inherently unstable, in flux, and made up of the traces of other signs and symbolic statements. Hence there can never be a clear, unambiguous statement of anything, including an intention or a meaning. (Denzin, 1989, p. 14)

Such a position calls into question the very possibility of representing a life in the form of text. To the question, "What does the text mean?", J. Bruner (1986) argues that the deconstructivist position leaves only two possible answers: anything or nothing. J. Bruner and others interested in life history and narrative (e.g., Clandinin & Connelly, 1994; Emihovich, this volume; Hawkesworth, 1989) see more hope in being able to create a meaningful representation of a person's life within a text. Understanding the poststructuralist stance gives researchers a framework for deconstructing their own work in ways that can improve the quality of the representations they produce.

Conclusion

It has been suggested over the years that qualitative researchers should undergo psychoanalysis before going into the field. The tongue-in-cheek rationale for such a strategy is to provide researchers with insights that will enable them to better monitor the impact of their own personalities on their work (see Langness & Frank, 1981). It may be that in the postmodern moment, narrative and life history researchers could use help working their way through what we see as a kind of "poststructural paralysis." The poststructuralist critique is difficult to deal with because it is complex and because it challenges the postpositivist assumptions that many qualitative researchers fought hard to legitimate (Hatch, 1995). Still, we believe it is time to move on from our paralysis and act.

Based on our review of manuscripts over several years, we see a strong tendency among scholars to reflect on their work and their place in it rather than to do the work, a tendency Patai (1994, p. A52) has labeled "nouveau solipsism." As a result, and despite the espoused goal of encouraging other voices to be heard, the loudest voice is that of the author. This is a dilemma for all scholars committed to life history and narrative inquiry, and its resolution is at the heart of all qualitative research.

In our best judgment, we are at a stage where we need a better balance between the examination of the methodological and personal understanding of life history and narrative procedures and the reporting of studies derived from this approach. Fine tuning our understandings of methods and ethics is vital to the quality of our work, but we need far more studies *utilizing* narrative and life history approaches based on our methodological consensus to date.

We believe the chapters in this book comprise a strong contribution to our understanding of life history and narrative inquiry. The questions raised and probed are critical to our craft. We are pleased to have brought them to print. In calling for more studies utilizing life history and narrative procedures, we are stating what we hope will be the next step in the evolution of the field. Geertz (1986) summarized our position well: "We cannot live other people's lives, and it is a piece of bad faith to try. We can but listen to what, in words, in images, in actions, they say about their lives. . . . It's all a matter of scratching surfaces" (p. 373). Postmodern malaise can be debilitating, but there is so much more to learn from the stories and lives of others. Even if we are limited to scratching the surface, the work itself may be the best methodological therapy. It provides the best way to break through to the next level of understanding.[6]

Notes

1. In response to our questionnaire, Lou Smith wrote: "In general I find it difficult to respond to questionnaires – even open ended ones. I think that there is always a context lurking around implicitly and a more general theoretical structure as well." We appreciate that Lou and the others who responded did so with some discomfort. We hope we have not decontextualized (or recontextualized) their words in ways that distort their intent.

2. We deeply appreciate the help of the individuals who responded to our questionnaire: William Ayres, Leslie Rebecca Bloom, Richard Butt, Pauline Chinn, Ardra Cole, Norman Denzin, Michelle Foster, Ivor Goodson, Mary Jean Herzog, Yvonna Lincoln, Peter McLaren, Petra Munro, Linda Tillman Rogers, Paul Schempp, Pat Sikes, Louis Smith, Lisa Smulyan, Andrew Sparkes, William Tierney, Rob Walker, Stanton Wortham, and Nancy Zeller.

3. In *Interpretive biography*, Denzin (1989) provides a chapter entitled "A clarification of terms" from which several of these terms were taken. Others have made attempts at clarifying terms, for example: Connelly and Clandinin (1990, 1994), Hauser (1995), and Polkinghorne (1988).

4. More detailed historical overviews of the development of life history are found in Watson and Watson-Franke (1985) and Langness and Frank (1981).

5. These issues are examined by Barone (1992), J. Bruner (1986, 1990), Connelly and Clandinin (1990), Denzin (1989), Emihovich (this volume), and Polkinghorne (1988).

6. We are grateful to our colleagues in the editorial offices of *QSE* for their help in completing this chapter. Thank you to Connie Settle for typing the questionnaire responses, Elisabeth Wright-Harrison for putting the appendices together, and Charlotte Duncan for her editorial work.

References

Agger, B. (1990). *The decline of discourse: reading, writing, and resistance in postmodern capitalism*. New York: Falmer Press.

Bakhtin, M. M. (1981). *The dialogic imagination: four essays*. Austin: University of Texas Press.

Barone, T. (1992). A narrative of enhanced professionalism: educational researchers and popular storybooks about schoolpeople. *Educational Researcher, 21*(8), 15–24.

Bruner, E. M. (1984). The opening up of anthropology. In E. M. Bruner (Ed.), *Text, play, and story: the construction and reconstruction of self and society* (pp. 1–18). Washington, DC: The American Ethnological Society.

Bruner, E. M. (1986). Introduction: experience and its expressions. In V. W. Turner & E. M. Bruner (Eds.), *The anthropology of experience* (pp. 3–30). Urbana: University of Illinois Press.

Bruner, J. (1986). *Actual minds, possible worlds.* Cambridge, MA: Harvard University Press.

Bruner, J. (1990). *Acts of meaning.* Cambridge, MA: Harvard University Press.

Butt, R., Raymond, D., McCue, G., & Yamagishi, L. (1992). Collaborative autobiography and the teacher's voice. In I. F. Goodson (Ed.), *Studying teachers' lives* (pp. 51–98). New York: Teachers College Press.

Casey, K. (1993). *I answer with my life: life histories of women teachers working for social change.* New York: Routledge.

Clandinin, D. J., & Connelly, F. M. (1994). Personal experience methods. In N. K. Denzin & Y. S. Lincoln (Eds.), *Handbook of qualitative research* (pp. 413–427). Thousand Oaks, CA: Sage.

Connelly, F. M., & Clandinin, D. J. (1990). Stories of experience and narrative enquiry. *Educational Researcher, 19*(5), 2–14.

Crapanzano, V. (1980). *Tuhami: portrait of a Moroccan.* Chicago: University of Chicago Press.

Denzin, N. (1989). *Interpretive biography.* Newbury Park, CA: Sage.

Denzin, N. K. (1992, April). *Deconstructing the biographical method.* Paper presented at the American Educational Research Association Annual Meeting, San Francisco.

Denzin, N. K., & Lincoln, Y. S. (Eds.). (1994). *Handbook of qualitative research.* Thousand Oaks, CA: Sage.

Derrida, J. (1967/73). *Speech and phenomena.* Evanston, IL: Northwestern University Press.

Derrida, J. (1972). Structure, sign and play in the discourse of the human sciences. In R. Macksey & E. Donato (Eds.), *The structuralist controversy: the languages of criticism and the sciences of man* (pp. 247–265). Baltimore: Johns Hopkins University Press.

Dollard, J. (1935/1949). *Criteria for the life history, with analysis of six notable documents.* New York: Peter Smith.

Etter-Lewis, G. (1993). *My soul is my own: oral narratives of African-American women in the professions.* New York: Routledge.

Fisher, W. R. (1989). *Human communication as narration: toward a philosophy of reason, value, and action.* Columbia: University of South Carolina Press.

Freeman, M. P. (1993). *Rewriting the self: history, memory, narrative.* New York: Routledge.

Geertz, C. (1986). Making experiences, authoring selves. In V. W. Turner & E. M. Bruner (Eds.), *The anthropology of experience* (pp. 373–380). Urbana: University of Illinois Press.

Goodson, I. F. (1992). Studying teachers' lives: an emergent field of inquiry. In I. Goodson, (Ed.), *Studying teachers' lives* (pp. 1–17). London: Routledge.

Grumet, M. (1988). *Bitter milk: women and teaching.* Amherst: University of Massachusetts Press.

Grumet, M. R. (1991). The politics of personal knowledge. In C. Witherell & N. Noddings (Eds.), *Stories lives tell: narrative and dialogue in education* (pp. 67–77). New York: Teachers College Press.

Hatch, J. A. (1995). Introduction. In J. A. Hatch (Ed.), *Qualitative research in early childhood settings* (pp. xix–xxv). Westport, CT: Praeger.

Hauser, M. E. (1995). Life history of a first grade teacher: a narrative of culturally sensitive teaching practice. In J. A. Hatch (Ed.), *Qualitative research in early childhood settings* (pp. 64–78). Westport, CT: Praeger.

Hawkesworth, M. E. (1989). Knowers, knowing, known: feminist theory and claims of truth. *Signs: Journal of Women in Culture and Society, 14*, 533–557.

Langness, L. L., & Frank, G. (1981). *Lives: an anthropological approach to biography.* Novato, CA: Chandler & Sharp.

Lincoln, Y., & Guba, E. (1985). *Naturalistic inquiry.* Beverly Hills, CA: Sage.

Lincoln, Y., & Guba, E. (1986). But is it rigorous? Trustworthiness and authenticity in naturalistic evaluation. In D. D. Williams (Ed.), *Naturalistic evaluation* (pp. 73–84). San Francisco: Jossey-Bass.

Lyotard, J.-F. (1984). *The postmodern condition: a report on knowledge* (G. Bennington & B. Massumi, Trans.). Minneapolis: University of Minnesota Press. (Original work published 1979)

McLaren, P. (1993). Border disputes: multicultural narrative, identity formation, and critical pedagogy in postmodern America. In D. McLaughlin & W. G. Tierney (Eds.), *Naming silenced lives: personal narratives and the process of educational change* (pp. 201–235). New York: Routledge.

Measor, L., & Sikes, P. (1992). Visiting lives: ethics and methodology in life history. In I. F. Goodson (Ed.), *Studying teachers' lives* (pp. 209–233). New York: Teachers College Press.

Michelson, T. (1925). *The autobiography of a Fox Indian woman.* Bureau of American Ethnology, Fortieth Annual Report. Washington, DC: Smithsonian Institution.

Patai, D. (1994, February 23). Sick and tired of scholars' nouveau solipsism. *The Chronicle of Higher Education*, p. A52.

Personal Narratives Group (Eds.). (1989). *Interpreting women's lives: feminist theory and personal narratives.* Bloomington: Indiana University Press.

Popular Memory Group (1982). Popular memory: theory, politics, method. In R. Johnson, G. McLennan, B. Schwarz, & D. Sutton (Eds.), *Making histories* (pp. 240–256). London: Hutchinson.

Phillips, D. C. (1994). Telling it straight: issues in assessing narrative research. *Educational Psychologist, 29*(1), 13–21.

Polkinghorne, D. E. (1988). *Narrative knowing and the human sciences.* Albany: State University of New York Press.

Radin, P. (1926). *Crashing thunder: the autobiography of an American Indian.* New York: Appleton.

Ricoeur, P. (1991). *From text to action: essays in hermeneutics, II* (K. Blamey & J. B. Thompson, Trans.). Evanston, IL: Northwestern University Press. (Original work published 1986)

Sapir, E. (1932). Cultural anthropology and psychiatry. *Journal of Abnormal and Social Psychology, 27,* 229–242.

Sartre, J.-P. (1964) *Nausea.* Norfolk, CT: New Directions. (Original work published in 1938)

Smith, L. M. (1994). Biographical method. In N. K. Denzin & Y. S. Lincoln (Eds.), *Handbook of qualitative research* (pp. 286–305). Thousand Oaks, CA: Sage.

Thomas, W. I., & Znaniecki, F. (1920/1927). *The Polish peasant in Europe and America.* New York: Alfred A. Knopf.

Watson, L. C. (1976). Understanding a life history as a subjective document: hermeneutical and phenomenological perspectives. *Ethos, 4,* 95–131.

Watson, L. C., & Watson-Franke, M. B. (1985). *Interpreting life histories: an anthropological inquiry.* New Brunswick, NJ: Rutgers University Press.

Witherell, C. (1991). The self in narrative: a journey into paradox. In C. Witherell & N. Noddings (Eds.), *Stories lives tell: narrative and dialogue in education* (pp. 83–95). New York: Teachers College Press.

Witherall, C., & Noddings, N. (Eds.). (1991). *Stories lives tell: narrative and dialogue in education.* New York: Teachers College Press.

Wood, D. (Ed.). (1991). *On Paul Ricoeur: narrative and interpretation.* London: Routledge.

Appendix A: Selected works about life history and narrative

Bakhtin, M. M. (1986). *Speech genres and other late essays.* Austin: University of Texas Press.

Blumer, H. (1969). *Symbolic interactionism: perspective and method.* Englewood Cliffs, NJ: Prentice Hall.

Bowen, C. D. (1959). *Adventures of a biographer.* Boston: Little, Brown.

Brown, C. S. (1988). *Like it was: a complete guide to writing oral history.* New York: Teachers & Writers Collaborative.

Chow, R. (1993). *Writing diaspora: tactics of intervention in contemporary cultural studies.* Bloomington: Indiana University Press.

Clandinin, D. J., & Connelly, F. M. (1994). Personal experience methods. In N. K. Denzin & Y. S. Lincoln (Eds.), *Handbook of qualitative research* (pp. 413–427). Thousand Oaks, CA: Sage.

Clifford, J. (1970). *From puzzles to portraits: problems of a literary biographer.* Chapel Hill: University of North Carolina Press.

Coles, A., & Knowles, G. (in press). A life history approach to self-study: methods and issues. In I. Russell & F. Korthagen (Eds.), *The reflective teacher educator.* Lewes, UK: Falmer Press.

Cortazzi, M. (1993). *Narrative analysis.* Lewes, UK: Falmer Press.

Denzin, N. (1989). *Interpretive biography.* Newbury Park, CA: Sage.

Dollard, J. (1935). *Criteria for the life history.* New Haven: Yale University Press.

Eco, U. (1990). *The limits of interpretation.* Bloomington: Indiana University Press.

Edel, L. (1985). *Writing lives: principia biographica.* London: W. W. Norton.

Ellis, C. (Ed.). (1987). *Investigating subjectivity: research on lived experience.* Thousand Oaks, CA: Sage.

Freeman, M. P. (1993). *Rewriting the self: history, memory, narrative.* New York: Routledge.

Goodson, I. F. (Ed.). (1992). *Studying teachers' lives.* New York: Teachers College Press.

Krieger, S. (1991). *Social science and the self: personal essays on an art form.* New Brunswick NJ: Rutgers University Press.

Langness, L. L., & Frank, G. (1988). *Lives: an anthropological approach to biography* (4th ed.). Novato, CA: Chandler & Sharp.

Linde, C. (1993). *Life stories: the creation of coherence.* New York: Oxford University Press.

McEwan, H., & Egan, K. (Eds.). (in press). *Perspectives on narrative and teaching.* New York: Teachers College Press.

McLaren, P. (1993). Border disputes: multicultural narrative, identity formation, and critical pedagogy in postmodern America. In D. McLaughlin & W. G. Tierney (Eds.), *Naming silenced lives: personal narratives and the process of educational change* (pp. 201–235). New York: Routledge.

McLaughlin, D., & Tierney, W. G. (Eds.). (1993). *Naming silenced lives: personal narratives and the process of educational change.* New York: Routledge.

Middleton, S. (1993). *Educating feminists: life history and pedagogy.* New York: Teachers College Press.

Miner, E. R. (Ed.). (1992). To tell a free story: narrative, theory and practice. *William Andrews Clark Memorial Library Seminar Papers.* Los Angeles: University of California.

Mishler, E. G. (1986). *Research interviewing: context and narrative.* Cambridge, MA: Harvard University Press.

Mitchell, W. J. T. (1981). *On narrative.* Chicago: University of Chicago Press.

Munro, P. (1993). Continuing dilemmas of life history research: a reflexive attempt of feminist qualitative inquiry. In D. Flinders & G. Mills (Eds.), *Theory and concepts in qualitative research: perspectives from the field* (pp. 163–177). New York: Teachers College Press.

Personal Narratives Group. (Eds.). (1989). *Interpreting women's lives: feminist theory and personal narratives.* Bloomington: Indiana University Press.

Plummer, K. (1983). *Documents of life*. London: George Allen & Unwin.

Polkinghorne, D. (1988). *Narrative knowing and the human sciences*. Albany: State University of New York Press.

Portelli, A. (1991). *The death of Luigi Trastulli and other stories: form and meaning in oral history*. Albany: State University of New York Press.

Reissman, C. K. (1993). *Narrative analysis*. Newbury Park, CA: Sage.

Runyan, W. (1982). *Life history and psychobiography*. New York: Oxford University Press.

Smith, L. (1993). Notes toward theory in biography: working on the Nora Barlow papers. In D. Flinders & G. Mills (Eds.), *Theory and concept in qualitative research* (pp. 129–140). New York: Teachers College Press.

Smith, L. (1994). Biographical method. In N. K. Denzin & Y. S. Lincoln (Eds.), *Handbook of qualitative research* (pp. 286–305). Thousand Oaks, CA: Sage.

Sparkes, A. (1994). Life histories and the issue of voice: reflections on an emerging relationship. *International Journal of Qualitative Studies in Education*, 7, 165–183.

Stake, R. (1994). Case studies. In N. Denzin & Y. Lincoln (Eds.), *Handbook of qualitative research* (pp. 236–247). Thousand Oaks, CA: Sage.

Witherall, C., & Noddings, N. (Eds.). (1991). *Stories lives tell: narrative and dialogue in education*. New York: Teachers College Press.

Wolcott, H. (1994). *Transforming qualitative data*. Newbury Park, CA: Sage.

Wood, D. (Ed.). (1991). *On Paul Ricoeur: narrative and interpretation*. London: Routledge.

Appendix B: Selected examples of life history and narrative work

Ayres, W. (1989). *The good preschool teacher: six teachers reflect on their lives*. New York: Teachers College Press.

Ball, S., & Goodson, I. (Eds.). (1985). *Teachers' lives & careers*. Lewes, UK: Falmer Press.

Barlow, N. (Ed.). (1933). *Charles Darwin's diary of the voyage of the H.M.S. Beagle*. Cambridge: Cambridge University Press.

Barlow, N. (Ed.). (1946). *Charles Darwin and the voyage of the Beagle*. New York: Philosophical Library.

Bateson, M. (1990). *Composing a life*. New York: Penguin.

Behar, R. (1933). *Translated woman: crossing the border with Esperanza's story*. Boston: Beacon Press.

Belenky, M. F., Clinchy, B. M., Goldberger, N. R., & Tarule, J. M. (1986). *Women's ways of knowing: the development of self, voice, and mind*. New York: Basic Books.

Berger, J. (1981). *A seventh man*. New York: Writers & Readers.

Berger, J., & Jean, M. (1967). *A fortunate man: the story of a country doctor*. New York: Holt, Rhinehart & Winston.

Berger, J., & Jean, M. (1982). *Another way of telling*. New York: Pantheon.

Bowen, C. D. (1944). *Yankee from Olympus*. Boston: Little, Brown.

Bowen, C. D. (1950). *John Adams and the American Revolution*. Boston: Little, Brown.

Brown, K. (1991). *Mama Lola: a voodoo priestess in Brooklyn*. Berkeley: University of California Press.

Casey, K. (1993). *I answer with my life: life histories of women teachers working for social change*. New York: Teachers College Press.

Clark, S. P. (with Brown, C. S.). (1986). *Ready from within: Septima Clark and the civil rights movement*. Navarro, CA: Wild Tree Press.

Cohen, R. M. (1991). *A lifetime of teaching: portraits of five veteran high school teachers*. New York: Teachers College Press.

Crapanzano, V. (1980). *Tuhami: portrait of a Moroccan*. Chicago: University of Chicago Press.

Cruikshank, J. (1990). *Life lived like a story: life stories of three Yukon elders*. Lincoln: University of Nebraska Press.

Denzin, N. (1987a). *The alcoholic self*. Newbury Park, CA: Sage.

Denzin, N. (1987b). *The recovering alcoholic*. Newbury Park, CA: Sage.

Desmond, A. J., & Moore, J. R. (1992). *Darwin*. New York: Warner Books.

Eco, U. (1983). *The name of the rose*. San Diego: Harcourt Brace Jovanovich.

Etter-Lewis, G. (1993). *My soul is my own: oral narratives of African-American women in the professions*. New York: Routledge.

Freedman, S. (1990). *Small victories: the real world of a teacher, her students and their high school*. New York: Harper & Row.

Gruber, H. (1981). *Darwin on man: a psychological study on scientific creativity* (2nd ed.). New York: Harper & Row.

Gwaltney, J. L. (1980). *Drylongso: a portrait of black America*. New York: Vintage Books.

Haug, F. (1986). *Female sexualisation: a collective work of memory*. London: Verso.

Kidder, T. (1989). *Among schoolchildren*. Boston: Houghton Mifflin.

Kotlowitz, A. (1991). *There are no children here: the story of two boys growing up in the other America*. New York: Doubleday.

Nyman, E., & Leer, J. (1993). *Brought forth to reconfirm the legacy of a Taku River Tlingit clan*. Fairbanks: University of Alaska, Alaska Native Language Center.

Orlans, K., & Wallace, R. (Eds.). (1994). *Gender and the academic experience*. Lincoln: University of Nebraska Press.

Rosengarten, T. (1989). *All God's dangers*. New York: Vintage Books.

Sarton, M. (1976). *The small room: a novel*. New York: Norton.

Schempp, P., Sparkes, A., & Templin, T. (1993). The micropolitics of teacher induction. *American Educational Research Journal, 30,* 447–472.

Shostak, M. (1983). *Nisa: the life of a !kung woman.* New York: Vintage.

Sikes, P., Measor, L., & Wood, P. (1985). *Teachers' careers: crises and continuities.* Lewes, UK: Falmer Press.

Sparkes, A. (1994). Self, silence and invisibility as a beginning teacher: a life history of lesbian experience. *British Journal of Sociology of Education, 15*(1), 93–118.

Talayesva, D. C. (with Simmons, L. W.). (1942). *Sun Chief: the autobiography of a Hopi Indian.* New Haven: Yale University Press.

Thomas, D. (in press). *Teachers' stories.* Washington, DC: Open University Press.

Tierney, W. (1993). Self and identity in a postmodern world: a life story. In D. McLaughlin & W. G. Tierney (Eds.), *Naming silenced lives: personal narratives and the process of educational change* (pp. 119–134). New York: Routledge.

Warner, S. A. (1963). *Teacher.* New York: Simon & Schuster.

Wolcott, H. (1983). Adequate schools and inadequate education: the life history of a sneaky kid. *Anthropology and Education Quarterly, 14*(1), 3–32.

Wolfe, T. (1983). *The right stuff.* New York: Bantam Books.

X, M. (with Haley, A.). (1965). *The autobiography of Malcolm X.* New York: Grove Press.

Notes on Contributors

Liz Barber is Assistant Professor at Lynchburg College. Her work focuses on literacy development in time and space and on the connections between uses of reading and writing in school and in the community. She has published in the *Virginia English Bulletin, Harvard Educational Review,* and elsewhere.

Correspondence to Liz Barber, College of Education, Lynchburg College, Lynchburg, VA 24501, USA

Thomas E. Barone is Professor of Curriculum and Instruction in the College of Education at Arizona State University. He received his doctorate in Design and Evaluation of Educational Programs from Stanford University in 1979. Barone currently teaches graduate-level courses in curriculum studies and qualitative research methodology. In his writing, Barone explores the possibilities of a variety of narrative and arts-based forms of educational discourse. His articles and chapters have appeared in books and in journals such as *Daedalus, Journal of the American Academy of Arts and Sciences; Educational Researcher; Curriculum Inquiry; Journal of Curriculum Theorizing; Phi Delta Kappan; Educational Leadership;* and *Journal of Teacher Education.*

Correspondence to Thomas Barone, Arizona State University, College of Education, Tempe, AZ 85287–1911, USA

Leslie Rebecca Bloom is Assistant Professor of Curriculum and Instruction at Iowa State University. She is teaching courses in curriculum theory and qualitative research. Her research focuses on feminist methodology and interpretive practices for understanding narrative data. Her current project focuses on postmodern theories of sexuality, identity, and representation. She has published articles in *Human Studies* and *Teaching Education* and is completing a book, *Feminist Interpretation and Methodology.*

Correspondence to Leslie Rebecca Bloom, Department of Curriculum and Instruction, N157 Lagomarcino Hall, Iowa State University, Ames, Iowa 50011, USA

Donald Blumenfeld-Jones, Assistant Professor of Curriculum and Instruction at Arizona State University, has recently published in the *Journal of Curriculum Theorizing, Education in Asia,* and the *Journal of Thought.* He practices research in philosophy of education (including work in issues of research methodology and the relation of forms of classroom discipline to learning) and teacher beliefs (in the areas of pleasure and learning, teacher authority, and community in the classroom and school).

Correspondence to Donald Blumenfeld-Jones, College of Education, Division of Curriculum and Instruction, Arizona State University, Tempe, AZ 85287–1911, USA

Catherine Emihovich is director of the Buffalo Research Institute on Education for Teaching (BRIET) and Associate Professor of Educational Psychology in the Department of Counseling and Educational Psychology at the University of Buffalo, State University of New York. She has published papers on topics related to sociolinguistic studies of computer discourse, culture and education, and qualitative research and evaluation methods. She has guest edited special issues of *Theory Into Practice, Education and Urban Society, The Urban Review,* and is the editor of *Anthropology and Education Quarterly.* *Correspondence to Catherine Emihovich, University at Buffalo, Department of Counseling and Educational Psychology, 409 Baldy Hall, Buffalo, NY 14260, USA*

Ivor Goodson is Professor at the University of Western Ontario and the Frederica Warner Professor in the Graduate School of Education and Human Development at the University of Rochester. At Western, he is a member of the Faculties of Graduate Studies, Education, Sociology, and The Center for Theory and Criticism. He is the author of a range of books on curriculum and life history studies. They include *School Subjects and Curriculum Change, The Making of Curriculum, Biography, Identity and Schooling* (with Rob Walker) and *Studying Teachers' Lives.* He is the Founding Editor and North American Editor of *The Journal of Education Policy* and the Canadian Editor of *Qualitative Studies in Education.*
Correspondence to Ivor F. Goodson, Faculty of Education, University of Western Ontario, London, Ontario N6G 1G7, Canada

J. Amos Hatch is Associate Professor of Inclusive Early Childhood Education at the University of Tennessee, Knoxville. He has published widely in the areas of children's social behavior, qualitative methods, and educators' perspectives on early childhood theory and practice. He is currently involved with four teachers in a collaborative investigation of the appropriateness of "Developmentally Appropriate Practice" for inner-city early education settings. He is editor of a new book, *Qualitative Research in Early Childhood Settings* (Praeger, 1995), and is co-editor (with Richard Wisniewski) of the *International Journal of Qualitative Studies in Education.*
Correspondence to J. Amos Hatch, Inclusive Early Childhood Education Unit, College of Education, University of Tennessee, Knoxville, TN 37996, USA

Petra Munro is Assistant Professor in the Department of Curriculum and Instruction and Women's and Gender Studies at Louisiana State University. She teaches courses in qualitative research, curriculum theory, and secondary social studies. These interests converge in her research collecting the life histories of women educators. She is currently engaged in collecting life history narratives of retired Southern educators. She has published articles in the *Journal of Curriculum and Supervision, Journal of Curriculum Theorizing,* and is completing a book, *Rereading "Women's True Profession": Women's Life History Narratives and the Cultural Politics of Teaching.*
Correspondence to Petra Munro, Department of Curriculum and Instruction, Louisiana State University, Baton Rouge, LA 70803, USA

Jan Nespor is Associate Professor in the Department of Curriculum and Instruction at Virginia Polytechnic Institute and State University. His work centers on practices of knowledge and knowledge production in settings ranging from elementary schools to universities. He has published articles in the *American Educational Research Journal, Journal of Curriculum Studies, Educational Researcher,* and elsewhere.
Correspondence to Jan Nespor, Department of Curriculum & Instruction, Virginia Tech, Blacksburg, VA 24061–0313, USA

Donald E. Polkinghorne is Professor of Counseling Psychology at the University of Southern California. His research interests include the relation between theoretical and practical knowledge and the epistemological bases of qualitative and narrative approaches to research. He is the author of *Methodology for the Human Sciences* and *Narrative and the Human Sciences.*
Correspondence to Donald E. Polkinghorne, Waite Phillips Hall – 503G, University of Southern California, Los Angeles, CA 90089–0031, USA

Richard Wisniewski is Professor and Dean of Education at the University of Tennessee, Knoxville. His particular interests lie in the restructuring of educational institutions, particularly colleges of education. His academic home is in the sociology of education and he has long been a supporter of qualitative research. For the past four years, he has served as co-editor (with Amos Hatch) of the *International Journal of Qualitative Studies in Education.* *Correspondence to Richard Wisniewski, College of Education, University of Tennessee, Knoxville, TN 37996, USA*

Nancy Zeller completed her PhD in Educational Inquiry Methodology at Indiana University (1987). A faculty member in the department of Foundations and Research at East Carolina University since the fall semester of 1992, Zeller previously served as a policy analyst for the Indiana Commission for Higher Education. Her research and teaching interests include qualitative research methodology, the rhetoric of research in the human sciences, and higher education policy. *Correspondence to Nancy Zeller, East Carolina University, School of Education, Speight Building, Greeneville, NC 27858–4353, USA*

Index